The Crime Fiction
Handbook

Blackwell Literature Handbooks

This new series offers the student thorough and lively introductions to literary periods, movements, and, in some instances, authors and genres, from Anglo-Saxon to the Postmodern. Each volume is written by a leading specialist to be invitingly accessible and informative. Chapters are devoted to the coverage of cultural context, the provision of brief but detailed biographical essays on the authors concerned, critical coverage of key works, and surveys of themes and topics, together with bibliographies of selected further reading. Students new to a period of study or to a period genre will discover all they need to know to orientate and ground themselves in their studies, in volumes that are as stimulating to read as they are convenient to use.

Published

The Science Fiction Handbook
M. Keith Booker and Anne-Marie Thomas

The Seventeenth-Century Literature Handbook
Marshall Grossman

The Twentieth-Century American Fiction Handbook
Christopher MacGowan

The British and Irish Short Story Handbook
David Malcolm

The Crime Fiction Handbook
Peter Messent

The Crime Fiction Handbook

Peter Messent

WILEY-BLACKWELL

A John Wiley & Sons, Ltd., Publication

This edition first published 2013
© 2013 John Wiley & Sons Ltd.

Wiley-Blackwell is an imprint of John Wiley & Sons, formed by the merger of Wiley's global Scientific, Technical and Medical business with Blackwell Publishing.

Registered Office
John Wiley & Sons Ltd, The Atrium, Southern Gate, Chichester, West Sussex, PO19 8SQ, UK

Editorial Offices
350 Main Street, Malden, MA 02148-5020, USA
9600 Garsington Road, Oxford, OX4 2DQ, UK
The Atrium, Southern Gate, Chichester, West Sussex, PO19 8SQ, UK

For details of our global editorial offices, for customer services, and for information about how to apply for permission to reuse the copyright material in this book please see our website at www.wiley.com/wiley-blackwell.

The right of Peter Messent to be identified as the author of this work has been asserted in accordance with the UK Copyright, Designs and Patents Act 1988.

Library of Congress Cataloging-in-Publication Data

Messent, Peter B.
  The crime fiction handbook / Peter Messent.
      p. cm.
  Includes index.
  ISBN 978-0-470-65703-4 (cloth) – ISBN 978-0-470-65704-1 (pbk.)
    1. Detective and mystery stories – History and criticism. 2. Detective and mystery stories, English–History and criticism. 3. Detective and mystery stories, American–History and criticism. 4. Detective and mystery stories, Swedish–History and criticism. I. Title.
  PN3448.D4M435 2011
  809.3'872–dc23

                                                                            2012008956

A catalogue record for this book is available from the British Library.

Cover image © UpperCut Images / Getty
Cover design by www.simonlevyassociates.co.uk
Part opener image © optimarc / Shutterstock

Set in 10/13pt Sabon by Thomson Digital, Noida, India.
Printed in Malaysia by Ho Printing (M) Sdn Bhd
1   2013

Contents

Acknowledgments

Thanks, first of all, to David Schmid and Chris Routledge, both of whom took time out of their busy schedules to read major sections of this work. Their comments make this a much better book than it would otherwise have been, and their encouragement was much appreciated. Thanks too to others who read individual sequences in the book: Charlotte Fallenius (who kept a close eye on my generalizations about Swedish culture), John Harvey, and Andy Pepper. Again, their critical input was greatly appreciated. Any mistakes or stupidities left are mine alone. Dave Murray, as so often in past cases, said things about the subject as we casually talked that opened my eyes to new angles on it and new ways of thinking about it. Thanks, too, to the students who have taken my crime fiction module in the American and Canadian Studies Department at my home university (Nottingham) over the last decade. It is that teaching, and the ideas that came from those classes and in essay work, that have enabled me to get a much better grasp on these materials than I would otherwise have. Thanks to my son and daughter, William and Alice, and step-daughters, Ella and Leah, for their interest and support. And thanks as always, and love, to my wife, Carin, for her encouragement – even though I have never quite been able to persuade her that crime fiction is a good thing.

Some of the material in this book is based on earlier work. My section on "The Police Novel," in particular, is a re-working of the essay with that same name in Charles J. Rzepka and Lee Horsley's *A Companion to Crime Fiction* (Wiley-Blackwell, 2010). I have also drawn on my other previous publications in the field, but – in all cases – considerably updated and revised them. These include the introduction to my own edited book, *Criminal Proceedings* (Pluto, 1997); two essays on Patricia Cornwell, one in Warren Chernaik et al. (eds.), *The Art of Detective Fiction* (Macmillan, 2000) and the other in *Clues: A Journal of Detection* (Winter 2000); an essay on Thomas Harris that first appeared in Philip Sutton (ed.), *Betwixt-and-Between: Essays in*

Liminal Geography (The Gateway Press, 2002) but that has been published several times since in updated forms; and two pieces on Cornwell and Harris in Michael D. Sharp's edited collection, *Popular Contemporary Writers* (Marshall Cavendish, 2006).

I could not have asked for a better copy-editor than Hazel Harris as we worked to prepare the book for publication. I recognize all the hard work she put into this task, and appreciate it greatly. Again, my thanks.

I dedicate this book to the memory of Phil Melling, who died of cancer just as I was completing it. He was a very good friend from our university days onward, a fine academic (and much more), and a man of many passions. I will miss him greatly.

Introductory Note

In this book, I refer to crime fiction across the U. S. and European spectrum. But I recognize my limitations. This is not a handbook of global crime fiction and, even within Europe and the Americas, I leave many traditions (Canadian, French, Italian, South American, Spanish, and others) unexamined. My own teaching experience is mainly in the field of U. S. crime fiction, and I rely on this area for a good many of my examples. I am relatively happy to do so because of both the importance and the popularity of that writing. I write in the belief that what I say here will be useful to those interested in authors and countries that either I do not mention or to whom/which I give short shrift. The critical approaches I take will, I hope, transfer across – to some degree at least – to that other material, though I recognize the importance of cultural and historical context; the impossibility, too, of giving blanket rules for the reading of all instances of the genre. My chronological reach in this study is also limited. I am well aware of a fuller history than that I give, which can be traced in the work of such critics as Stephen Knight and Charles J. Rzepka. But I focus here on the best-known examples of the genre, particularly in a twentieth- and twenty-first-century context but with some attention to its nineteenth-century pre-history. My decision to start with Edgar Allan Poe and Sherlock Holmes follows that logic. I thought long and hard about the fourteen texts on which I focus in Part 3 of this book but fully recognize the arbitrary nature of my choices. There are many other texts that cried out for the same kind of attention. Those I have chosen, however, do allow me to refer back to the earlier parts of the book, exemplifying a good number of the different approaches I lay out there. Crime fiction is one of those

The Crime Fiction Handbook, First Edition. Peter Messent.
© 2013 John Wiley & Sons, Ltd. Published 2013 by John Wiley & Sons, Ltd.

areas that either fosters compulsive readers or deters those who find the genre shallow and of little or no interest. While I recognize that is it the former who will have the most interest in this book, I am hoping that some of the latter may read it too, and even alter their opinion of the genre as a result. Its enormous present-day popularity is a measure of its cultural importance and influence.

Part 1

Introduction

. . . [W]ith an expression of interest, [Sherlock Holmes] laid down his cigarette, and, carrying the cane to the window, he looked over it again with a convex lens.

"Interesting, though elementary," said he as he returned to his favourite corner of the settee. "There are certainly one or two indications upon the stick. It gives us the basis for several deductions."

Doyle (2003: 6)

This short passage from Conan Doyle's *The Hound of the Baskervilles* (1902) immediately inspires sparks of recognition for many readers. We assume almost without question that Holmes is talking here to his slightly obtuse companion and chronicler, Dr. Watson. And we automatically recall the phrase "Elementary, my dear Watson" – in fact absent from the original written texts but present in their film versions – that traditionally accompanies Holmes' detections and explanations and has passed as a commonplace saying into the (English) language. We recognize Holmes' "deductions," too, as the sign of his genius: the logical and analytic skills that enable him to coolly link cause to effect; that "marvellous faculty" (Doyle 2001: 12) that enables him, for instance, to trace the history of a watch and give detailed characteristics of its former owner, even despite its recent cleaning, in the opening chapter ("The Science of Deduction") of *The Sign of Four* (1890). The "convex lens" is, of course, part of what has become in consequent representations a magnifying glass, one of Holmes' most valued tools and the very icon of detective fiction – as instantly recognizable in his case as the deerstalker hat that has come to be synonymous with his

The Crime Fiction Handbook, First Edition. Peter Messent.
© 2013 John Wiley & Sons, Ltd. Published 2013 by John Wiley & Sons, Ltd.

professional attire and role. The cigarette, too, hints at a certain leisure-class loucheness, or bohemianism as Watson calls it, confirmed elsewhere by Holmes' use of morphine and cocaine – drugs he praises as "transcendently stimulating and clarifying to the mind" (Doyle 2001: 6).

Detective fiction has a long history and, in its modern form, is usually traced to a handful of stories by Edgar Allan Poe: "The Murders in the Rue Morgue" (1841), "The Mystery of Marie Roget" (1842–1843), and "The Purloined Letter" (1845). All three feature Monsieur C. Auguste Dupin, the French detective whose deductive intelligence provides the model for Conan Doyle's protagonist. But it is Doyle's creation of Sherlock Holmes that first gave detective fiction its enormous popular currency and began to make it such a resonant part of our cultural consciousness. Following, in one way or another, in his footsteps are writers such as Agatha Christie, Dashiell Hammett, Raymond Chandler, Georges Simenon, Patricia High-smith, Henning Mankell, and Stieg Larsson (to name a significant few) – with Larsson being the first writer to sell over a million copies of his books in Amazon's Kindle electronic bookstore. This type of sales figure, and the popularity (and often quality) of the various film and television spin-offs that have followed on the heels of the publication of such authors' books, signifies the massive cultural appetite for, and importance of, crime fiction (the larger generic category to which detective fiction belongs) in the Western world from the late nineteenth century to the present.

The question immediately raised is why crime fiction should have had such a massive impact and be so popular? And why, for instance, should we "enjoy" such best-selling novels as Thomas Harris' *The Silence of the Lambs* (1988), with its scenes that include Hannibal Lecter's savage removal of a policeman's face (he uses it to mask his own as he escapes imprisonment) and references to his cannibalism and shocking violence – his biting off (or so the implication is), for instance, of the tongue of a nurse who gets too close to him? In the punning relationship between Lecter's name and the French word for "reader" (*lecteur*), as well as in Lecter's own distinctive mix of refined sensitivity and predatory blood-letting, Harris may be suggesting that the line that divides the apparently "civilized" audience that consumes his books from its (normally firmly repressed) primal and savage instincts and tastes is thinner and more permeable than we think.

But there are other explanations available, too, for such readerly interest in crime and its often bloody and violently macabre manifestations – some of which complement the one just given, others quite different. Critic David Stewart (1997) writes about non-fiction crime writing in a much earlier period, examining the reportage of urban crime in mid-nineteenth-century

America. But his focus on urban life and a rapidly expanding capitalist economy offers a helpful prompt for thinking about crime fiction too, and the nature of its appeal, both in the nineteenth century and later. Stewart sees the "relish" (681) with which the crime literature of that period was consumed in terms of an ambivalence about criminality and its relation to the dominant social order. The popular appeal of such writing, he suggest, lies in the way it "eroticized urban experience" (684) – that is, provided a necessary and thrilling release from the disciplinary procedures of capitalism, the "laws and behavioral practices" (689) sustaining an increasingly regimented social order. The "exhilaration" (688) associated with criminal danger and the darker underbelly of life in the city consequently stood as a direct and exciting contrast to a daily experience "that was, for the vast majority of city-dwellers, constraining, confining, and mind-numbingly dull" (684).

But Stewart also argues that crime writing engaged quite opposite emotions too, feeding on a popular *fear* of crime and the threat to the reader's own security contained in such "narratives of violation" (682). Thus, to modify one of his remarks, "[g]ore defacing [urban and textual] space [is] still gore, and potentially the reader's own." Fears of "real urban danger" (697), then, inhabit these texts alongside the other emotions they trigger: the reader's desire for transgressive excitement balanced by her or his need for security and safety. In identifying such ambivalences, Stewart offers, perhaps, a larger lesson: that the appeal of (usually) violent crime – in both non-fiction and fiction – has a multitude of (sometimes common but often contradictory) causes. In the second part of this book, in which I offer a brief overview of the politics of crime fiction and of some of its main forms and key concerns, I extend this argument to indicate the wide range of reasons for the popularity of this type of fiction, and the complexity of their mix.

I return, though, to the violent and bloody episodes in Harris' novel and the pre-history to them implied in Stewart's essay. For Stewart also identifies in his ante-bellum subject matter another crucial, and related, tension – the way in which the qualities of rational control and logical explanation that crime reportage then, and (as I draw my own analogies) crime fiction now, associates with law-bringers – be they detectives or police – are undermined and contrasted with the descriptions of the spilling of blood, of sexual abuse, and of physical suffering that excessively inhabit many examples of such writing. He identifies a curious connective logic to this relationship as he looks at one particular newspaper story, "Horrible and Mysterious Murder in Broadway," published in *Frank Leslie's Illustrated Newspaper* on August 2, 1856. Focusing on the detailed description of the corpse in this case, "the victim of bodily opening and exposure," which extends right down to the exact measurements of the deep razor slashes made on it, Stewart asks:

> What, if any, of the information [the descriptions of bodily disfiguration] is in fact evidence? . . . And more disturbing: Why is it important to differentiate among drops, clots, and pools [of blood]? What is the depth of a razor slash evidence of? . . . Prurient excess would seem to undermine the strict task of productive looking. More to the point, productive looking seems to lead all too irresistibly to prurient excess. (695)

How, then, are we to understand these – in Stewart's words – "nonproductive desires associated with violence" (694) and the attraction, but also the abhorrence, of readers to them? Why is so much textual time spent giving those excessively bloody details that are irrelevant to the scientific business of detection? Do such excesses again signify (for the reader) some psychological compensation for a "behavioural regime" (696) that restricts human behavior, in terms of day-to-day social practice, into its most productive channels?

There are no easy answers to these questions, and any explanation of the popularity of crime writing – and of crime fiction in particular – will be complicated, multi-faceted, and sometimes paradoxical, and will take in various types of historical, sociological, and psychological circumstance. My intention in this book is to indicate some of the elements responsible for such a popularity, but in the knowledge that there is no simple or straightforward key to be found. Stewart's focus on New York in the 1850s and the conditions and pressures of its everyday life is, though, suggestive in indicating the importance to crime writing both of the rise of the city and of the living and working conditions of those situated within a fast-modernizing Western capitalist system. This is not, however, to say that all such writing must be urban-based (for that is patently wrong) nor that a modernized Western economy is a necessary condition for its production. But it is to suggest that city life – its institutional structures, its economic life, and its policing – are vital factors in the development and importance of the genre.

Crime fiction writer Austin S. Camacho (2008) points out on the "Criminal Minds at Work" website (run by a group of crime novelists) that the present enormous popularity of the crime fiction genre is a relatively recent phenomenon: "Did you know," he asks,

> that crime novels account for somewhere between 20 and 25 percent of the fiction sold around the world? At least what's published in English. It makes you wonder why books about murder and other evils that men do are so popular . . . . The popularity of crime fiction is a fairly recent phenomenon.

20 or 30 years ago, you didn't see crime novels on the bestseller list. Today they regularly account for half of it. But what accounts for this love of mystery fiction?

We are reminded here that the appeal of popular fictional genres changes in response to particular historical circumstances. This is true both of novels and films, with – in that latter case – Hollywood centrally involved in such a process. Thus, the western, for example, was at the peak of its popularity from the late 1940s to the early 1960s – a period in which the belief that it had been white America's historical destiny to spread westward across the continent, with a continued mission (both home and abroad) to defend and protect liberty, family, and democracy against whatever outside threat might appear, still (mostly) retained its currency. In turn, horror fiction, and particularly film, saw a period of ascendancy in the 1970s and 1980s, a period when the promise of American society was undermined by a whole series of cultural and political tensions, and when the sanctity and importance of the family (taken for granted in the western), its patriarchal assumptions, and its role in maintaining the status quo were subject to searing critique. Clearly the relationship between social and political realities on a transnational (as well as purely North American) scale and the changing popularity of generic tastes in fiction and film is a complex business and, in considerable part, beyond the scope of this book. The present popularity of crime fiction cannot, however, be divorced from such factors.

If I were to start to identify some of the reasons for such an upsurge, I would point to a whole range of factors concerning our (as readers) contemporary sense of identity and social agency; our understanding of gender, both masculinity and femininity, and the roles we attribute to each; our fears and vulnerabilities as far as our physical bodies are concerned; our larger sense of the social networks that position us, and the relationship accordingly played out between individual autonomy and the power of the state; our attitudes to lawlessness and the law, and the relationships of both to the greater social compact and our awareness of the tensions and injustices that exist there; and our anxieties about the power of officialdom and its supervisory authority. What I basically suggest here is that crime fiction confronts the problems of the everyday world in which we live as directly as any form of writing can. It allows its readers – though sometimes indirectly and obliquely – to engage with their deepest social concerns, their most fundamental anxieties about themselves and their surrounding world. This engagement, though, can vary in intensity, and vary too in any explicit recognition by the reader of its presence.

At its most basic level, crime fiction works as a highly accessible fictional form and one that functions best in the grip it holds on its reader in terms of basic narrative structure. Who is the criminal and how will he or she get caught? Will the victim – where a living victim is involved – escape the criminal's clutches? How will the detective or police team solve the mystery established in the text? For many readers any further social or cultural resonance a text may have will remain below their conscious radar and unexplored – and none the worse for that. As a critic, however, my intention is to explore those further levels, (hopefully) to assist those who read this book to see something more of the cultural value and importance of the genre.

Part 2

The Politics, Main Forms, and Key Concerns of Crime Fiction

The Politics of Crime Fiction

*The door was invented by the bourgeoisie to protect the individual;
now it becomes a threat; one is advised never to turn the key. . . . This
is the totalitarian aspiration towards a transparent society: "My dear
fellow," says Holmes to Watson, "if we could fly out that great
window hand in hand, hover over this great city, gently remove the
roofs, and peep in at the queer things which are going on . . . " ("Case
of Identity"). Holmes exists because Peter Pan does not: it is not yet
possible to fly through keyholes.*

Franco Moretti, "Clues" (1983: 136)

There are many ways of approaching crime fiction. Here, I focus on an
issue of central importance to the way crime fiction works and the cultural
issues it engages. While I refer to a number of critics working in the field
(and to the work of Franco Moretti in particular), my intention is not to
weigh down my argument with too much theoretical matter, nor to give a
comprehensive overview of the critical writing on this subject. I rather
highlight ways of thinking about the politics of crime fiction that I have
found useful, in the hope that this will start to open up the area in productive
ways for others, too. I return in more detail to some of the topics raised in this
chapter as the book continues.

Franco Moretti's chapter "Clues" in his book *Signs Taken for Wonders*
(1983) provides a good starting point for thinking about crime fiction and its
social and political implications. For one of the most productive ways of
thinking about the genre is its relationship to the dominant social system: to
the hierarchies, norms, and assumptions of the particular area, country, and
historical period it represents, and to the power and authority of the state

The Crime Fiction Handbook, First Edition. Peter Messent.
© 2013 John Wiley & Sons, Ltd. Published 2013 by John Wiley & Sons, Ltd.

that ultimately upholds that system. To say this is immediately to recognize here a certain slippage. For, on the one hand I am referring to the internalization of a general set of social norms and values that condition day-to-day lives in any given culture: its generally accepted rights and wrongs, its patterns of social organization, and the relationships between the individual, the family, and the larger community. On the other, any allusion to the power of the state is a reminder of the coercive powers – the police, the secret service, the justice system, and law – used by a dominant ruling class to discipline the larger social group and to keep anti-social and/or anti-establishment tendencies in check. To recognize this move between accepted social norms and the machinery of the law, and the varying and often tricky nature of that relationship, is crucial to an understanding of all that now follows.

I see crime fiction as a genre that can be used for conservative ends, to protect and sustain the dominant social order, but that can also (often, paradoxically, at one and the same time) work in a more radical and challenging way. I agree with Catherine Nickerson (1997) that crime fiction is a genre that can release "explosive cultural material" (756); that it is:

> deeply enmeshed with most of the thornier problems of the Victorian, modern, and postmodern eras, including gender roles and privileges, racial prejudice and the formation of racial consciousness, the significance and morality of wealth and capital, and the conflicting demands of privacy and social control.

I would, accordingly, echo her words – that the genre "represent[s] in a generally realistic style the most anxiety-producing issues and narratives of a culture" (744–745).

There may be tendency at this point to say, so what? Isn't this, after all, what we expect from any novel to a lesser or greater extent? This may be true, but what makes the crime fiction genre so distinctive is its direct relationship to the law, and to the fracturing of the social system that it supports and protects. The crucial business of detective fiction (specifically) consists of the solving of crime and the restoration of normality and the rule of law: so, accordingly, Dennis Porter argues that "[i]n a detective story . . . the law itself is never put on trial" (1981: 122). As I later show, this statement is not always true. But, where it *is* the case, how then does the form release its "explosive cultural materials," and can such a release be any more than temporary and provisional before the final containment of the disruptive forces that have been released? There are no hard-and-fast answers to these questions, but it is in the putting and exploring of them that the fascination and the power of crime fiction can be most clearly seen.

Franco Moretti has been praised by John Sutherland (2006: n.p.) for

tak[ing] English studies by the scruff of the neck, refusing to observe the distinctions between high and low literature, between academic and common-reader approaches. He can talk (at machine-gun speed) about Sherlock Holmes and Joyce's Ulysses in the same breath.

I use Moretti's written, not his spoken, work here but one of the reasons I do so is because of that same (refreshing) breakdown of literary categories, one that is at the heart of my own critical enterprise too. This does not mean, however, that Moretti is particularly easy to read and understand. An Italian Marxist by origin, he looks to position crime fiction in its socio-political and historical context. And, in "Clues," he focuses primarily on Sherlock Holmes to show how we can read this master detective as a defender of the status quo, "interested only in *perpetuating* the existing order" (140). "Detective fiction," Moretti writes, "is a hymn to culture's coercive abilities" (143). As this last sentence indicates, his argument may focus on a particular type of crime fiction (he directly mentions Agatha Christie as well as Holmes) but claims a wider application. And he provides (to my mind) a good starting point from which we can move to consider the genre's more radical possibilities – its ideological tensions, its ability to challenge established conventions and norms and to ask questions about the larger condition of the society, its values and systems of authority.

Moretti calls Sherlock Holmes "the great *doctor* of the late Victorians, who convinces them that society is still a great *organism*: a unitary and knowable body." Holmes' "science," he continues, "is none other than the ideology of this organism" (145). The authoritative knowledge of this doctoring figure, then, comes about due to the *"unproblematic"* (144) nature of the relationship between [this] "science" and the larger social order – unproblematic (in Moretti's eyes) because of Holmes' total ("ideological") commitment to that order and to the status quo. Holmes, then, is the controlling figure who, whatever his personal eccentricities, represents established values and can (relatively) easily and clearly solve any crime or "mystery" (145) he faces, because of its exceptional or aberrant quality – its existence as a highly visible sign of discord and disturbance in an otherwise settled and holistic social world.

The assumption underlying the detective stories featuring Holmes and Christie's Hercule Poirot – and, by extension, many other detective protagonists – is that the social body, representing the existing, and desired, good, is always the "innocent" victim (144) of the individual criminal act. And innocence and guilt here are measured, crucially, in terms of the contrast between stereotypical normality (all who live under the umbrella of the dominant value system) and individualism (the sign of danger and of difference, of the failure to conform). Thus, "[i]nnocence is conformity; individuality, guilt. . . . Detective fiction . . . exists expressly to dispel the doubt that guilt might be impersonal, and therefore collective and social" (135).

Society, in such a view, is never guilty. "Because the crime is presented in the form of a mystery [and focusing on the interaction between the criminal and the victim], society is absolved from the start: the solution of the mystery proves its innocence" (145). The two quotes I have just used may sound puzzling, but this is a product of Moretti's rather epigrammatic style. In fact, what he is saying is quite simple: I explain, accordingly, as I go on. Social science has long seen the functioning of society as a complex business, with an "*infinity* of causal factors [conditioning] the occurrence of [any one] individual 'event'" (sociologist Max Weber, qtd. in Moretti 1983: 144). Detective fiction, rather, "aims to keep the relationship between science and society *unproblematic*" (144), to reduce complexity to simplicity. The criminal and the crime he or she commits become, within the framework of genre, as Moretti portrays it, the *only relevant cause* of social upset. There is little interest in what may cause criminality, nor in the energies released in a fast-modernizing social world that might affect that world's ("organic") unity and settled hierarchies – and that in reality make any type of full and proper social control problematic, even "impossible" (143). So, for instance:

> Money is always the motive of crime in detective fiction, yet the genre is wholly silent about *production*: that unequal exchange between labour-power and wages which is the true source of social wealth. . . . The indignation about what is rotten and immoral in the economy must concentrate on . . . phenomena [such as] . . . thefts, con-jobs, frauds, false pretences, and so on. . . . As for the factory – it is innocent, and thus free to carry on. (139)

The rightness, justice, and value of the everyday social world – the world of stereotype, conformity, fitting-in, de-individualization – is taken for granted here. The possibility that there may exist exactly in that world a site for enquiry into warping injustice, and even forms of violence, is occluded by the genre's focus on the wholly exceptional individual act. So, Moretti asks us to think about Agatha Christie's *The Mysterious Affair at Styles* (published in 1921 but written in 1916), claiming that in the detective novel anything "*repeatable* and *obvious*" cannot, of its very nature, "be criminal" or worth investigating. So, accordingly, "Agatha Christie's first book is set at the same time as the massacres of the Great War, yet the only murder of interest occurs on the second floor of Styles Court" (135). Flaws and failures in the Western (capitalist) socio-political order are ignored, in other words, in favor of single individual acts that threaten the status quo and, most especially, the lives, money, and property of the privileged classes.

There is an obvious Marxist thrust to this analysis (the "innocent" factory), and also a Foucaultian one. (Fuller discussion of Foucault will wait until my chapter on "Vision, Supervision, and the City.") All I need to say in terms of the latter here is that Moretti associates Sherlock Holmes, even despite his unofficial status, with the notion of the policing and the *supervision* of society (my emphasis). A major issue at stake is that of privacy – directly related to the already-mentioned subject of individualism. Liberal ideology believes in the right and benefit of a certain individual "'freedom from' . . . the interference of society" (136). This assumption is challenged and reversed (so Moretti argues) in detective fiction, where the locked door – a favored traditional motif in the genre – no longer signifies that protective barrier behind which the citizen can exercise this freedom and his or her individual difference. Rather, the genre "treats every element of individual behavior that desires secrecy as an offence" (135–136). Such secrecy is seen as a threat to the controlling authority of the doctoring state and its representatives – an evasion of conformity and full social belonging (Moretti argues that Holmes' own individualism is suppressed in the service of his detective work). Such secrecy, too, is posited as the unwelcome opponent of society's need for transparency and the benefits of that supervisory authority that the detective represents. This is why, in the introductory quote to this chapter, Moretti alludes to Holmes as a Peter Pan figure, able to keep a controlling eye on the whole panorama of urban space and seemingly able even to peer into locked private rooms. This, too, is why he describes detective fiction as that hymn to a culture's "coercive abilities," and the detective himself as "the figure of the state in the guise of 'night watchman,'" whose limited role lies in "assuring respect for laws" (154–155).

I have spent some time on Moretti because he offers the type of sociological perspective on crime fiction rarely encountered elsewhere, and one that is powerful and provocative in its implications. Moretti also discusses the *narrative structure* of the type of detective fictions on which he focuses, seeing this structure as confirming the conservative nature of the form. I use Agatha Christie's *The Mysterious Affair at Styles* to provide my own textual example as prelude and bolster to Moretti's more abstract arguments. The murder of Mrs. Inglethorp, the crime that drives Christie's novel, occurs early on – in chapter three – of the novel. The rest of the book is dedicated to the investigation and solution of this mystery. In essence, then, the whole unfolding textual process focuses around, and takes us back to, this early narrative point as Poirot works out who committed this crime and why, and explores the time before, and leading up to, the murder to uncover the sequence of events that caused it. Ultimately, his detective work restores the social order as it existed *before* that crime occurred, with everything once more in its former proper place – though, of course, with victim and criminal now removed. In fact, not only does Poirot do this, he also manages to repair certain fissures previously affecting this "orderly and hierarchical world," returning "the Inglethorp fortune to its rightful owners, [and] . . . restor [ing] conjugal happiness to the marriage of John and Mary Cavendish" (Malgrem 2010: 154–155).

There is, to put this another way, little interest in character development here. What we have instead – and this takes us back to my earlier point – is a world of stereotypes: a cast of "innocent" characters marked out as such by their social and cultural conformity. These stereotypes, for Moretti, only "come alive" (137), take on visibility and importance, when the crime that ruptures the smooth pattern of this social world is committed. The whole thrust of the detective novel, then, is *"to restore an earlier state of things"* (Freud, qtd. in Moretti: 137), to "[r]einstate a previous situation, return to the beginning" – in Christie's case to a relatively unchanging, privileged, and upper-class English country-house existence. The movement of the narrative of detection is regressive, "from crime to prelude" (Moretti 1983: 137). There is no growth to this story: "In detective fiction, as in law, history assumes importance only as *violation* and as such, must be ultimately repressed. . . . [T]he ideal is for nothing to happen" (138–139).

Moretti's description of the way in which Doyle's and Christie's detective fiction supports and endorses the status quo, and how the backward-looking structure of the genre endorses this political and social vision, is generally convincing. It makes one of the strongest cases for the reactionary nature of the form, and stands as one pole in any exploration of the way the genre works. But Moretti ignores hard-boiled crime fiction in his essay. And, in the conventional critical view, it is here that the other pole to his way of seeing detective fiction is to be found – where anxieties about the existing social order are much more apparent, and where such anxieties are reflected, too, in its different narrative structure. I show how this argument works before then suggesting that, if the opposition constructed here between two types of crime writing – one at the conservative end of the spectrum, the other challenging the social status quo – contains a general truth, we should be wary of simplification, of falling into an overly reductive way of thinking. To categorize in this way does not do full justice to what is a much more complicated and diverse generic panorama.

I return at this point to Nickerson's comment on the genre's ability to express "explosive cultural material." Holmes may be seen as protecting the health of the Victorian social organism, reinforcing its conventional patterns and practices through his detective work. But, by the 1920s, and in the United States, his role as a "consulting detective" (Doyle 1981a: 23), working out of intellectual interest rather than material need, had been replaced by that of the professional private eye or detective, working to make a living: in the case of Raymond Chandler's Philip Marlowe, "twenty-five dollars a day and expenses" (Chandler 1979: 94). And the detective's relation to the dominant social order had taken a different turn: serving as an individual example of (by and large) honesty and integrity in a modernized urban world generally associated with greed, chicanery, and political corruption. The notion of the social system as a healthy organism was by now, and in this modern American environment, nothing but a bad joke. The crime novel became, instead, a tool to dissect society's flaws and failures, and to expose the wrong turns that a capitalist economy, and the political structures to which it was allied, had taken. The strained relationship between the protagonist and his surrounding social world took on a highly critical – and sometimes radical – edge here, as "the significance and morality of wealth and capital" was held up for serious, and usually damning, review.

I illustrate my meaning here through a reading of Dashiell Hammett's *Red Harvest* (1929), a novel that set the benchmark for such hard-boiled crime fiction. I am aware of the mismatch in setting my earlier summary of a particular critical approach against a text-based analysis. But I see this as the best way to make an argument that persists, in a variety of ways, throughout this book. The tone of *Red Harvest* is set by the laconic and cynical wit of its narrator, whose only identity, the Continental Op, is determined, significantly, by his professional role as an employee of the Continental Detective Agency. Entering the city of Personville (or Poisonville, as it has come to be known), the Op describes what he sees:

> an ugly city of forty thousand people, set in an ugly notch between two ugly mountains that had been all dirtied up by mining. Spread over this was a grimy sky that looked as if it had come out of the smelters' stacks.
>
> The first policeman I saw needed a shave. The second had a couple of buttons off his shabby uniform. The third stood . . . directing traffic, with a cigar in one corner of his mouth. After that I stopped checking them up. (9)

Physical description quickly takes on a metaphorical cast here, as the urban landscape and its industry are associated with pollution, a spreading stain affecting every feature of the natural environment that frames it. And the swift move from the city to its law enforcers and their casual and slapdash turnout and behavior immediately prepares us for a civic world in which things are very much awry. The fact that the narrator is a stranger to the town where he is now to be employed, and describes it from that perspective, implies the absence of any strong commitment to its norms and values on his part, and suggests, instead, a certain self-protective wariness of the world he is about to enter.

The first thing that happens to the Op in Personville is that Donald Willsson, the liberal and reformist local newspaper publisher who has paid for his services (but whom he has not yet met) is murdered. The Op quickly finds out that Personville is a city riddled with corruption, violence, and criminality. This situation had its original cause in a labor dispute between the local miners, supported by the IWW (International Workers of the World) and Elihu Willsson, Donald's father, "the man who had owned Personville, heart, soul, skin and guts . . . president of . . . the Personville Mining Corporation, ditto of the First National Bank, owner of the . . . city's only newspapers" (13). Political, industrial, and financial power and a press monopoly are, then, figured in this one man. In order to break the resulting strike, Elihu had "hired gunman, strike-breakers, national guardsmen and even parts of the regular army." But, in defeating the miners and the "wobblies" (the slang name for the radical IWW) supporting them, Elihu "lost his hold on the city and the state. To beat the miners he had to let his hired thugs run wild. When the fight was over he couldn't get rid of them. . . . [T]hey took [Personville] over" (14). Donald had been unwittingly set up by his father to start a reform campaign in the town, and thus potentially to drive out its power-sharing criminal element. With his death, the Op takes up Elihu's challenge to "clean this pig-sty of a Poisonville for me, to smoke out the rats," but on his own less melodramatic terms: "If you've got a fairly honest piece of work to be done in my line, and you want to pay a decent price, maybe I'll take it on. . . . But I'm not playing politics for you. . . . [Y]ou're going to get a complete job or nothing" (38, 40).

There are already a number of things to be said here. Hammett gives us an exaggerated parable of the U. S. industrial and political complex (as he saw it) in the representation of Personville. Everyday normality and social life is conspicuous by its absence as he focuses almost solely on issues of politics, power, and criminality. The hostility of capitalism to labor is endorsed by the larger state apparatus – Elihu's use of the national guard and army to break the strike. The final impotence of labor against such institutional odds, and in the violence of the conflict that occurs, is accordingly pretty much inevitable, whatever the justice of its case and strength of its campaign: "When the last skull had been cracked . . . organized labor in Personville was a used firecracker" (14). Elihu's reliance (in part) on state power, as well as the knowledge that he "owned a United States senator, a couple of representatives, the governor, the mayor, and most of the state legislature" (13), make it clear that the civic issues Hammett engages extend well beyond Personville's city limits.

The view of "the kind of capitalist state personified by Elihu Willsson's Personville/Poisonville" (Pepper 2010a: 145), then, is a bleak one. Willsson is the untrustworthy father figure (for the personal, when it does briefly appear, endorses the political), one who wishes once more to have complete authority as "Czar" (15) over his city, as well as over the son he uses "for his monkey" (14). Labor and the rights of common working men have been rendered irrelevant in this America, where they are judged merely a hindrance to the larger operations of the economic and institutional system. As the Op enters the scene and begins "stirring things up" (70), we are shown a city in which the police are open to bribery ("Buy us a get-away, Jerry. . . . A uniformed copper held the back gate open," 48) and where the police chief, Noonan, is hand in glove with gangsters involved in a variety of illicit activities – Pete the Finn (illegal liquor), Max Thaler (gambling), and Lew Yard (stolen goods). And these are the three men who, alongside Willsson and Noonan, both run the town and "own the courts" (95). As Noonan tells the Op, explaining the nature of the resulting alliances, "I got to play with them that play with me. See what I mean?" (81).

In this poisonous atmosphere, the Op himself – as he looks to open the town up "from Adam's apple to ankles" (55) as a way of cleaning it up – is himself metaphorically "poisoned" (123). Playing a game of deceit and double-cross, he gets caught up in the mayhem around him, becomes party to the killings involved, and even finds himself "getting a rear out of planning deaths" (123), going "blood simple like the natives" (121). He is also implicated in the death of Dinah Brand, the one person for whom he has a genuine emotional attachment. Indeed, initially, he fears that it is he himself who has buried the "six-inch needle-sharp blade" of the ice-pick she owns (128) in her breast. Hammett is representing a world here in which decent intent, and the actions that follow from it, are swiftly and inevitably compromised. He also shows that – in a situation where the normal checks and balances (the press, labor organizations) have failed, and where law is bought and sold (attorney-at-law, Charles Proctor Dawn, is "the guy that the joke was wrote about: 'Is he a criminal lawyer?' 'Yes, very,'" 144) – it is only the Op's pragmatic individualism, however morally suspect it then becomes, that can have any effect in addressing the general corruption. The irony is, of course – and here we come to the rub of so much crime fiction – that all the Op can finally do is to restore the previous, and highly unsatisfactory, status quo as the national guard are once more called in, and the Op finally gives Personville back into Elihu Willsson's hands, "all nice and clean and ready to go to the dogs again" (157). But Willsson himself is implicated in the general criminality – the material his son had obtained just before his death "would have put his old man in jail with the rest of them" (35). He has, too, it seems, both initially obtained and held on to his autocratic power in this town by similar illegal and/or immoral methods. When the Op calls him an "old pirate," he replies, "Son, if I hadn't been a pirate I'd still be working for the Anaconda [the Anaconda Copper Mining Company] for wages, and there'd be no Personville Mining Corporation" (119).

What we then see in Hammett's brilliant novel is a clear illustration of the deep anxieties about capitalism and political and economic power, and their relation to corruption and violent criminality, in late 1920s America. And, if the Continental Op finds his own sense of moral integrity highly compromised in his attempt to bring some kind of order to the "damned burg" (121) in which he works, that does not affect his distaste for both its original, and its final, governance. Nor does it affect his final re-establishment of his day-to-day professional role at a clear remove from the extreme actions and personal compromises to which it has led him in this particular case. Andrew Pepper, one of the most perceptive critics of Hammett's work, sees the writer's "dark vision" here as anticipating such writers as Chester Himes and James Ellroy, and suggests two possible readings of the book's final message:

> [I]nsofar as [Hammett's] own politics would take a more radical turn in the decade following the publication of *Red Harvest*, it might be possible to read the anger that lies behind the Op's rhetoric [at the end of the novel] not simply as an expression of nihilistic despair but also as a spur to action on the part of his readers. That said, given the expanded nature and reach of state power in the novel, one could just as well see and read [it] as a harbinger of the kind of even more repressive constellations of political and economic power characteristic of the post-Second World War era.
>
> (Pepper 2010b: 349)

We see here, then, a gap between the role of the individual detective and his values and the socio-political status quo that is very different to the complementary relationship Moretti establishes in Doyle's and Christie's case. Moreover, here, and in hard-boiled detective fiction generally, we see a very different formal structure employed. The classical detective story, as previously discussed, is backward-looking, with the detective engaged in solving a crime (usually) committed either before or soon after the chronological start of the text – and with much of its focus on his or her analytic skills in recovering and recreating the backstory of that crime and the motives of the criminal(s) involved. Knight refers to it aptly as "the death-detection-explanation model" (2004: 136). The hard-boiled crime novel is progressive rather than regressive, tracing an ongoing chain of violent criminal action, the way it proliferates, and its relationship to a contaminated larger social body, rather than foregrounding the exceptional and relatively discrete nature of the (often) single criminal act as in the classical case. To some degree at least, then, and certainly in Hammett's case, the way the hard-boiled works reflects its different political positioning. There is much more emphasis, too, on the detective protagonist's involvement in the ongoing and violent action at the text's center, rather than on his ability to stand separately, at one analytic remove from that world. I will return to this in my next chapter.

Hammett's novel, though, can tell us more about how the formal differences between the two types of detective fiction work. In *Red Harvest*, the initial case, the murder of Donald Willsson, is in fact relatively swiftly solved – as a crime of passion. Albury, an assistant cashier at the First National Bank, has misunderstood the nature of the check Willsson has taken to Dinah Brand (whom Albury himself is "cuckoo over," 51) as a sign of romantic involvement between the two, in accordance with Dinah's reputation as a "strictly pay-as-you-enter" (28) woman. In fact, the money is a pay-off for information given on the criminal corruption in the town. But, by the time this one case is solved and the murderer revealed, we have started to move on to that latter and larger intrigue, with the Op already hired by Elihu for his clean-up job. And it is as he acts to fulfill this contract that he gets caught up in the city's violence and deceit, foments and manipulates more of it for his own final ends (to cleanse the town), and causes the body count to escalate accordingly. The Op is right in the middle of the action here, making sense of what happens as best he can – and at times losing the ability to do so – on a pragmatic moment-by-moment basis. The brevity of Hammett's action-packed chapters entirely suit this process (and would provide a highly influential model for future crime fictions).

As I have said, the one person with whom the Op has a personal relationship of any intimacy, Dinah Brand, is caught up in the chain of violence he instigates and is herself murdered. Chapter twenty-one, in which her death occurs, is titled "The Seventeenth Murder," reducing her to just another statistic as the town is "bust[ed] . . . open" (118). And more deaths are to follow. This sense of rapidly developing, and often confusing, ongoing action, and the denial of the reflective calm and lack of personal involvement so common in its classical form, make up a large part of hard-boiled crime fiction's distinctive difference.

We can then arrive at some general conclusions. Hard-boiled crime fiction is more likely to release "explosive cultural materials" – those that raise direct and challenging questions about the values of the dominant social order and our status both as individuals and community members within it – than its classical equivalent. The very forms of the two types of fiction, what is more, facilitate these different effects. This general political difference between the classical and hard-boiled variants of detective fiction stands as a foundation point for much of the discussion that follows, and mirrors the basic chronological development of the genre. In the remainder of this chapter, though, I add a series of necessary qualifications to the rather black-and-white reading of the genre, and the concentration on – and separation of – its two main variants I have thus far given, even as I remain committed to the general truth above.

The first thing to say here is that simply to oppose the politics of classical and hard-boiled detective fiction in the way I have so far done is far too simple. We have learned in a post-structuralist age to distrust stark oppositions – binary readings of the world – and crime fiction is no exception to this rule. Hard-and-fast rules about the politics of crime fiction are extremely difficult to make. Texts following a hard-boiled model may, as I have argued, have more obvious potential for radical social commentary than those in the classical tradition. But, as Lee Horsley comments, and writing about all forms of the crime novel:

> The genre itself is neither inherently conservative nor radical: rather, it is a form that can be co-opted for a variety of purposes. There has always been within it a capacity for socio-political comment, and using it in this way is facilitated by the very nature of crime fiction. . . . [T]he genre itself contains characteristics that lend themselves to political and oppositional purposes. (2005: 158–159)

I agree with this, even as I distinguish between the different political potential of the classical and hard-boiled forms.

It is at this point that I recall Pepper's comments on the ending of *Red Harvest* and the two possible responses to it: that it might act as a spur to individual political action to oppose political and economic corruption; or that it might simply serve to confirm the way things are – the repressive nature of state power in the modern age, and our general inability to do much about it. In other words, while there is much about the novel we can read as "oppositional," there is nonetheless a counter-movement that is more accommodating to the status quo. This contradiction is a repeated characteristic of crime fiction novels of all types. So even here – in a novel written by a writer with known left-wing sympathies and that depicts a particularly morally and politically dysfunctional urban reality – the detective ends up restoring the prior social order more or less as it existed before the crimes that he investigates were committed, with only a very qualified possibility for social change (dependant, if we follow Pepper, on the political response of the individual reader). Classical and hard-boiled crime fiction, then, share a final underlying formal similarity. While differences may exist in terms of the *explicit recognition* on the part of any one or other writer of the problematic nature of the social reality he or she depicts, and in her or his *commitment to (or disaffiliation from) the existing socio-political order*, this generally has little influence on the final narrative results, as the status quo, however unsatisfactory, is restored. Criminal and anti-social activity occurs only (normally) for the immediate problem(s) to be resolved, with little or nothing having been done to alter the dominant social reality and whatever the faults there evident. This pattern is present in almost all variants of the crime fiction genre and tends consequently to mute some of the political differences between them.

Indeed, simply to contrast a hard-boiled crime writing (generally American) that challenges the existing social order with a classical detective tradition (generally British) whose conservative politics finds a mirror in the formal strategies it uses is, again, too reductive. Hard-boiled American fiction can certainly work to conservative ends, as any number of examples illustrate (Ed McBain and Joseph Wambaugh jump to mind). Similarly, it is difficult to imagine any type of detective novel – classical or hard-boiled, American or British – that does not explore the cultural anxieties of its time and place, and in a way that challenges (though to varying degrees) the existing social order. So, Doyle's Sherlock Holmes is not just the figure Moretti makes him, totally committed to the ideologies and social structures of his Victorian period, but also himself contains "almost uncontainable contradictions" and self-divisions (Horsley 2005: 31) that reflect back accordingly, and in a critical way, on the society in which he lives. And, in twinning him with his arch-enemy Moriarty and in giving both men similar characteristics, Doyle anticipates other such doublings across the crime fiction spectrum (as that of Will Graham and Hannibal Lecter in Thomas Harris' 1981 novel, *Red Dragon*) that undermine the clarity of the boundaries between a social virus and its doctoring vaccine.

That nostalgically conservative glow, too, that is so often associated with Agatha Christie's fiction is not without its complications: that glow is unsettled, at least in part, in its gentle challenge (in the Miss Marple stories) to fixed and conventional gender roles; unsettled, too, in "the . . . frisson of anxiety" that comes from

> the deadly potential embedded in even the most mundane domestic situation. Parents, children, spouses all prove to be lethal family members, while apparent bastions of society – doctors, politicians, wealthy manufacturers . . . – could also be dangerous. Christie's texts assume that anyone can be a murderer, no one is exempt, no one totally to be trusted.
>
> (Makinen 2010: 417)

The whole fabric of inter-war English social life is, in fact, more precariously balanced than a first and superficial reading of Christie's work might suggest (see, especially, Light 1991; Peach 2006). Gill Plain identifies clear structural and thematic similarities shared by Christie's and Chandler's work that tend to blur any too-firm boundaries between their supposed "conservative feminine and ground-breaking masculine" difference (see Horsley 2005: 68). Not all classical detective novels, either, are as formally alike as Moretti suggests. For a good number of such texts "disrupt such apparently predictable elements as the reliable narrator and the reliably 'fixed' triangle of characters – detective, victim, criminal" (Horsley 2005: 41). A good number, too, do address the "thornier problems" of their historical period even when their central narrative thrust is, to recall Moretti, "*to restore an earlier state of things.*" I explore such issues further in the cases of both Doyle and Christie later in this book.

The boundaries containing the two forms (classical and hard-boiled) are then – to a certain degree – permeable. A number of critics indeed have questioned the accuracy of classifying types of crime fiction in this way in the first place. They suggest that to do so is over-dependent on, and under-critical of, Raymond Chandler, who used his highly influential essay "The Simple Art of Murder" (1944) (see my next chapter) as "a way of positioning the American model as being more truth-telling and indeed more masculine" than its British counterpart (Knight 2004: 111). They point, too, to the distortions that result in focusing on key figures such as Doyle and Christie, Hammett and Chandler, who represent only a fraction of the full range and variety of the crime novel and who bring an occluded timescale to its critical history.

While I recognize all these things, and despite such reservations, I stick to my earlier argument: that hard-boiled fiction was (primarily) an American form of writing, dating from the late 1920s and 1930s, that offered much more of an explicit challenge to the social and political status quo than its (mainly British) classical detective counterpart. As Horsley says: "Whereas the golden age writers [Christie et al.] can be said to have created detective fiction that *encodes* the socio-political anxieties of their time, hard-boiled writers addressed the problems of their society explicitly" (Horsley 2005: 68). But – and this is crucial – as time has passed, the contours of crime fiction have changed. As they have done so, generic lines of division have blurred, at the same time as different variants of the genre have developed and flourished. Accordingly, the very terms "classical" and "hard-boiled" have come to be, to a certain degree, outmoded. We are, however, still able to identify – to varying degrees – crime novels in such terms, and judge their politics accordingly. Even if Conan Doyle and Agatha Christie's novels illustrate anxieties about the traditional social order, they remain committed to it. And the gap in social vision between their fiction and that of Dashiell Hammett remains enormous. So, in a more recent period, we see a similar gap between (say) P. D. James and James Ellroy. The hard-boiled texts of Hammett and Ellroy (and those who write in their mould) provide the deeper and much more damning critique of the social world they represent and have by far the greater political "bite."

But I want to return here to another earlier point: that to talk of crime fiction in terms of two variants, the classical and hard-boiled detective novels (however important these two forms are), is reductive. The astute reader will already have noticed the fuzziness of my terminology thus far: I have introduced the very term "detective fiction" in a rather one-dimensional way, and have used it interchangeably with the wider generic label "crime fiction." I address this issue further in my next chapter. But, for now, I need to widen and clarify my definitional boundaries, for crime fiction is more various than I have thus far suggested, and to qualify my previous analysis accordingly.

First, and this connects with what I have just said about the historical development of the genre, the type and number of detective fictions that have been written have (unsurprisingly) changed over time. The detective writing I have so far mainly been discussing features the private – amateur or professional – detective, who may or may not ally himself with the police, but who is not a policeman, is not employed by the state. But we also need to take into account the category of the police novel – a form of crime fiction that became increasingly popular from the 1950s onward. It would be easy to assume that here – where crime is solved by what we might clumsily call the apparatus of the state – that the more conservative implications of crime writing would become increasingly and necessarily apparent. For, in such fiction, the system of law and its representatives are, in theory, one and the same, with established institutions and social norms protected and upheld by the policemen and women featured in such texts.

In England, Colin Dexter's *Inspector Morse* series (1975–1999) provides a good example of such a model, modified only (as is not unusual in such texts) by Morse's personal eccentricities and curmudgeonly anti-authoritarian atti- tudes. It may also be significant that Dexter's conservative use of the police novel form connects strongly with the classical detective tradition of Conan Doyle and Christie. His emphasis on a picture-postcard hierarchical and traditional Oxford world where Morse tackles the case on which he works (in *The Jewel that Was Ours*) "like some fiendishly devised crossword" (Dexter 2007: 141) confirms the nature of such a connection, and its difference from the rawness and ever-present violence of the hard-boiled form.

The police novel is necessarily structured around the protection and re-establishing of the existing social order. It can, however, still be used to challenge that status quo – and increasingly has been. The best explanation for this apparent paradox lies in the powerful effect that the hard-boiled tradition has had on so many authors working in this field – its gritty realism where violence and corruption are part and parcel of society as a whole and in which the police themselves are affected, and often infected, by such forces. The ten novels (1965–1975) by Maj Sjöwall and Per Wahlöö, written to expose the social and political fissures and failings of the Sweden of their time, were to prove highly influential here. (For, as I have already suggested, we cannot just identify the classical form with British and European fiction and the hard-boiled with American. Both traditions have had their wider transnational influence.) The connection Andrew Pepper makes (mentioned earlier) between Hammett and police novel writer James Ellroy is also highly suggestive. For, Ellroy, in his *LA Quartet*, exposes a deeply depraved system of male-driven economic, social, and political authority and power even while he confirms its continuing corrupt vitality.

But there is another main form of crime writing that is still unmentioned – one that is not police or private detective (private eye) fiction, and in which we shift away from a narrative structured round the process of detection to one driven by the *actions and motivations of the criminal*, and what then follows from them. Scaggs calls such novels crime or noir thrillers (2005: 105–121); Horsley, "literary noir" (2010: 39); Knight, "the crime novel" (2004: 125). Unsurprisingly, given the focus put on the figure of the transgressor here, such fictions tend to foreground flaws and insufficiencies in the social fabric and possible reasons for individual alienation rather than the beneficial value of the dominant social order and its operating structures. But a curious, though understandable, double logic (similar to that found so widely in the crime fiction genre as a whole as to become almost a condition of its production) often operates in these texts too. For the exposure of fractures in the social compact here, too, tends to go hand in hand with the firm re-establishing of the disrupted status quo at the text's end (though see Patricia Highsmith's Ripley novels for a notable exception). Thus, the radical potential of such novels is – usually – cancelled out in their closures. I return to many of the issues considered above in the readings of individual novels in the final part of this book.

The Types of Crime Fiction

In this chapter, I build on what I have said previously as I lay out – and define more directly – the different categories into which crime fiction can be divided. I then go on, in the remainder of Part 2, to identify certain key topics central to the genre, and to explicate their importance.

Classical Detective Fiction

The mental features discoursed of as the analytical are, in themselves, but little susceptible of analysis. We appreciate them only in their effects. . . . As the strong man exults in his physical ability, delighting in such exercises as call his muscles into action, so glories the analyst in that moral activity which *disentangles*. He derives pleasure from even the most trivial occupations bringing his talent into play. He is fond of enigmas, of conundrums, of hieroglyphics; exhibiting in his solutions of each a degree of *acumen* which appears to the ordinary apprehension praeternatural. His results, brought about by the very soul and essence of method, have, in truth, the whole air of intuition.
(Edgar Allan Poe, "The Murders in the Rue Morgue," 2000: 527–528)

In "The Murders in the Rue Morgue" (1841), the first in a series of three detective stories featuring C. Auguste Dupin, Poe sets the ground for Sherlock Holmes and for the classical detective story as a form. The disquisition on the analytical ("the very soul and essence of method") is one of a piece with Holmes' description of his "exact science" at the start of *The Sign of Four*. So Holmes, too – like Dupin (as Poe's narrator describes him) – derives his pleasure from bringing his talents into play:

"My mind," [Holmes] said, "rebels at stagnation. Give me problems, give me work, give me the most abstruse cryptogram, or the most intricate analysis, and

The Crime Fiction Handbook, First Edition. Peter Messent.
© 2013 John Wiley & Sons, Ltd. Published 2013 by John Wiley & Sons, Ltd.

I am in my own proper atmosphere. . . . But I abhor the dull routine of existence. I crave for mental exaltation. That is why I have chosen my own particular profession, or rather created it, for I am the only one in the world."

"The only unofficial detective?" [Watson] said, raising my eyebrows.

"The only unofficial consulting detective," he answered. "I am the last and highest court of appeal in detection. When Gregson, or Lestrade, or Athelney Jones are out of their depths – which, by the way, is their normal state – the matter is laid before me. I examine the data, as an expert, and pronounce a specialist's opinion. I claim no credit in such cases. My name figures in no newspaper. The work itself, the pleasure of finding a field for my peculiar powers, is my highest reward.

(Doyle 2001: 6–7)

The direct line from Poe to Doyle is obvious here. So the unnamed narrator in Poe's tales fills the same function as Watson, narrating the cases that his detective friend takes on and serving as his companion as he looks to solve them. The analogy Holmes draws between his own work and the cryptogram is similar to the emphasis on the pleasure taken in "enigmas, . . . conundrums, . . . hieroglyphics" that Poe's narrator describes – further elaborated in the later references to draughts and whist (or a card game very similar in kind). The idea here of an amateur or unofficial detective testing his own skills in a ludic manner emphasizes the gap – crucial in this form of the crime novel – between the mental enjoyment and exercise of the detectives and the excessive physical violence of, and emotional disturbances caused by, the crimes he investigates: in "The Murders in the Rue Morgue," one corpse stuffed up a chimney and the other that of an "old lady, with her throat so entirely cut that, upon an attempt to raise her, the head fell off" (538).

This gap between the detective's playful enjoyment – as he or she solves the relevant conundrum – and the serious personal and social consequences of the (often monstrous) criminal act is highlighted in Dorothy L. Sayers' first Lord Peter Wimsey novel, *Whose Body?* (1923), a story very much in the classic detective mode. Discussing the (probable) murder of Sir Reuben Levy (a famous Jewish financier) with Inspector Parker (the Scotland Yard detective with whom he teams up), Wimsey weighs up his mixed feelings: both a liking for and suspicions about a potential suspect, John Milligan. When he confesses that, in doing so, he doesn't feel he is "playing the game somehow," Parker replies: "Look here, Peter, . . . suppose you get this playing-fields-of-Eton complex out of your system once and for all. . . . If Sir Reuben has been murdered, is it a game? and is it fair to treat it as a game?" Wimsey then answers: "That's what I'm ashamed of, really. . . . It *is* a game to me, to begin with, and I go on cheerfully, and then I suddenly see that somebody is going to be hurt, and I want to get out of it" (n.d. [1923]: 157).

The games-playing aspect of the detective's investigations is confirmed later in the same text where the narrator (a stand-in for the author) speaks of the crime or crimes being investigated here as "two grotesque conundrums," and compares them to an anagram. Speaking of two different types of detection, she explains how COSSSSRI is identified as an anagram of SCISSORS either through the trying out of "all the permutations and combinations [of the letters] in turn" or through a more unconscious and instinctive process (166–167). In other texts, such a solving of the puzzle faced by the detective is described in terms of chess (see, for instance, Pérez-Reverté 1990) – though Poe sees draughts and whist as the more accurate analogy, Ellery Queen uses algebra (1947: 251), and so on. While the idea of the detective as a games player is open to moral critique (as indicated in the Lord Peter Wimsey example above), the idea of the investigative case as a mental challenge dependent on quick wits, an analytical mind, and the making of connections, usually within some type of confined spatial limits, is nonetheless crucial to the classical detective form. The detective here is distanced from his investigative material, treating its various pieces (to take one of the previous analogies) as figures on a chess board, to be studied and sometimes made to move.

A good number of such mysteries are, accordingly, of the "locked room" variety, where the corpse is discovered alone in a room with no apparent means of exit (see "The Murders in the Rue Morgue," Doyle's "The Speckled Band," or Christie's *The Mysterious Affair at Styles*) or (in a variant) where one particular enclosed location – a train, for instance, in Christie's 1934 novel *Murder on the Orient Express* – contains both the victim of a crime and all its possible suspects. Such settings intensify this sense of the detective pitting his wits against the killer within certain well-defined boundaries; solving a puzzle that is deliberatively positioned at one remove from the pressures and tensions of an ongoing historical reality. All of this tends to confirm Moretti's analysis of the genre as described in my last chapter.

The sense of a closed ludic territory associated with the classical detective novel is commonly also extended to the implied contract in such fictions between the author and the reader. When we read such a novel, in other words, we too take part in a game with certain fixed rules and procedures. While we recognize that, as readers, we are closer to the obtuse Watsons of this fictional world than the brilliant Holmeses, we nonetheless expect to be able to follow the series of clues that lead from the crime to the exposure of the murderer, and look even to anticipate that detective's final act of criminal unmasking (though, of course, the whole skill of such crime writing is in preventing this from happening). This contract, then, is of an unusual type.

For we expect the classical detective novel to follow certain rules that assure the reader that he or she is engaged in a fair contest with the detective protagonist in the solving of a crime, even while we would be disappointed, and judge the novel a failure, if we reached the correct solution to that puzzle much (if at all) before the detective revealed it.

This sense of generic expectation in the way that the classical crime puzzle works, and the nature of its contract with the reader, has on a number of occasions been formalized into a set of rules – twenty, in the case of American detective writer S. S. Van Dine, writing in 1928. I give just two by way of example:

> The culprit must be determined by logical deductions – not by accident or coincidence or unmotivated confession. To solve a criminal problem in this latter fashion is like sending the reader on a deliberate wild-goose chase, and then telling him, after he has failed, that you had the object of his search up your sleeve all the time. Such an author is no better than a practical joker . . . .

> A detective novel should contain no long descriptive passages, no literary dallying with side-issues, no subtly worked-out character analyses, no "atmospheric" preoccupations. Such matters have no vital place in a record of crime and deduction. They hold up the action, and introduce issues irrelevant to the main purpose, which is to state a problem, analyze it, and bring it to a successful conclusion. To be sure, there must be a sufficient descriptiveness and character delineation to give the novel verisimilitude. (1928: 190–192)

The following year, fellow American Ronald Knox set out his "Detective Story Decalogue" – just ten rules this time. These included the following: "*The detective must not himself commit the crime*" and "The detective must not light on any clues which are not instantly produced for the inspection of the reader" (1946: 196).

There may be a certain irony here in the presence of such rules given that the continued interest and vitality of (any) crime fiction lies in its variation and difference from any too-static and predictable form. But, in fact, this often makes for a productive interplay between formal expectation and its subversion. The fact that the narrator of one of Agatha Christie's most successful novels, *The Murder of Roger Ackroyd* (1926), is also its murderer makes an immediate nonsense of Knox's first rule ("*The criminal must be someone mentioned in the early part of the story, but must not be anyone whose thoughts the reader has been allowed to follow,*" 1946: 194). It is exactly through such rule-bending, though, that the detective novel form has been able to retain its energy and interest.

There is more to be said about classical detective fiction. For the present, though, I keep my further commentary relatively brief and identify just three other aspects of the form. First – and I return here to the earlier Sherlock

Holmes quote – such fiction often portrays a relationship between the private or amateur detective and the official police force (professional detectives Gregson, Lestrade, and Athelney Jones in Holmes' case). The analytic brilliance and ability to think "outside the box" of the detective who is not constrained by institutional boundaries is, accordingly, commonly contrasted, and often to comic ends, with a plodding officialdom: police detectives "out of their depths – which, by the way, is their normal state." This is one of the most common motifs in the classical detective novel, further emphasizing the flair and insight of the detective hero while suggesting a certain lack of confidence in the normal procedures of the law and its administrative routines.

A second thing to note is the way in which classical detective fiction is limited in terms of its spatial and class environments. "Golden Age" detective fiction – the name usually given to British detective fiction written in the period between the two world wars working within the classical tradition – can be set in either a rural or an urban environment, but there is usually little attempt to portray a full social panorama, and such settings are usually very restricted in type. So, Christie is conventionally associated with the British country house murder, an act committed in a well-off setting and for purely private ends, and lacking any connection to the pressing social problems of the day (S. S. Van Dine's rule nineteen reads, "The motives for all crimes in detective stories should be personal," 192). Styles Court in *The Mysterious Affair at Styles*, despite references to the village and farms nearby, is pretty much a self-enclosed entity, inhabited by the upper-middle class, their immediate dependents, and their servants. The map of the house (42) and descriptions of its grounds suggest the privileged nature of the social world we enter here.

Christie, in fact, draws deliberate attention to the house's status as a place apart from the pressures of public history when she has Hastings, her narrator, describe the house's "flat Essex country" setting as "lying so green and peaceful under the afternoon sun, it seemed almost impossible to believe that, not so very far away, a great war was running its appointed course" (13). The fact that Poirot identifies Alfred Inglethorp – an "absolute outsider" to Styles and its family, and marked out by his (villainous) "great black beard" (12) – as the murderer of his wife (in cahoots with his cousin, Evelyn Howard) further confirms the novel's nostalgic attraction for this bounded and attractive social and family space, and confirms too the conservative politics underlying its (temporary) pollution by an invasive and money-grabbing dark and threatening "other."

If the Golden Age detective novel works within well-defined spatial and social boundaries, it also tends to self-reflexivity – a self-conscious awareness of the very tradition it works within. Thus, when Hastings is asked at the beginning of *The Mysterious Affair at Styles* what profession he secretly desires, he says "I've always had a secret hankering to be a detective!" Further asked, "The real thing? – Scotland Yard? Or Sherlock Holmes?" he immediately chooses the latter. His interlocutor, Evelyn Howard, then explicitly comments on the artificiality of the classic detection form: "Like a good detective story myself. . . . Lots of nonsense written, though. Criminal discovered in the last chapter. Every one dumbfounded. Real crime – you'd know at once" (19). Lord Peter Wimsey, too, defines himself in the Holmes tradition. Looking in the mirror as he prepares to take up the case of the dead body in the Battersea bath in *Whose Body?*, he envisions the grey suit he will wear on the job: "enter Sherlock Holmes, disguised as a walking gentleman" (11).

This self-reflexivity carries over to the matter of narrative form, and what Moretti defines as the "anti-novelistic" features of the genre. For the classical detective story (normally) tends to follow well-worn lines, having a simpler basic structure than its hard-boiled variant – and essentially working through the provision of a lengthy delay between the criminal act and its solution. Doctor Watson's narrative role in the Sherlock Holmes stories is paradigmatic here, and is almost exactly reprised by Captain Hastings in Christie's later novels (both, too, share the role of documenting their detective-friend's case histories). Watson's function in the Holmes stories (and this is to complicate the Van Dine "rule" previously quoted) is obfuscatory, and slows the narrative resolution. He is what Moretti would call a "naturalist" writer, holding a mirror up to the world, *"accumulat[ing] useless details"* (147). In other words, Watson describes all the elements of the scene around him but, lacking Holmes' analytic and deductive skills, never sorts out the essential detail from the surrounding irrelevancies. The more he tells us, the less (when it comes to solving the crime) we know. So, Moretti reminds us, Watson carefully spends a couple of pages describing a room in "The Speckled Band," "but he does not even mention the false bell-pull which is the only clue" (1983: 147).

To extend this idea a little, we might also think about how this type of crime fiction makes considerable use of narrative delay in other ways, and through false leads in particular. Moretti suggests that such narratives of detection have "the structure of the short story" (146). For, the move from criminal act to its detection is structurally a very short and simple one. The narrative, though, becomes a novel through all the extra (and – in terms of its final resolution – useless) information we are given, all the red herrings, wrong turns, holdings back of knowledge, and building up of suspense that occur before Holmes or Poirot (in the cases I am speaking of here) cut through the confusion and the excess of detail and information given in the text to solve the mystery; to show the – often simple – relationship between effect (the crime) and cause (its motivation).

Dennis Porter sees a principle of "deliberately impeded form" here (he is quoting from Victor Erlich) – and suggests the "pleasure" on the part of the reader that "results . . . from the repeated postponement of a desired end." The very success of such novels, he argues, depends upon the way in which the author manages to create suspense by balancing the move toward the solution of the puzzle (the progressive) against all the delays that impede that realization – the regressive "crooked path to knowledge" (1981: 30–32, 46). Moretti is less forgiving, seeing a gap between literariness (all the possible motives, suspicions, and possibilities the narrative explores) and the scientific (the clear vision and deductive perspicuity of the detective, able to bypass such a maze). Classic detective fiction then, as Moretti describes it, is *"literature that desires to exorcise literature,"* in that the whole narrative meaning of the text essentially lies in that final moment when the detective ends the "long *wait*" (148) that makes up all the middle part of the book – the narrative delay separating crime and its solution.

I conclude this section with a few brief general points. Thus, if Doyle and Christie both belong within the classical tradition, there are clear differences in the types of spatial and class boundaries represented in their work, and the impact this has on it. The fact that so many of the Sherlock Holmes stories use London as their setting almost inevitably means that a more extensive range of social types is introduced. Additionally, though, and as Martin Kayman points out, "Holmes' London has established itself as stereotypical vision of Victorian London" (2003: 43). More than his Golden Age successors, Sayers and even Christie (who also set some of her fictions in London), Doyle's representation of a modern urban world raises issues of scale, identity, social belonging, and change that impact on the whole range of crime fiction that followed.

It is, similarly, quite possible to see Christie's work in terms of threats to, and fractures in, the established social order. However, her use of "closed" country house settings and their like, and emphasis on family or small group relationships, tends to take attention away from their more subversive potential. So, too, her very foregrounding of the playful potential of the fictional form she uses – her move, for instance, from *Murder on the Orient Express*, with its contrived and confined exotic setting and international cast of characters, to *And Then There Were None* (1939), with its nursery-rhyme echoes, as ten protagonists, the only guests on the novel's island setting, are all one-by-one mysteriously murdered – is very much to downplay any possible socio-historical intent.

In focusing on Poe, Doyle, Christie, and Sayers in this chapter, I leave more or less unmentioned a whole host of other writers working in the classical tradition. Of these, G. K. Chesterton and his Father Brown stories, Michael Innes, Ngaio Marsh, Ellery Queen, Josephine Tey, and S. S. Van Dine are perhaps the best known. All of these writers have their distinctive voices and concerns and would deserve attention in their own right in a longer book than this. So, such differences suggest the dangers of generalizations about the form. We should note, too, that classical detective fiction did not come to an end with Golden Age fiction but continued beyond World War II, and indeed to the present time. Writers such as Colin Dexter, Erle Stanley Gardner, Elizabeth George, P. D. James, and Ruth Rendell – among many others – all take elements from, and are clearly influenced by, the tradition. But crime fiction has changed enormously since the 1920s and 1930s, increasingly influenced by the hard-boiled form, the police novel, and a changing social and moral landscape. Criminal behavior and its relation to the culture of which it is a part have accordingly been generally recognized as far more complex than was the case in this previous literary age. Thus, the term itself, and the standard opposition made with hard-boiled writing, has lost both power and relevance for a late-twentieth-century and twenty-first-century audience. Crime writing has changed as the boundaries between law and order, normative values, and criminal behavior have become increasingly problematic, and as the genre has increasingly been used to tackle an ever-widening series of social issues. The length of current crime fiction (commonly now more than four hundred pages) is indicative of the growing range and complexity of such texts – texts that increasingly stand alongside the traditional novel as reflective investigations into the state of contemporary society. We are a long way here from the clear lines, moral blacks and whites (whatever the complications then introduced), and games-playing analogies of the classical detective form.

Hard-Boiled Detective Fiction

In "The Simple Art of Murder" (1944), Raymond Chandler launched his famous attack on the classical detective novel, particularly as it manifested itself in its Golden Age form, and proclaimed the merits of its "hard-boiled" opposite – which he specifically associates with the work of Dashiell Hammett. Sherlock Holmes is dismissed early in the essay ("Sherlock Holmes after all is mostly an attitude and a few dozen lines of unforgettable dialogue," Chandler 1962: 5). The complexity of Poirot's mental processes, as he works out the whys and wherefores of a murder, are also denigrated as "guaranteed to knock the keenest [reader's] mind for a loop" (9). Attacking what he saw as the artificiality, exoticism, mental gymnastics, and elaborate props of Golden Age fiction, Chandler praised Hammett for his realism, and his move away from the baroque complications of an upper-middle-class or aristocratic world: the type of "Cheesecake Manor" where "somebody stabbed Mrs. Pottington Postlethwaite III with the solid platinum poniard" (9).

"Hammett," Chandler resonantly said, "took murder out of the Venetian vase and dropped it into the alley." His represented world, for Chandler, was different from that of Christie and Sayers and their like, since "it had a basis in fact; it was made up out of real things." (Reality, of course, is not confined to back alleys, but for Chandler the artificial plots of an essentially English model of detective fiction went hand in glove with its world of upper-class privilege to final unconvincing effect.) Hammett, he continued,

> wrote at first (and almost to the end) for people with a sharp, aggressive attitude to life. They were not afraid of the seamy side of things; they lived there. Violence did not dismay them; it was right down their street. Hammett gave murder back to the kind of people that commit it for reasons, not just to provide a corpse; and with the means at hand, not with handwrought duelling pistols, curare, and tropical fish. He put these people down on paper as they are, and he made them talk and think in the language they customarily used for these purposes. . . . [Hammett] was spare, frugal, hard-boiled, but he did over and over again what only the best writers can ever do at all. He wrote scenes that seemed never to have been written before. (12–13)

Chandler, then, sees Hammett's writing as the epitome of the hard-boiled, taking murder out of the drawing-room and into the streets, and representing crime as part and parcel of – and not as an exceptional and often exotic alternative to – everyday life. Such a response came out of, and reflected, the changing conditions of the American world in which both men lived. For, again to quote Chandler,

> The realist in murder writes of a world in which gangsters can rule nations and almost rule cities, in which hotels and apartment houses and celebrated restaurants are owned by rich men who made their money out of brothels, in which . . . the nice man down the hall is a boss of the numbers racket; a world where a judge with a cellar full of bootleg liquor can send a man to jail for having a pint in his pocket. . . . (14)

The hard-boiled crime novel, then, was a product of its America: a form more appropriate than the classical model to a society that seemed out of joint; when anxieties about crime, capitalism, and the conditions of urban life were increasingly and urgently pressing.

"Hard-boiled" referred to a style of writing but it also came to stand for a style of life on the part of the protagonists of such fiction. To read *Red Harvest*, Hammett's first novel, is to be struck by its use of American vernacular, of a linguistic toughness and terseness exactly suiting the street-wise Op and the world of bent cops and politicians, mercenary women, and hard-nosed criminals and killers through which he moves. "[L]ay off Max," Dinah Brand says to the Op, "I'll give you enough on Noonan to nail him forever" (83). Reno Starkey, realizing that Dinah has "turned rat" on Whisper Thaler, tells her that "throwing in with a dick and cracking the works to him is kind of sour" (108). And, when Bill Quint growls at the Op, "So you're a gumshoe," the Op replies, "That's the bunk. . . . I come all the way down here to rope you, and you're smarted up" (29). This must have been like a foreign language for the British reader at the time of the book's first publication, but it is one that effectively represents both the depicted environment and its tough-guy inhabitants.

There is little room for expansive forms of expression or elaborate and poetic language here, and when Elihu Willsson does launch into metaphor ("this pig-sty of a Poisonville") his words are rejected by the Op as "a lot of foolishness" (38). Hammett's style is, as many commentators have noted, similar to Hemingway's (if developed separately), with an emphasis both on dialogue to move the narrative forward and on the rapid description of scene and action with little acknowledgment of feelings and emotion. This further contributes to the impression of a protagonist – in the Op's case, "a fat, middle-aged, hard-boiled, pig-headed guy" (70) – facing the world behind a carefully constructed and self-protective shield. As in Hemingway, too, any (rarely glimpsed) sign of emotion is expressed obliquely, here in slight changes in the paratactic pattern of the sentences, their "This happened. Then this happened" sequential drive. So, when Dinah is murdered, the commencing adverbs used, and the hesitations between words and phrases, in the sentence "Slowly, gently, as if afraid of awakening her, I let go of the ice pick" (128), as well as the formal and drawn-out quality of the multi-syllabic "awakening," form the linguistic space in which the Op's emotions show through (the "awakening her" introduces a pause in the flow of words, a brief moment before the death is finally acknowledged, and before time then beats on with the removal of the hand from the pick). Similarly, his feelings for Dinah, and any physical intimacy that may or may not have occurred when they spend the night together in the one-bedroom shack outside Personville, is concealed by the temporal ellipsis at that point. The unusual sentence construction and brief emphasis on their intimacy that occurs just previously ("The girl shivered with her cheek warm against mine," 111) signals, however, that there is a considerable emotional charge at stake here.

The Op's emotions, then, are by and large concealed behind the hard-boiled mask and the style that represents it. But Hammett's work represents just one version of the hard-boiled – though a particularly effective one. And, if he has come to represent a type of model for the form, there remain a host of writers within this tradition with a different stylistic signature – Chandler himself perhaps being one of the most distinctive. However, these writers usually still have something in common in a strong reliance on dialogue, a protagonist whose laconic wit forms her or his standard response to the surrounding world, and sometimes (though not in Chandler's case) a minimalist prose that on the whole eschews ornamentation and metaphorical flourish.

But the hard-boiled form is identified too with the type of world it represents, where criminality is no longer exceptional and where "violent rupture is not routinely healed by a re-establishment of life's reassuring patterns" (Horsley 2005: 67). A number of critics (including Horsley) have pointed out that Chandler's version of the classical/hard-boiled divide is an exaggeration and simplification of a more complex literary reality. But there is nonetheless a basic truth to his argument – that at this historical point, and in this modern American urban world, there was a significant and necessary re-working of the detective fiction form. And part of this shift resulted from a new focus on the professional "private eye" rather than on the amateur detective (in the Holmes, Miss Marple, Poirot, and Wimsey tradition) – and on the style of life associated with that P. I. as he (in Hammett and Chandler's case) negotiates a world where trust is in very short supply and where violent criminality is endemic.

In "The Simple Art of Murder," Chandler insists on the realistic nature of hard-boiled detective fiction. But his depiction of the private eye protagonist, in the best-known section of his essay, is noticeably romantic:

> down these mean streets a man must go who is not himself mean, who is neither tarnished nor afraid. The detective in this kind of story must be such a man. He is the hero, he is everything. He must be a complete man and a common man and yet an unusual man. He must be, to use a rather weathered phrase, a man of honour. . . . He is a relatively poor man, or he would not be a detective at all. He is a common man or he could not go among common people. . . . If there were enough like him, I think the world would be a very safe place to live in, and yet not too dull to be worth living in.
>
> (Chandler 1962: 14–15)

This rather odd combination of realism and romance is repeated within Chandler's own work where Marlowe's sharp irony and defensive wit go hand in hand with a clearly romantic sensibility. I explore this at greater length in my reading of *The Big Sleep* in Part 3.

But the main point here is that, in the labyrinthine city world through which the protagonists of these fictions move and where danger and physical violence are constant threats, it is the single honest and heroic man who is portrayed as the possible savior of an entire society (indeed of an entire world). While this is undoubtedly a romantic and unrealistic conception, it fits firmly into a larger American tradition (one need only think of the western) where the *agency* of a single individual provides the means to redeem an environment threatened by moral and social disorder. It is this focus on redeeming action and the difficulties in realizing it that helps to bring us to the heart of the hard-boiled form and what I see as its ambivalences about individualism and its limits.

For, if individual agency – its potential and its limitations – lies at the heart of all crime fiction, it becomes an especially problematic issue in its hard-boiled form. In theory, to follow Chandler, the hard-boiled hero is associated with a self-sufficient masculinity: so the American novelist Joyce Carol Oates calls Chandler's main protagonist, Philip Marlowe, "the essence of virility . . . all that other men are not" (1995: 34). He is the tough guy, one who knows how to use his fists and his gun, but a "man of honour," strong enough to withstand the wiles of the female sirens that tempt him and the lure of monetary riches held out by the criminal world through which he moves. In a world where the usual moral checks and balances of the economic, legal, political, and social system have broken down, the detective – and he alone – becomes the protector of liberal value previously entrusted to the state (see also McCann 2000 here). He is also unattached, his solitary nature and often spartan existence a sign of his difference from the surrounding world, of his ability to remain untainted by it. His ability to withstand the physical violence he inevitably meets, to retain linguistic authority (through his wisecracks and quick wit) over those around him, to solve crime and to put the world back to order in its wake (however temporarily), are all signs of successful agency – to act, and in acting, to change the surrounding society for the better.

But this is only half of a much more complex story. What, for example, happens to the idea of individual agency in *Red Harvest*? Here, as John Whitley points out, the Op's identity as a fully realized subject disappears into a type of void, swallowed up by the professional role that is the only thing that defines him (we never know his name) and by the wariness of his personal relationships (even taking into account his feelings for Dinah Brand – a woman killed, after all, as a result of his activities). The Op is defined by his professional, not personal, agency – or, to put this another way, the professional and the personal become almost indistinguishable as the job (the operation) defines the man (the operative). His is a world of very little meaning, as the Flitcraft parable shows, where the best anyone can do is adjust and readjust to the uncontrollable illogic of reality, to iron beams that accidentally fall and then stop falling in random and unpredictable ways. In such a context, the Op becomes a shape-shifter, taking on whatever identity enables him to complete his job, to negotiate the "indifferent, violent [and] deceptive world" (Madden 1968: xvii) through which he moves – by and large adopting the same qualities as that world in order to do so successfully.

Moreover, the toughly minimalist speech and overt display of masculine self-sufficiency practiced by the hard-boiled protagonist are at often at odds with his personal vulnerability, a vulnerability that we would normally code as "feminine." If Oates focuses on the powers of recovery of the Chandler hero, her description of the way he is "repeatedly 'sapped' on the head . . . , shot at, beaten, kicked. Choked, drugged, trussed up and left for dead" (1995: 35) tells another story. For, men such as Marlowe, despite an active engagement with their urban world as crime busters, must finally be seen as passively contained within its deterministic limits. Their work produces, in the last analysis, very little – perhaps the solving of a particular crime, but (with it) the restoration of a social reality that remains untenable. Marlowe's homophobia disguises a longing for homosocial intimacy, some kind of real comradeship to combat the predatory/cash-oriented nature of most of those associated with the normative heterosexual world (or at least the way this world functions in terms of the relationships in which he is usually involved). The hard-boiled protagonist does the best job he can (and his life is predicated on that basis) but, to use a vulgar but effective contemporary metaphor, he is pissing in the wind, merely placing a plaster on a festering urban sore – and, what is more, he knows it.

What we get then in hard-boiled detective fiction is a peculiarly schizo-phrenic fictional world in which constant action and the desire for social improvement goes hand in glove – though in varying ratios – with passivity and powerlessness and the knowledge of a deep-lying social disease for which no foreseeable remedy is possible (W. H. Auden would describe Chandler's Los Angeles in 1948 as "a criminal milieu, the Great Wrong Place," n.p.). The image of Sherlock Holmes as a doctor working on behalf of a healthy social body that is cured of its temporary blemishes by his ministrations, when that proves necessary, has little relevance here.

After Hammett and Chandler, their contemporaries, and those influenced by them (Carroll John Daly, James Ellroy, Chester Himes, Ross Macdonald, William McIlvanney, Walter Mosley, Sara Paretsky, Robert B. Parker, Ian Rankin, and many, many others), any straightforward return to Golden Age fiction, or to the classical and analytic form from which it developed, became very tricky – at least, not without considerable adjustments involved. And, if any simple definition of hard-boiled is problematic, it is often (though not always) associated with the use of a first-person vernacular narrative voice with an emphasis, not on emotion, but on dialogue and spare description – on what Ogdon calls "a specific way of speaking and seeing" (1992: 71). Plot, the crux of classical detective writing, gives way to "an emphasis on *scene itself*," often (but again not always) a complex and labyrinthine urban world that, of its very nature, always remains partially unknown, "to be grasped only in a fragmentary way" (Horsley 2005: 71). The common focus in such texts on pervasive violence and a raw sexuality are signs of a larger social disease, a disease by which the detective protagonist is often, at least in part, infected. As I have argued earlier, the vision of the world represented in such fiction gives this sub-genre a greater potential for radical enquiry into the nature of, and flaws in, the dominant social structure than the classical model, but that is not to say that the politics of such texts are uniform: far from it – for one of the basic assumptions of this book is that the crime fiction genre (whatever its particular form) can house any number of different political and social perspectives.

Once Hammett and Chandler (working in the wake of Hammett, but – as I show later – in quite different a way) had started writing their hard-boiled texts, crime fiction would never be the same. The patterning I have traced, with the classical detective novel (including Golden Age fiction) on the one side and hard-boiled writing on the other, provides a useful way of distinguishing between traditions. But, following World War II – though the dating is somewhat arbitrary – thinking in terms of a classical/hard-boiled binary becomes increasingly pointless. Many of those writers working broadly in the classical tradition were influenced by the style and vision of hard-boiled crime, while the (by and large) comfortable attitudes and hierarchies of Golden Age detection became increasingly irrelevant to the social and political realities of the later-twentieth-century and twenty-first-century world.

Meanwhile, over the nineteenth and twentieth centuries, crime fiction developed in a number of different directions, two of which deserve particular attention. First is the major shift in the genre away from amateur detective or private eye fiction to the police novel, a form that can follow classical conventions but more usually, nowadays, stays closer to the assumptions and outlook of the hard-boiled form. Also – and (often) connected to the hard-boiled – there are transgressor fictions: a form of crime fiction that we can trace to late 1920s and 1930s America, and one that has come to have considerable influence since. I describe these forms of writing in more detail below.

The Police Novel

> From 1997 on, I've written about cops. I consciously abandoned the Private
> Eye tradition that formally jazzed me. Evan Hunter wrote: "The last time a
> Private Eye investigated a homicide was never." The Private Eye is an iconic
> totem spawned by pure fiction. The American Cop is the real goods from
> the gate.
>
> (Ellroy 1994: n.p.)

Ellroy's words help to explain the recent popularity of the police novel.
Joyce Carol Oates argues along similar lines: "private detectives are rarely
involved in authentic crime cases, and would have no access, in contemporary times, to the findings of forensic experts." Thus, "the police procedural"
has prospered accordingly (1995: 34).

If I have so far spoken of crime fiction in terms of its classical and hard-
boiled modes, another way of classifying the genre might be (as both Ellroy
and Oates suggest) through its two kinds of detectives: private eye and
police. The private eye, often an ex-cop, is a self-employed detective who
works outside the official legal system and is not as bound by the procedures
and constraints of those working as part of an official police body. The
protagonist or protagonists of the police novel are part of the system of law
and officially subject to its disciplines, but with access to the resources and
authority of the profession (and the government that supports it) that the
private eye lacks. If the police novel has been a popular form since at least
the early-to-mid-nineteenth century (see Knight 2004), it has now become
the dominant form of crime fiction.

Rather than Oates' descriptor, the "police procedural," I use here its more
inclusive variant, the police novel. The former term suggests a certain
narrative structure – with criminal act, detection, and solution in orderly
sequence. It also assumes that significant attention will be paid (as in
Ed McBain's ground-breaking sequence of 87th Precinct novels) to the
way policing functions, the day-to-day "procedures" that compose its
professional life – investigative processes, command and communication
structures, and the way knowledge is shared and institutional resources are
used (see Panek 2003a, 2003b). More recently, such procedural detail has
focused especially on the fast-developing scientific and technological aspects
of detection – forensics, psychological profiling, IT support systems, and the
like (see the work of Patricia Cornwell, among many others). Such novels, in
Priestman's words, "shift our attention" away from the type of apparent
"magic" associated with the exceptionally gifted detective able to penetrate
what, for others, remains a mystery, "to the process . . . of policing."

"Police work," in its procedural context, accordingly loses many romantic elements found in other forms of detective fiction; it is "collective, grim and often untidy, rather than . . . merely an elegant intellectual exercise" (Priestman 2003b: 179).

But such defining features do not always figure in police novels – and thus my choice of the different term. Joseph Wambaugh, for example, often downplays the "criminal act, detection, solution" paradigm. Speaking of his *Hollywood Station* (2006), he distances himself considerably from the "procedural" label, and the "meticulously plotted genre story" it implies: "In my stories it usually turns out that only the reader knows the truth of the matter and the cop ends up with part or none of the answer" (Wambaugh 2007: n.p.). Thomas Harris' *The Silence of the Lambs* (1988) similarly disrupts the normative narrative conventions of the procedural, with the double narrative that follows the reader's early knowledge of the identity of the criminal (Jame Gumb), its representation of psychological intimacy between Clarice Starling and Hannibal Lecter (a second serial killer, to one side of the novel's main investigative center), and its conclusion in which a focus on Lecter's new freedom undermines the closure and sense of containment we might normally expect in a "procedural" text. So, the police novel provides a more flexible and inclusive term to use.

The police novel, in its various forms, is now a strongly established branch of crime fiction, and has seen a massive growth in popularity in the post-World War II period, and especially the more recent past. It is this timespan on which I concentrate here. Perhaps the most significant American writers at the start of this post-bellum history were Ed McBain, whose *Cop Hater* was published in 1956, and (writing from an entirely different and racially oriented perspective) Chester Himes and his 1957 novel *A Rage in Harlem*. Since then, the major figures that can be (loosely) grouped under such a heading would include those already named – Cornwell, Ellroy, Harris, and Wambaugh – together with the likes of James Lee Burke, Michael Connelly, Robert Crais, Tess Gerritsen, Tony Hillerman, James Patterson, and Kathy Reichs.

The post-war British police novel, too, reaches back to the 1950s with J. J. Marric (John Creasey) and his George Gideon novels. A number of British police novels tend to follow a different path than their American counterparts, as I have suggested in the case of Colin Dexter, with a stronger reliance on the classical detection model. But British crime writing, too, has been increasingly affected by the influence of the American hard-boiled tradition of gritty realism and (to varying degrees) social disarray – diminishing accordingly the relevance of classifying such fiction by national type. Significant British writers across the genre include Michael Dibdin (whose

Inspector Zen novels are set in Italy), Elizabeth George (an American writer whose Inspector Lynley novels are set in the United Kingdom), John Harvey, Reginald Hill, P. D. James, H. R. F. Keating, Val McDermid, William McIlvanney, David Peace, Ian Rankin, and Peter Robinson. But to name names is only to be aware of the injustice done to the many thus omitted. The police novel, too, is an important form in mainland European crime fiction. George Simenon's seventy-five Maigret novels (published from 1931 onward) have been extremely influential. So, too, in their different way, have the ten novels by Swedish writers Maj Swöjall and Per Wahlöö, in the highly regarded Martin Beck series (1965–1975). Contemporary writing on the European mainland – Arnaldur Indridason, Henning Mankell, Jo Nesbø, Håkan Nesser, and Fred Vargas are just a few examples – is unimaginable without such precedents.

There are many types of police novels – novels of detection, thrillers, psychological and/or sociological novels, narratives reliant on gothic effects, and so on – but all focus on crime and police work. A narrow definition of the form might focus on the way such narratives represent a distinctive police culture – the "unique impact . . . crime and police work have . . . on the way men and women work as well as the way they live" (Panek 2003b: 156). But, in line with my previous chapter on the politics of crime fiction, I put my own emphasis more strongly on the larger frameworks within which the police, and other law enforcers, work. The strength and importance of modern police fiction, then, lies in its institutional and systemic context – its representation of policing as a central part of a larger "state apparatus" (Winston and Mellerski 1992: 2). This allows, in turn, a broader definition of the police novel than one that just includes the uniformed police force and its (plain-clothed) detective counterpart. Policing in our Western world, the protection and defense of the larger interests of the state, takes place, rather, at a variety of levels and across a number of organizations. So, I see both Patricia Cornwell's and Thomas Harris' work as police novels, despite Kay Scarpetta's position, in Cornwell's earlier books, as Chief Medical Officer of Richmond, Virginia, and Clarice Starling's as F.B.I. agent.

To see the police novel through an institutional lens focuses attention on our relation (as private citizens) to the larger social network that contains us, and on any doubts and anxieties we might have about the nature of its organization and operations. Such anxieties may center on the meaning of, and relationship between, such terms as justice, morality, community, and law, and on the nature and extent of our commitment to the values of the social authorities that are normally assumed to operate on our behalf. So, Ian Rankin, asked why the form suits his needs as a writer, emphasizes the police detective's position as one who has "open access to all layers of society, from the oligarchs to the dispossessed":

> I wanted to write about contemporary urban Britain, and couldn't think of a better way of doing it than through the medium of the detective novel: I would, after all, be positing questions about the "state we're in," and reckoned a cop could act as my surrogate.
>
> (Rankin 2007: n.p.)

Rankin's tone is modest but his claims are significant. The police novel is a form that, at its best, has mutated – depending on its particular setting – into an ongoing (serial) enquiry into the state of the nation, its power structures, and its social concerns. If the genre of crime fiction as a whole can make much the same claim (after all, it is the "detective novel" to which Rankin refers here), the fact that these particular detectives are part of the official power structures of the state does make a difference. James Ellroy, in his distinctively hyperbolic style, captures something of the contemporary relevance and importance of the police novel when he speaks of "cops as the up-close in-your-face voyeuristic eyes of a public that senses epic dysfunction all around them, and wants to know why" (Ellroy 1994: n.p.). He is talking about real-life cops here, but the words carry over to their fictional equivalent.

To approach the police novel in terms of its institutional context is to take a three-way focus: first, on individual law enforcers and the policing communities to which they belong; second, on the exercise of state power and bureaucracy (the way society is policed); and third, on the general health, or lack of it, of the social system thus represented. These factors complement any emphasis on realism alone (cops as "the real goods from the gate') in explaining the growth in popularity of the form. Much of the success of the majority of police fictions depends on the reality-effect suggested – on the accurate reflection of "real" police work conveyed. But a changing social and institutional environment has also played its part here, for the rise of the police novel, in Winston and Mellerski's words, undoubtedly

> suggests a response [after World War II] to the technological penetration and increased bureaucratic complexity of post-industrial society which operates by proposing a squad of individualized detectives, each possessing certain crucial skills which enable them to work collectively to investigate the same systemic evil that the hard-boiled detective nostalgically confronted alone. (1992: 6)

But this quote raises almost as many questions as it answers. It fails to account for police novels where the central detective is a maverick and, as in the cases of John Rebus, or of Bucky Bleichart (in Ellroy's ground-breaking

1987 novel, *The Black Dahlia*), conducts investigations to one side of, or parallel to, what Rankin calls "the team effort." It also leaves that resonant term "systemic evil," and where precisely it is to be discovered, unexplained.

There is here, however, a clear indication of the way the police novel is generally associated with notions of state bureaucracy, collective agency, and forms of social monitoring and control (reinforced by high-level technological and scientific support); an emphasis on the corporate symptomatic of its surrounding late-capitalist context. Such centralized systems of policing, the procedures used, and the resources accordingly available are, moreover, seen as increasingly necessary in uncovering criminality in "the anonymous and transient society that [has] become a feature of late twentieth-century [and early twenty-first century] life" (Priestman 2003b: 157). It is easy then to see police novels as reflecting an increasingly invasive monitoring on behalf of the state of any threat to the established social order. So, in Patricia Cornwell's *Unnatural Exposure* (1997), a military C17 plane – a "monstrous flat-gray machine" (304) – transports the camper van/laboratory belonging to the novel's murderer for forensic examination at the U. S. army's Utah "test facility for chemical and biological defense" (294). The description of the plane's descent, with its suggestion of an alien invasive force (302), serves as a reminder of the authority and supervisory power wielded by the federal government that reinforces Kay Scarpetta's detections, while the management by Lucy, Scarpetta's niece, of the F.B.I.'s Criminal Artificial Intelligence Network, and her monitoring of the e-mail messages being passed from Crowder (the criminal) to Scarpetta, also indicates panoptic control (see my chapter on "Vision, Supervision, and the City"). The solution of the crime (an attempted release of a deadly infection on the American people), the role of the detective, and the power and best interests of the state, then, go absolutely hand in hand in this particular case.

But the police novel often takes a different form from this, and works in more complicated and ambivalent ways. There are, Lee Horsley argues, two main types of police novel. In one, an emphasis is placed on the investigative efforts of a group of police operating as a team (Joseph Wambaugh's novels, for instance, largely work like this). In the other, the focus is on the individual detective, often something of a non-conformist, and resistant both to official procedures and interests. There are certainly cases where any difference between such types is blurred – where, for instance, this one detective, who tends to have scant regard for established rules, systems, and values, reconciles his (or her) methods and point of view with the larger police team. Nonetheless, when the main protagonist is this often-abrasive, individual figure – marked by some significant degree of self-sufficiency and independence, even within her or his police setting – we are also more likely to find (in Horsley's words) "narratives that move towards an exposure of the injustices and failures of the official machinery of law and order." Drawing parallels between the various types of detective fiction, she continues:

> Much contemporary detective fiction, both private eye and police procedural, does underwrite the values of [what one critic has called] "the controlling agencies of modern society". . . . But there are many writers who use these forms to explore the contradictions of contemporary existence, creating . . . a "discontinuous" tradition that in a variety of ways has challenged normative thinking (existing social and racial hierarchies, the assumed power structure, establishment values). (2005: 102)

In exploring these issues further we can usefully move our attention from policing as an abstract quality, expressing the power and authority of the state, to particular law enforcers – such as Rebus in Rankin's novels and Wallander in Henning Mankell's – who represent "the human face of state power" and who mediate "the spectre of absolute state control . . . [and] fears of an overextended and inhumane police power" (Winston and Mellerski 1992: 6–7). Detectives of this type may, then, represent the larger state, but they also stand apart from it, motivated (and the extent of such mediating activity varies from text to text) by their own particular set of moral and social values. Such protagonists are often aware of individual rights and communal responsibilities that (abstract) law can compromise or overlook. They are aware too that the system they represent can be flawed, with its own forms of corruption, moral fault-lines, and large-scale injustices – even if, sometimes, such injustices are themselves sanctioned by the law and/or the government. In other words – and to return to a previous point – the "systemic evil" detectives investigate can refer to the criminal elements on the margins of society that prevent its smooth functioning. But it can also refer to other forms of immorality, hypocrisy, social injustice, and abuse of power at that society's very heart. Crossovers between both such forms are also possible, with criminal conspiracies protecting key establishment interests.

The police detective, then, can stand as a mediating figure between the authority of the law (and the social order it upholds) and an emphasis on an individual or alternative sense of moral responsibility, social justice, and freedom of expression. It is, accordingly, possible to identify a range of positions emerging within the police novel form. First, there is the police-woman or man who carries out her or his professional role with no qualms about the law and justice s/he represents. Second, there is the cop, detective, or F.B.I. agent (usually one of the last two) whose social values – often what we might call "progressive" – lead her or him deeply to question that system, and/or whose independence, intelligence, and emotions distance that protagonist considerably from the larger policing group of which s/he is a part. Third, there is the range of different positions available between such poles.

I would briefly note that there is more to be added here. For Horsley's division of police fiction into two main types – that of the police team and of the individual and non-conformist detective who challenges "normative thinking" – is not comprehensive. What she says is both accurate and astute, but we should note that police novels can also challenge an established social system in other ways. Authorial intervention, for example, can represent a critical position not through character identification but rather through third-person description or simply through the juxtaposition of different modes of dialogue and points of view (both methods are used in Sjöwall and Walhöö's novels). Such a critique can also operate through the shaping and handling of narrative form and tone (as in the very different cases of Elmore Leonard and Chester Himes). In some police novels (Ellroy's would be a good example), the sense of social malaise, of crisis and large-scale social dysfunction, is so strong that the normal binaries structuring the genre – good and evil, law and criminality, the civilized and the savage – collapse in on themselves completely. This is also true in the work of Thomas Harris (and, increasingly, other writers), where gothic conventions and forms undermine the rational aspects of the conventional novel of detection. Thus, Harris' "pointe[d] abandon[ment of] the framework of the police procedural about two-thirds of the way through [his 1999 novel] *Hannibal*" (Horsley 2005: 146) suggests the failure of the police novel adequately to continue to represent his worldview and to serve his artistic needs, and signals his virtual abandonment of the crime novel's conventional structuring vision.

But I return to the more common instance of the police novel, and to the idea of mediation: how the authority of the law (and the social order it upholds) is balanced against the individual law enforcer's judgments and values. I have already implicitly suggested that the type of novel focusing on police teamwork, on the police as an "extended family" (Panek 2003b: 170) following a regular set of procedural routines, is less likely to question the dominant social system than novels that feature just one or two individual protagonists (though, again, both Ellroy's and Sjöwall and Walhöö's work provides a notable exception to this rule). We can see this in the example of Joseph Wambaugh's novel *Hollywood Station* (2006). Wambaugh is an important figure in the history of the ensemble police novel. An ex-policeman himself, he is at his best in representing American cop culture: the way cops work, the routines and dramas of the job, their conversations and jargon, their eccentricities and indulgences. He shows how the demands of the profession affect his protagonists' emotional lives and relationships, and highlights the procedural constraints that condition, and hamstring (as he would argue), their effective performance.

Wambaugh's sympathies in his novels (and *Hollywood Station* is no exception) lie with "the cops on the street" (Wambaugh 2007: n.p.). He puts strong emphasis on the constraining absurdities of a U. S. system in which police actions are systematically monitored by other regulatory agencies, so negating their ability to perform a tough, dangerous, and emotionally traumatic job, and to do it well. As Flotsam (one of the cops on the Hollywood Station team) remarks: "being an LAPD cop today is like playing a game of dodgeball, but the balls are coming at us from every-fucking-where" (2006: 128). The main agenda in the novel is, consequently, clear: a critique of the way the police are pressured from above, subject to the demands of political correctness (see, for instance, 66), and – in the wake of the Rodney King incident and parallel cases (see 52–55) – monitored by investigative and supervisory agencies such as the Internal Affairs Group and bound by mandates such as the federal consent decree agreement (Wambaugh's particular *bête noire*). The Oracle, the sergeant and father figure to the station personnel, sums up what is clearly the authorial position too: "Aw shit, . . . How're we supposed to police a city when we spend half the time policing ourselves and proving in writing that we did it?" (137).

Wambaugh exposes some key anxieties of modern American urban life in the novel, and most particularly those clustering around the subject of race. Indeed, racial and ethnic tension is one of the book's main subjects. But, because the focus of, and commitment in, his novel is so closely tied to his cop protagonists, there is no challenge to the existing social system and the "normative thinking" that upholds it. Things are the way they are and, however unfortunate that may be, there is no hint of an avenue for change, or even a sense that it might be particularly necessary. The only challenge to existing institutional or social structures here has to do with the arrangements governing police life. The description in the book of the Rodney King incident, which had such serious repercussions for the LAPD, is particularly revealing:

> That was a bizarre event wherein a white sergeant, having shot Mr. King with a taser gun after a long auto pursuit, then directed the beating of this drunken, drug-addled African American ex-convict. That peculiar sergeant seemed determined to make King cry uncle, when the ring of a dozen cops should have swarmed and handcuffed the drunken thug and been done with it. (53)

This is not Wambaugh's own voice but one of his cop characters. However, in its larger novel-length context, this version of events endorses what is clearly the book's main message: that the King incident was a one-off error of judgment (rather than a sign of systemic racism) and that the city government's response (via the Christopher Commission) has unnecessarily hampered a police force that would operate more effectively without such "outside" controls. The one-sided version of the event given here, however, suggests the dangers inherent in such an approach – in too close a commitment to the ground-level cop point of view, and too little concern accordingly with the larger system – to those spaces in society where law and justice fail. (James Ellroy is interesting on the King case, suggesting the way that a voyeuristic public depend on the police for the operation of the law, but also how police actions and attitudes expose that public's prejudices and assumptions: "We love cops for getting us close. We hate cops for getting us too close. Rodney King brought us into collective guilt range. Four cops took the literal rap but our complicity was undeniable," Ellroy 1994: n.p.)

I wait until Part 3, on individual novels, to examine Ian Rankin's *The Naming of the Dead* (2006), and to show how the type of police novel that puts its emphasis on the individual detective (in Rankin's case, John Rebus) can lead to that "exposure of the injustices and failures of the official machinery of law and order" (Horsley 2005: 102) previously mentioned. But, in contrasting Wambaugh and Rankin, I am *not* saying – as Winston and Mellerksi seem to imply – that British (and other European) police novels tend necessarily to be "more sophisticated than [their] American counterpart" in terms of their "ideological and political" engagement (1992: 14). There may be some element of truth to this as a general rule, but writers such as Chester Himes, and more recently James Ellroy, certainly disprove such blanket assumptions. Ellroy, indeed, undermines conventional boundaries between officialdom and criminality to even more disruptive effect than Rankin, asking penetrating questions about the workings of the American social order as he does so. His reconfigurations of the history and geography of Los Angeles of the late 1940s and 1950s in his *L. A. Quartet* (1987–1992) serve as entry points to a fictional world of collapsing boundaries, uncanny doublings, and identity slippage, where political, economic, and media interests powerfully combine in the suppression of any version of the "truth," and where the law (and the investigative actions of Ellroy's cop protagonists) are usually subordinate to such interests.

In their general form, and in many of their concerns, American and European police novels have much in common: Ian Rankin, for instance, is clearly indebted to Ellroy (see Plain 2002: 14, 34–35), and David Peace even more so. But they also differ, both in terms of local geographical, institutional, and cultural specifics and in "the ideological space of the cultures from which they derive" (Winston and Mellerski 1992: 10). There remains much work to be done to determine the cultural and ideological differences between the police fictions set in a variety of European countries, *and* how these European fictions differ in turn from their U. S. counterparts. My hope is that the arguments made in this section, and in the study of individual texts both here and later in the book, will provide a foundation for further work on this subject.

Transgressor Narratives

The final type of crime novel discussed is what we can call "transgressor narratives." The term is an awkward one but is, I think, the best available to fit the form. Literary categorizations are rarely completely watertight or satisfactory. So, for instance, when I previously traced the move from private eye to police fiction, I was aware that figures such as Sherlock Holmes, Hercule Poirot, and Lord Peter Wimsey cannot really be described as "private eyes," for the term applies to a more professional world than that to which they belong. My discussion of police fiction makes it clear, too, that there is an overlap, in a large number of cases, between that form of crime fiction and the previously defined hard-boiled category.

Lee Horsley uses the term "literary noir" in her discussion of transgressor narratives, and speaks of the form as "explor[ing] the psychopathology of killer protagonists, revenge-seekers, and those murderously determined on achieving upward mobility" (2005: 113). Elsewhere, she writes that

> [noir's] quintessential figures are individual transgressors and victims. Com-
> promised, ineffectual masculinity has . . . been a recurrent theme in twenty-
> first century noir. . . . McCoy and Cain [two authors particularly associated
> with the beginnings of an American noir tradition in the 1930s and 1940s]
> create characters who are the antithesis of the iconic private eye – morally
> deficient, lacking all effective agency and representing traumatized masculinity
> at its most vulnerable. (2010: 39)

There is some slippage in these two descriptions between violent agency (killer protagonists) and ineffectual passivity (traumatized male victims). While this does, in part, speak to the paradoxes of transgressor fiction, it may also suggest the wider resonances of the term "noir" itself. Indeed, the fact that the word is often applied more widely, and to the whole American hard-boiled crime tradition, makes its use in a more specific manner problematic. And, although many fictions of transgression do undoubtedly focus on ineffectual masculinity, clearly not all do (think Hannibal Lecter). It is noticeable, accordingly, that critics, generally, have struggled to find a satisfactory categorization for these types of fiction. Knight uses the general category of "the crime novel" (as opposed to "the private-eye tradition") for such texts (2004: 125–127). Glover includes them under the catch-all title "the thriller" (2003: 135–153). Scaggs (coming close to Horsley) refines this descriptor to "the *noir* thriller" (2005: 108–117).

I start with the leading characteristic in Horsley's description – that this form of crime narrative explores "the psychopathology of killer protagonists." It is this that prompts my use of the term "transgressor fiction." I recognize that there are various types of transgressor fictions, not all of which I explore here. So, I omit gangster and Mafia novels: texts from W. R. Burnett's *Little Caesar* (1929) through Paul Cain's *Fast One* (1933) to Mario Puzo's *The Godfather* (1969). I also put to one side narratives such as *Pimp: The Story of My Life* (1969), an "autobiographical novel" by Iceberg Slim (Robert Beck). Echoing, even as it ideologically challenges, the rags-to-riches narratives of the dominant white mainstream, this last-named book (and others of its type) powerfully documents African American underclass life and the pimping and drug-peddling that can bring success (of a certain type) in this deprived environment. While I recognize the presence and importance of such books, I focus on narratives of *personal* alienation, on those in which individuals' motivations and/or desires lack connection with the social values of their larger group, and lead accordingly to transgressive action. I see such fiction as closer to the heart of the crime-writing tradition as I have explored it so far than the other types of narrative referred to above – narratives that are more *professional* in kind, whether they deal with gangsters, pimps, prostitutes, or with any others who make their living in a sustained way through criminal activity. (I make this distinction even as I recognize the difficulty of making hard and fast rules here.)

In many cases, transgressor fiction overlaps with broader categories – that (rather amorphous) literary noir, and hard-boiled crime fiction. We can see the connection with the hard-boiled in the work of James M. Cain, called, indeed, by David Madden, "the twenty-minute egg of the hard-boiled school" (see, for instance, Madden 1967). So, Cain's 1934 novel, *The Postman Always Rings Twice*, starts with the words:

> They threw me off the hay truck about noon. . . . [T]hey saw a foot sticking out and threw me off. I tried some comical stuff, but all I got was a dead pan, so that gag was out. They gave me a cigarette, though, and I hiked down the road to find something to eat.
>
> That was when I hit this Twin Oaks Tavern. (5)

The emphasis on fact and action, along with the use of the first person narrator and of a colloquial language marked by its limited range are all familiar hard-boiled attributes. And the book's Depression setting (America in the 1930s) indicates the same type of social malfunctioning common to other hard-boiled texts of the time.

But Cain is often, too, spoken of as a "noir" writer. Noir and hard-boiled, though not always coterminous, can have much in common. Both terms take in a particular vision of the world. The former, however, carries heavily deterministic implications and often takes the form (as in films in this genre) of a retrospective and doom-laden narrative told from the death cell, or its equivalent. There is also a strong emphasis in "noir" texts on raw sensuality – on the instincts and feelings that drive the protagonist, and the violence that commonly follows in their wake. But I do not want to over-complicate my argument here and the term "transgressor fiction" suits my present needs. Where such fiction shares noir traits, though, I comment accordingly.

I return now to Horsley's earlier definitions, and the apparent paradox that emerges as, on the one hand, she speaks of "killer protagonists . . . and those murderously determined on achieving upward mobility" while, on the other, of "victims," "compromised, ineffectual masculinity," and those who lack "all effective agency." There is an interesting tension here between the idea of self-assertive agency and its passive lack that provides a useful springboard for examining a literary tradition, transgressor fiction, that reaches at least as far back as the eighteenth-century *Newgate Calendar* stories (Scaggs 2005: 108–109), finds its modern incarnation in America in the 1930s, and morphs into the serial-killer novel of the contemporary period (with Thomas Harris as perhaps its most notable practitioner).

By far the majority of the modern forms of transgressor fictions focus on what Horsley calls "damaged sel[ves]." But that term does not really fit Harris' main protagonist, Hannibal Lecter – or at least not in the first two novels in the tetralogy. Horsley's fuller description that such fiction depicts "the psychological states of those who stand outside (but might pretend conformity to) mainstream society [thus providing] a means of exploring social and psychological malaise" (Horsley 2005: 117) does, however, take in Lecter. And she points usefully here to the fact that transgressor fictions can be associated even more strongly and clearly with social or/and ideological critique than other forms of crime fiction. But it is the idea of agency (or its lack) that is crucial to this type of fiction. I consequently use it as my entry point to the texts I discuss, structuring much of what I say around notions of the active and/or passive subject.

Transgressor fiction in the 1930s and 1940s is often (to repeat) heavily deterministic, its protagonists caught in a trap that inevitably springs closed in the narrative's course. Such entrapment is built into the narrative structure of many such texts. So, both of James M. Cain's major novels, *The Postman Always Rings Twice* (1934) and *Double Indemnity* (1936), take the form of confessions, with Frank Chambers, in the first-named novel, ending the book with the words "I'm in the death-house, now, writing the last of this" (Cain 1947: 94), as he completes his backstory.

This sense of inevitability shaping the individual subject's fate is even stronger in Horace McCoy's powerful novel *They Shoot Horses, Don't They?* (1935). The novel opens with the words "The prisoner will stand" (1970: 5), with the protagonist, Robert Syverten, being sentenced for his "crime." It then shifts to its more-usual first person narrative (italicized in this instance), as Robert takes the reader back to the moment when he shot Gloria Beatty: "*I stood up. For a moment I saw Gloria again, sitting on that bench on the pier. The bullet had just struck her in the side of the head; the blood had not even started to flow*" (7). The narrative then rapidly moves back in time to its chronological beginning, "It was funny the way I met Gloria" (15), then to develop from that starting point as it tells of Robert and Gloria's friendship and their partnership in a marathon dance competition. (Such competitions were one of a number of popular "entertainments" in the 1930s, where the competitors got at least a chance to make – usually a little – money, and where the spectators could watch those less fortunate than themselves often literally "out on their feet," in their attempt to remain standing, and dancing, over the marathon's course.) At regular points in the telling of this story, however, there are brief interludes in which the words of the judge as he sentences Robert to death are starkly displayed. As this occurs, the text's typescript gets gradually larger, to finally appear in bold, and climaxing with the final words of the book: " . . . may God have mercy on your soul . . . " (125).

Artist Philip Evergood's visual representation of a dance marathon (see the painting of that title from 1934, readily available online) is uncannily similar in its motifs to McCoy's novel of the following year, though working in an exaggerated and expressionistic way. Evergood's depiction of the wooden boards of the dance floor suggests a spider's web, and this same sense of the individual dancer, down on his (and her) luck and caught in a trap from which there is no way out, dominates the novel too. Gloria (and Robert) might be "trying to get into pictures" (15) – just like Cora, initially, in Cain's *Postman* – but neither can get registered by the Central Casting Bureau and, in Gloria's case, Robert can see why: "She was too blonde and too small and looked too old" (17). Robert is an almost entirely *passive* figure, identified as a dreamer from the first and going along with the various demeaning events arranged by the marathon organizers with little or no questioning of their dehumanizing effect. When the "rather pretty" girl (52) whom Robert only knows by her marathon number (seven) tries to engage him in sex, he is slow on the uptake, and the liaison is interrupted anyway. He sees and describes the events around him but with no sense at all that he might influence them in any way. The one thing he does actively *do* is to shoot Gloria, though even this act is driven by her will. Cynical and disillusioned, her point of view is of one who recognizes the pointlessness of a life where she never gets the breaks, and where the painful and demeaning business of the marathon dance provides the metaphor for the only life Depression America offers her and those like her: "This whole business is a merry-go-round. When we get out of here we're right back where we started" (72).

Finally, Gloria asks Robert to shoot her ("Shoot me. It's the only way to get me out of my misery," 123), which he then does. And, when a policeman asks him why he did it, he says (in the final line of the book prior to the "may God have mercy" sequence), "They shoot horses, don't they?" (124). What Robert sees as mercy killing, his society sees as murder. And McCoy's talent is in getting his reader to question the line between the two, given Gloria's despair and the economic and social conditions that seem to determine its permanent continuation. Both Robert's individual agency and masculinity are heavily compromised here – his "crime," in his mind, an entirely rational response to the world of a damaged individual (Gloria) from whom all hope has been stripped away.

This is an extreme representation of ineffectual and affectless male subjectivity – but it indicates a sense of social and economic entrapment common in the 1930s and crucial to transgression fictions of the period (and to literary noir). James M. Cain's protagonists in *The Postman Always Rings Twice* may be far more active, but the strength of his novel and much of its impact lies in the tension between the extremes and excesses of their behavior and the inevitability of their final fate. Much of the focus of the novel is on the pace and violence of Frank's actions, and the raw sensuality invoked in that process. Thus, at the opposite extreme from classical detective fiction, with its coolly analytic protagonists, here, and in a good number of transgressor narratives, we have protagonists driven by raw impulse – their "recklessness," directly linked to the narrowness and frustrations of the "wrecked opportunities" and "blind contingencies of everyday [Depression] life" (Glover 2003: 145).

Cain wrote that "I think my stories have some of the quality of the opening of a forbidden box" (qtd. in Bradbury 1988: 90). In his novels, the actions of his characters result in the box's lid being taken off – releasing lust, sexuality, and violent mayhem, sometimes unexpectedly combined. Finally, though, the force of law and social authority are finally exercised to snap that lid firmly back in place, and with equal violence – at the cost of the transgressor's life. In the opening short two chapters of *Postman*, Frank's first sight of Cora (running Twin Oaks Tavern alongside her husband Nick) triggers a violent sexual response: "her lips stuck out in a way that made me want to mash them in for her" (6). The combination of this desire and the sweet Greek wine given him by Nick then acts on him like a body blow, physically expressed in his vomit: "I let everything come up. It was like hell, the lunch, or the potatoes, or the wine. I wanted that woman so bad I couldn't even keep anything on my stomach" (9). And, by his second day at Twin Oaks, his and Cora's relationship is consummated in the sado-masochistic violence that serves as prelude to sexual consummation: "I sunk my teeth into her lips so deep I could feel the blood spurt into my mouth. It was running down her neck when I carried her upstairs" (11).

This is powerful stuff, especially for the period in which Cain was writing. Frank and Cora kick over all the ordered rules of their surrounding social world, moving rapidly from adultery to murder. Frank cracks Nick's skull open with a wrench: "I brought down the wrench. His head cracked, and I felt it crush" (36). He then turns his violence toward Cora – ripping her clothes and "hit[ting] her in the eye as hard as I could" – as they stage a car "accident" to explain Nick's death. This violence then quickly becomes an elemental sexual urge, acted out beside Nick's still-dying body:

> She was down there [at my feet], and the breath was roaring in the back of my throat like I was some kind of a animal, and my tongue was all swelled up in my mouth, and blood pounding in it. . . . I had to have her, if I hung for it.
>
> I had her. (38)

In this depiction of murderous brutality, intense passion, and quick-fire action, the reader's attention is all on Frank and Cora's agency, their ability to change their immediate world to meet their instinctual needs. Rational thought almost completely disappears here as instinct and action coalesce – no sooner is an impulse brought to consciousness than its enactment then occurs.

Frank's active masculine urgency, though, is highly compromised. For his actions are "contained" by a larger force, by the authority systems and normative social orderings that he and Cora look to disavow. The French psychoanalyst Jacques Lacan wrote that "[l]aw and repressed desire is one and the same thing" (qtd. in Johnston 1980: 102). Here, sure enough, law – that which structures accepted and acceptable social behavior – obliterates transgressive desire to snuff out Frank and Cora's agency. Frank is tried and condemned for a supposed murder (Cora's) that he has not in fact committed: pregnant, she is killed accidentally in a second car crash (the heavy repetition-effects in the book reinforce its determinism) when Frank is in fact rushing her to hospital after she is taken ill while swimming. His and Cora's act of setting up their false family (based on a murder) and of pursuing their sexual and financial urges (for Cora gets Twin Oaks and a fat insurance settlement with Nick's death), whatever crossings of conventional moral and legal boundaries this takes, is thus symbolically punished, and cancelled out, at the novel's end. Cain is (like McCoy) highly aware of the type of dreams American culture encourages and the failure of the social system to allow their realization; of the immoralities of business (the insurance companies that manipulate Frank and Cora's guilt to their own best monetary ends); and the inadequacies of the law. It is such larger interests that finally master Frank's violence, and counter and suppress his animalistic desire. The success of Cain's novel, though, exists exactly in its tense counterpoint between the urgency of Frank's agency, his anti-social needs, and the normative (and repressive) social mechanisms that finally and firmly contain them.

Cain and McCoy lay the twentieth-century ground, then, for transgressor narratives, and play them out against the insufficiencies and failures of an existing social order – a Depression America, where the capitalist economy, with all its ideological concomitants, seemed to have failed. There are many writers who then follow in this tradition, including – in the period either side of World War II – David Goodis, Dorothy Hughes, Charles Willeford, and Cornell Woolrich. Perhaps the two best-known authors from this period writing in this tradition are Jim Thompson, known especially for his *The Killer Inside Me* (1952), and Patricia Highsmith, best represented by her *The Talented Mr. Ripley* (1955). The social conditions critiqued in both these texts are those of a later era – the deadening conformity of the Eisenhower presidency. So, the excessive and instinctual sexuality and physical violence of Lou Ford, in *The Killer Inside Me*, may be a result of his psychological abnormality, but are also a reaction to the dullness of his small-town Texas world, with its oil-refinery workers going through the motions of life, "plodding in to their jobs, and the other shifts plodding home . . . Driving home and . . . drinking beer and watching their television sets and diddling their wives . . . ." (181). Highsmith uses criminality in a rather different way, as a response to the failure of American life to satisfy any higher cultural and aesthetic need. And, while Thompson – at least in part – looks back to Cain, Highsmith anticipates a later generation of writers, led by Thomas Harris. I discuss Highsmith more fully in Part 3 but make brief introductory comment on her writing here.

But, what is also new in Highsmith's *Ripley* novels (and to lesser extent in Thompson) is the focus on the *series* of murders committed by their main protagonist. We tend to think of serial killing – despite earlier instances (Jack the Ripper is the most obvious) – as a recent phenomenon. Woody Haut reports that, factually, "[t]here was one serial killer [in the United States] during the 1950s, six during the 1960s, 17 during the 1970s, and some 24 within the first four years of the 1980s" (1999: 254). But Ripley, whose literary life begins in the 1950s, also belongs in this category. Highsmith accordingly provides an early model for the spate of enormously popular novels, dating (approximately) from the early 1980s, that focus on serial killing. (Jo Nesbø 's *The Snowman* and *The Leopard* (*Leopold's Apple* in the United States), both published in their translated versions in 2010, together with the other books in his Harry Hole series, are some of the latest bestsellers of this type.)

It is in Highsmith's novels that we see, too, a new focus on the *agency* of the killer – and an agency that is finally unaffected by the deterministic forces operating in the other texts so far considered here. Ripley is the killer-protagonist who gets away with it. A sophisticated art and music lover, who lives out of preference in Europe rather than the United States, he paves the way for Thomas Harris' Hannibal Lecter, the most notorious transgressor and serial killer of recent crime fiction. Like Lecter (and paradoxically) an attractive monster, Ripley's is the controlling perspective in the five High-smith novels that feature him (1955–1991). His civilized intelligence helps to throw the inanities and small-mindedness of conventional existence into high relief. His murderous activities, meanwhile, are represented as an amoral but oddly acceptable strategy to gain and retain his autonomy and social position (however precarious both may be) in a (fictional) world that lacks any satisfying alternative perspective or set of values. As Charles L. P. Silet comments,

> [t]hese are unsettling works of fiction, full of macabre humor and devilish insouciance, which play on the reader's fantasies of individual power and choice. In a universe so full of nasty people and random, uncontrollable events, it is strangely satisfying to watch someone exercise his personal will unfettered by the normal constraints of legality and civilized controls imposed upon the rest of us. (n.d.: n.p.)

In one sense, it is clearly worrying to have a protagonist such as Ripley held up for admiration. But one must remember that this is fiction, and that Highsmith uses Ripley's presence to challenge what she presents as the banalities of modern American existence, and the identity straitjackets and repressive structures of its normative social world. Something similar, but on a more baroque scale (for Highsmith's manner is usually low-key and matter-of-fact) occurs in the important and highly popular fictions of Thomas Harris.

I have already mentioned Harris in my section on police novels. But his novels – especially as they come to focus more and more on the mind and actions of Hannibal Lecter – are also (if not always wholly) fictions of transgression. (Generic and sub-generic categories in all forms of fiction tend to overlap and cross categories in this way, and crime fiction is no exception. James Ellroy's and David Peace's works, too, cross this same police novel-transgressor fiction boundary.) In *Red Dragon* (1981), however, the first novel in which Hannibal Lecter appears (though in a relatively minor role), it is a different serial killer who shares the novel's center stage. This novel, like Harris' next, *The Silence of the Lambs* (1988), works through the kind of double narrative increasingly common in contemporary crime fiction. If much of the focus is on the detective's quest to discover the identity of a killer, the reader *also* enters the consciousness of the transgressor – both that of the already imprisoned Lecter (commencing in chapter eight of *Red Dragon*) and, in a more sustained manner, that of the novel's main serial killer, Francis Dolarhyde (starting in chapter nine).

So, while we follow the twists and turns of detective Will Graham's hunt for the killer, we also come to know the latter's identity and motivation – the facial disfigurements and traumatic past family history that have helped to trigger his psychotic behavior. The novel eventually works itself out in relatively traditional manner, with Dolarhyde's death (shot by Graham's wife), but its gothic intensity and extremes of violence prepare us for the later novels in the sequence, which increasingly feature Hannibal Lecter. Harris' representation of Lecter focuses on the good taste, intelligence, physical power, and savage violence that come together, in his case, in such an unusual combination – and it is these qualities that work variously over the next two novels in the tetralogy to win Lecter his freedom and enjoy its fullest fruits, and to allow him (often contemptuously) to evade the cops and F.B.I. who seek his re-imprisonment. Lecter has regained his freedom by the end of *The Silence of the Lambs* – a novel in which it is Jame Gumb who this time plays the main role of serial killer. But it is Lecter's agency, barbaric violence, and freedom from normal legal or social constraints that ultimately dominate this novel (and the two novels to follow).

Harris moves into gothic territory here with his depiction of his main protagonist's monstrous presence. The emphasis on intense feeling (often sexual in kind) and bloody violence that we find in transgressor texts by the likes of Cain and Thompson takes another turn here. For Harris moves away from the brutal realism of the earlier writers to a more grotesque and highly dramatic type of visceral excess: Gumb in *The Silence of the Lambs* making himself a new womanly body from the skins of his female victims; the scenes in *Hannibal* (1999) – where Hannibal Lecter finally comes to take center stage – of monstrous facial disfigurement (Mason Verger), a mock crucifixion, and of general mayhem done to the human body by way of disemboweling, man-eating pigs, and the like. This generic crossover between crime fiction and the gothic has become increasingly common in recent crime fiction; has become part of the latter's armory as it looks to challenge normative assumptions about human behavior and identity, and the social orderings that conventionally contain them, by turning such assumptions and orderings completely on their heads.

Hannibal Lecter, Hannibal the Cannibal, dominates Harris' fictional landscapes. Lecter is a man of great "taste" – a word that, in its punning move between various meanings, resonates strikingly here. An aesthete who appreciates fine music and literature, Hannibal is also a gourmet. But he is, too, a savage serial killer and cannibal, who cooks and serves parts of his victim's bodies to his dinner guests. This crossing of the boundaries between the admirable and the abominable is highly disconcerting, a disruption of all that normally separates the "civilized" from the "savage." Moreover, by the end of *Hannibal*, the third novel in the sequence, any trust in the law as the antidote to Lecter's monstrous presence has completely failed. Lecter is on the loose, and now with "bride" – former F.B.I. agent Clarice – in tow. Infection here seems triumphant, with any notion of vaccine cancelled. Harris achieves genuine shock in this final vision of the world he represents. I look more carefully at the reasons for Hannibal Lecter's importance, and just why Harris should so radically destabilize the boundaries between the civilized and the savage, putting his emphasis on criminal transgression of the most excessive kind, in my later chapter on *The Silence of the Lambs*, in Part 3.

Transgressor fiction, then, is a powerful – though minority – strand of crime fiction, and one that tends to ask questions more openly than other types of crime novel about the nature, and the justice, of the dominant social order. It is perhaps the most shocking form of crime writing, not just in its often explicit violence and sexuality (for other crime fictions contain such elements too) but in the representation of criminal action from the inside (as it were), and the jolt that this can give the reader to his or her normative conceptions of innocence and guilt, good and evil, criminal act and victimization.

In the chapters that now follow, I turn away from the different forms of crime fiction to discuss some of the key and recurrent topics that have shaped its contours and development.

Vision, Supervision, and the City

Private eye. The term held a triple meaning for Quinn. Not only was it the letter "i," standing for "investigator," it was "I" in the upper case. . . . At the same time it was also the physical eye of the writer, the eye of the man who looks out from himself into the world and demands that the world reveal itself to him. For five years now, Quinn had been living in the grip of this pun.

(Auster 1988: 8–9)

Paul Auster, in his brilliant *The New York Trilogy*, pushes the crime fiction form far beyond its normal boundaries as he pursues a series of multi-layered themes (language and its relation to reality, the problematics of identity, the dynamics of urban space, knowledge and its limits) crucial to late-twentieth-century post-modernist concern. The passage above provides some illustration of his talent in the handling both of language and ideas. Quinn is his protagonist, a writer of private eye novels under the name of William Wilson (the title and main character, of course, of a Poe story). But, at the *Trilogy's* start, Quinn adopts the name of "Paul Auster. Of the Auster Detective Agency" (7) as he decides to take on the role of private eye himself. So, immediately, the twinned issues of personal and professional identity and the relationship of fiction to reality are foregrounded. And, as Quinn speculates on the pun inherent in that term "private eye," he (and the "real" Auster) take their reader in a direction of crucial relevance to the crime fiction genre and the way that it works.

First, at the simplest level, we have the abbreviation (P. I.) itself, and its fuller meaning in the professional role that Quinn adopts as private investigator. It is the phonetic slippage in the second initial, though, that gives the term its punning potential, and the consequent movement from "I" to "eye" is a particularly resonant and appropriate one. The individual subject, the detective

---

The Crime Fiction Handbook, First Edition. Peter Messent.
© 2013 John Wiley & Sons, Ltd. Published 2013 by John Wiley & Sons, Ltd.

at the crime novel's center, is that "'I' in the upper-case," both central subject and investigator, the focus and – usually in crime fiction – moral arbiter of the narrative. Auster then takes us from "I" to "eye" (to suit my purposes, I extend his referent from writer to detective) – from the physical presence of the detective subject to his vision (or eye): the way he sees the world and what that world reveals to the questing self, looking to uncover whatever mystery it holds. It is the seeing eye, indeed, that has become the very sign and signal of detection. So we recall the heightened vision of Sherlock Holmes as he used his magnifying glass. We remember, too, the iconic symbol of the major U. S. private detective agency, Pinkerton's – the unblinking eye that ornaments its Chicago central office and the promise of endless watchfulness contained in the words etched beneath, "We never sleep."

The punning link between the "I" and "eye," and the search for revelation in which both engage (note how "eye" slides into the man himself in Auster's passage), is suggestive of the close relationship between the two words, their conceptual inseparability. Rosemary Jackson associates the very notion of stable selfhood with the seeing eye. For, if "to see clearly" means to command a visual field through the dominance of the eye, it also means the sense-making ability and comprehension of the individual sovereign subject: "'I see' . . . [is] synonymous with 'I understand.' Knowledge, comprehension, reason, are established through the power of the *look*. Through the 'eye' and the 'I' of the human subject." Equally, as Jackson also points out, a loss of the sense of visual control (as constantly occurs in James Ellroy's fictions, for instance) implies a deep uncertainty about identity, the authority of the self, and the relationship between the self and the world (1981: 44–46).

The power of the seeing eye and the subjectivity it represents is crucially important in detective fiction. The placing of the Pinkerton's symbolic eye on its office frontage suggests, further, that this eye operates in two ways, not just privately but publicly too; not just in the interests of the individual but of the larger social group. The private eye is, traditionally, a solitary man or woman, serving (in theory) no one's interests but his or her own and that of the immediate client. Having said that, and as I have previously suggested, in doing this, he or she usually, and ultimately, also serves the best interests of the larger social structure and the laws that govern it – even while (commonly) remaining alienated from such dominant values. The police detective, though, even if sharing something of that same disaffection, works *directly* for the state as a *public* eye, and – as the idea of vision fuses with that of *supervision* – exercises both watchfulness and authoritarian control on its behalf. And, if Pinkerton's represented itself as a private detective agency, the public display of its sign overlooking the city street came to imply something more, as indeed the agency took on a public and political role, became an arm of hegemonic power. So it worked – for instance – for Carnegie to help defeat the union strikers in the 1892 Homestead Steel strike. That all-seeing eye, then, comes to stand as a metonymic representation of a larger and increasingly public monitor, operating on behalf of those committed to established social hierarchies and social order. The private and the public eye merge in such a move.

Vision and supervision in detective fiction are, though, crucially connected to location – and to *city space* in particular. Poe's "The Man of the Crowd" (1840) is prescient here in its use of the crowded streets of London in the early nineteenth century as its setting, and a narrator who starts as a spectator of this urban scene but who then becomes a type of detective immersed in its variety and movement. To focus on the city is not, of course, to say that crime cannot be committed anywhere and that fictional (and real) detectives do not function in rural settings – as modern crime fiction by the likes of Reginald Hill, Ruth Rendell, and Peter Robinson in the United Kingdom, and James Lee Burke, James Crumley, and Tony Hillerman in the United States, serves to illustrate. But it is to say that the growth of urban living brought its own particular problems of crime and its solution, and that when we think about twentieth-century crime fiction and its development it is usually in an urban context.

I return here briefly to Franco Moretti. Speaking of Sherlock Holmes, Moretti notes the problems and anxieties of an "expanding society" in the Victorian period, and the consequent difficulty of imposing "effective social control" (1983: 143). This relates particularly to the rapid urbanization of the time, for such difficulty "emerges fully in the *metropolis*, where anonymity – that is, impunity – potentially reigns and which is rapidly becoming a tangled and inaccessible hiding place" (143). As Kate Summerscale writes of Paddington Station in 1860 – then one of the new hubs of London life:

> Jack Whicher knew the place well – the thieves of London thrived on the surging, anonymous crowds in the new railway stations, the swift comings and goings, the thrilling muddle of types and classes. This was the essence of the city that the detectives had been created to police. (2008: xix)

Detection, then, as an activity, has a particular and powerful connection to the dense human conditions, particular physical geography, and multitudinous information networks of the modern urban landscape.

Vision and "active observation" (Benjamin, qtd. in Frisby 1994: 95) were necessarily key aspects of the detective's identity as he or she looked to unravel the crimes occurring in a crowded and confusing urban world and bring "effective social control" to it. But the words "observation" and "control" suggest (again) the close relationship between vision and supervision, as the police and other agents of the state (including, to varying degree, the P. I.) worked to keep a close eye on the activities of criminals (and others) who threatened its stability and best interests. This reminds us of Moretti's claim that secrecy is a type of offence and of his comment on the totalitarian desire for "a *transparent* society" – Sherlock Holmes existing because Peter Pan (and his ability "to fly through key-holes") is just a fantasy.

Moretti appears to acknowledge the influence of the work of Michel Foucault (1926–1984), French philosopher and intellectual historian, when – writing of the connection between detective fiction and a coercive culture – he says: "Every story reiterates Bentham's Panopticon ideal; the model prison that signals the metamorphosis of liberalism into total scrutability" (1983: 143). For Foucault, in his influential work on the development of the Western prison system, *Discipline and Punish* (1975), makes much of Bentham's Panopticon. Jeremy Bentham (1748–1832) was the English philosopher and social reformer who designed the Panopticon (literally, the "all-seeing') as his model prison. The concept behind this is that, rather than being enclosed in darkness, the traditional gloomy prison cell, all prisoners should be fully visible, and on a twenty-four-hour basis, to their guards. The guards would be centrally located in a tower, with the prisoners' cells configured around them, but invisible to the prisoners – the latter's uncertainty as to whether they were being watched or not crucial to the disciplinary process. The prisoners were to be separated from their neighbors by walls, but back-lit by windows to the outside of the cell. All in all, Bentham saw this as the ideal method for the surveillance and control of large numbers of criminals (or, by analogy – for Bentham – mental patients, workers, schoolboys, and the like). As Foucault would comment:

> The panoptic mechanism arranges spatial unities that make it possible to see constantly and to recognize immediately. In short, it reverses the principle of the dungeon; or rather of its three functions – to enclose, to deprive of light and to hide – it preserves only the first and eliminates the other two. Full lighting and the eye of a supervisor capture better than darkness, which ultimately protected. Visibility is a trap. . . . [T]he supervisor . . . is seen, but he does not see; he is the object of information, never a subject in communication. . . . And this invisibility is a guarantee of order. Hence the major effect of the Panopticon: to induce in the inmate a state of conscious and permanent visibility that assures the automatic functioning of power. (1991: 200–201)

This concept of powerful control through total scrutability applies (as suggested above) to much more than just a prison population. And, as Moretti indicates, it took on a particular and important emphasis when applied to the rapid urbanization that occurred in the West from the mid-nineteenth century on. In the contemporary period, panopticism seems to have become an ever-more all-encompassing fact of life, with the constant use of security cameras – the majority overhead – and other forms of surveillance to monitor buildings, streets, and public places (and, increasingly, private spaces too).

Ideas of scrutability and surveillance also inform the work of another French thinker, Michel de Certeau, in his 1980 book *The Practice of Everyday Life*. De Certeau uses an urban geography metaphorically to site forms and degrees of state regulation and control (but also, crucially, its avoidance). He describes looking down at the Manhattan cityscape from the (then still-standing) 110th-floor observation deck of the World Trade Center, and suggests that such a view indicates the panoptic domination of the managed city: a bird's eye view, or crystal-clear reading of the urban text seen from above, through what Steve Pile (one of his explicators) calls the "godlike eye of the powerful" (1996: 227). Opposed to this spectacle of the "city immobilised," however, de Certeau sets the visual activity associated with pedestrianism; the city seen from street level and as part of the crowd. Such pedestrians create metaphorically their own text of the city as they walk it, and are invisible to the panoptic eye, "involved" as they are "in the production of an unmappable space which cannot be seen from above" (Pile 1996: 225–226). "The ordinary practitioners of the city," then, "live 'down below,' below the thresholds at which visibility begins. . . . [T]hey are walkers . . . whose bodies follow the thicks and thins of an urban 'text' they write without being able to read" (de Certeau 1984: 93).

There is, in retrospect, something deeply ironic about de Certeau's use of the World Trade Center to figure panopticism – given that it was exactly here that the authority of the managed city was so catastrophically (and criminally) disrupted. But de Certeau's focus on the life of the individual citizen – very much a part of his overall project to re-examine culture through ordinary and everyday human practice – is useful here in suggesting both the limits of the panoptic and its interest in preserving the established, capitalist status quo (for the World Trade Center platform as well as its city seen/scene demonstrate what Pile calls "excesses of power and money," 1996: 225). I use the tension de Certeau draws between, on the one hand, the World Trade Center and the managed city metaphorically implicit in its view and, on the other, the alternative ground-level version of urban space ("below the thresholds at which visibility begins") – with hundreds of thousands of individual citizens creating the life of the city in their various journeys and the micro-narratives of which they speak – as a springboard for my own thoughts on urban space and visibility in the crime fiction genre.

While de Certeau's image of panopticism and the limits of its reach is a powerful one, it does need to be modified when applied to urban crime and its policing. The idea of the city spread out to view and managed from above makes a lot of metaphoric sense. For, this is the way the police would like to work: the modern detection equivalent of Peter Pan flying above the houses and peeking in would be the police helicopter buzzing over the city following criminals, monitoring potential and actual disturbances, supervising from above. And, indeed, security cameras, information from mobile phones, telecommunications monitoring, and the like do allow the police to keep – in reality – a watchful eye on the labyrinthine city streets (and, again rather like Peter Pan, even inside the homes which feed them).

The distinction between the tower and the street, then, with the ceaseless human movement and interactions of the city taking place in "spaces of darkness and trickery" (de Certeau 1984: 18) is both useful and relevant when we apply it to the policing of urban crime but, nonetheless, does not quite work. For we remember, too, that the state has its representatives at street level. So the private eye negotiates the street world, using his or her knowledge and watchfulness to illuminate that part of it through which s/he moves – and generally uses such knowledge to the ends of the existing social order, whatever alienation from it s/he may feel. The uniformed policeman, more simply, gives the state a highly visible street presence, while plain-clothes detectives, disguised police infiltrators, and the use of informers and the like open up street-level criminal activity to public inspection of various kinds.

What we have, then, is a more complicated situation than de Certeau's model might suggest, and one in which the forces of law and criminality exist in a particularly tense relationship. The state (in the guise of the police and others) can penetrate the street-level environment, where the ceaseless human movement and interactions of the city take place. Criminal activity can accordingly sometimes (though not always) become visible to the detectives (private agents or disguised public officials) who operate at this level, or – in the conventional parlance – "underground"; who have the technological means or know enough to read the fragmentary signs available on the streets (and indeed in more private places) and/or the trace evidence that the criminal leaves behind; who can penetrate both the spaces and the networks where the criminals normally hide.

But there is another side to this picture. For, in the complex urban maze or labyrinth (see Howell 1998: 363–364 on the differences between the two), the power of the public eye is necessarily limited. There are only so many spaces that can be supervised by security cameras and the like, and in many areas – as for instance the urban ghetto – where the police may not be trusted, there will be little co-operation with the law, and its most obvious security devices may well be vandalized. And security cameras, in particular, are of limited use, sometimes disabled by the criminal who looks to avoid their lens (remember the opening credit sequence of TV series *The Wire*, for instance, which gives a security camera-view of someone throwing stones at it, up to the point at which the camera is broken), sometimes too soon wiped clean of information, and producing images that may be crystal sharp but may also show fuzzy and indistinguishable figures. And the police and the detective cannot keep on top of all planned and actual crime – a good proportion of the multitude of urban crimes that occur will necessarily escape any watching or retrospective metaphorical radar.

Crime fiction generally mirrors such an understanding. As Philip Howell argues, it represents knowledge of the city as always partial and never complete:

> [E]ven when city solutions are offered, this seems often enough to be a never-ending, sisyphean task, whose ultimate worth is thoroughly in doubt. . . . The city's mysteries are ongoing, never conclusively confronted, and victories always partial and often pyrrhic. (364)

This inability finally to know the city is partly due to its labyrinthine quality – a place where a mass of people go about their various existences, often lacking any real sense of traditional community, and moving and living in a wide variety of locations, often in almost total anonymity. The very extent of, and the differences within, the urban landscape – its wealthy enclaves, ghettoes, slums, and class- or ethnically-divided neighborhoods; its streets, bars, offices, railway stations, and varied public spaces – similarly counter any full supervisory authority, the possibility of panoptic knowledge.

There are two other factors that should be mentioned, however briefly, in the picture I thus far draw. First, chronology must not be forgotten. The effectiveness of policing in the city has been highly dependent on technological advance. Detection in Sherlock Holmes' gas-lit London, with no security cameras or mobile phones and travel by horse-drawn hansom cab and the like, is a world away from the city as represented in most contemporary crime fiction. Second, the model with which I started (de Certeau's distinction between city tower and city street) fails to distinguish – in the case of crime – between the various types of space where crime is planned and occurs in urban settings. We might start to differentiate such places in terms of private homes, semi-public places (hotels, bars, restaurants, clubs, and shops), and public places (streets, public parks, and squares). Clearly, types of detection, and the possibilities for it, differ accordingly.

How does what I have said so far connect with the narrative form of crime fiction? (I acknowledge my debt to Phillip Howell as I look to answer this question.) Detective fiction normally tends to privilege the knowledge and authority synonymous with the seeing eye/I, and to use a first-person narration (or a third-person narration representing the detective's point of view) to do so. This undoubtedly constitutes a type of street-level knowledge but it provides just one single perspective on, and route through, a crowded urban scene that contains a multitude of other possible points of view and narratives – not just of those solving crime but of victims, criminals, bystanders, and others more indirectly affected. So, in a Chandler novel, for example, it is the first-person detective protagonist who maps the city of Los Angeles (and its surroundings) for the reader, and it is Marlowe's eye and laconic voice that takes us, at the start of *The Long Good-bye* (1953), from his "small hillside house on a dead-end street" in Laurel Canyon (Chandler 1962: 193) to the stores on Hollywood Boulevard, "already beginning [the week after Thanksgiving] to fill up with Christmas junk" (194), then to the "drive-in" where he takes Terry Lennox, "where they made hamburgers that didn't taste of something the dog wouldn't eat" (196). And generally in Chandler – even while we are made fully aware of the determining forces that limit Marlowe's agency – it is through the P. I.'s single lens that we see the city, with his meanings and vision of the world ultimately shaping the narrative he tells.

James Ellroy's *The Big Nowhere* (1988) is a more multi-dimensional text than any of Chandler's in the perspectives it employs – two cops and one disgraced ex-cop. His police context allows, moreover, for the type of knowledge and rapid processing of information that we can link, to a certain degree, with panoptic authority and control (though Ellroy's detailing of interdepartmental dispute and dirty police and city politics means that such authority is distinctly limited). I focus here, though, on the novel's opening sequence, channeled through the focalization (point of view) of Detective Deputy Danny Upshaw and represented by way of the third-person narrative voice. Again it is Los Angeles – this time on the New Year's Eve of 1950 – that composes the novel's urban environment, first described via Upshaw as he works the graveyard shift at the West Hollywood substation:

> At 12:03, a four-vehicle fender bender at Sunset and La Cienega. . . . At 12:14, an uninhabited vet's shack on Sweetzer collapsed in a heap of drenched prefab, killing a teenaged boy and girl necking under the foundation. . . . [T]hen . . . a slew of drunk and disorderlies as the clubs on the Strip let out; then a strongarm heist in front of Dave's Blue Room, the victims two Iowa yokels in town for the Rose Bowl, the muscle two niggers who escaped in a '47 Merc with purple fender skirts. (3–4)

Information here is being passed through to the local police headquarters where it is processed by (we gather) two-way radio. But it is fact and vision, not voice, that soon take primary interest. Upshaw is initially alone in the station, unsupervised, with "[n]o one to give him the fish-eye." When he hears of a new and startling case, he drives to "the weed-strewn vacant lot" on Allegro Street, to "loo[k] down" on the corpse that has been found there. He stops himself from vomiting at the grisly sight by moving into professional mode, and dictating the details of what he sees to a deputy in attendance: "Dead male Caucasian, nude. . . . The cadaver is lying supine. . . . There are ligature marks on the neck, the eyes have been removed and the empty sockets are extruding a gelatinous substance." As flashlights are then deployed to give Danny "some close-ups," he further reports that "[t]he genitals are bruised and swollen, there are bite marks of the glans of the penis." Light and vision, and its lack (those empty eye sockets), are emphasized here, not only in what the flashlights enable Danny to see – he is soon to move in "extra close" to see yet more bodily mutilation – but in the "profusion of cherry lights, flashlights and headbeams dart[ing] over the lot" and "the neon haze of Hollywood in the distance." And vision, knowledge, and the ability to think/see through the eyes of others are specified as the key to the success of the detective-protagonist, the mainspring of his professional identity: "If the detective is willing to sort physical evidence objectively and then *think* subjectively from the killer's viewpoint, he will often solve crimes that are baffling in their randomness" (4–7).

Here, as in Chandler, the process of detection, and the depiction of the urban environment in which it occurs, are tied to the perspective of the detective – a cop (this time), Danny Upshaw, with the resources of the larger organization behind him. Ellroy, though, unlike Chandler, in representing a proliferation of crime and denying reliance on a single subjective vision, both confuses and complicates any notion of a single story and point of view and resists the idea that it can contain the urban narrative he tells. The fact that two of his three main narrative filters are cops limits, however, both the perspective and the range of social positions he represents.

De Certeau suggests the importance of the criss-crossing of multiple individual journeys, and of the narratives they trace, in creating and representing urban space and its meanings. The formal correlative of this lies in a crime fiction that represents a plurality of perspectives, from a number of subject positions, giving its reader some picture not just of the variety of lives in the city and the ways in which they intersect but also of the different personal and social perspectives that compose them. The use of criss-crossing narratives of this type distances the reader from the single vision and worldview of the private eye or lone cop, and moves her or him beyond the shared common perspective of the police team. It allows, instead, a wider representation of urban reality, of the social anxieties and problems inhabiting that space, and of the conflicting psychologies and motivations of – and influences on – its denizens, be they police, criminal, victim, or bystander citizen. Such fictions – downgrading the narrative authority of the single detective or police team, and disturbing any unthinking acceptance of her/his or its values on the part of the reader – are increasingly common in contemporary crime fiction. They present the reader, in Howell's words, "with a formal analogue of the multiple stories, overlapping narratives, partial truths, and sheer contingency of city life": "[i]nsistence on the shared knowledge of place constructed in the everyday lives of the city's inhabitants," he continues, "is to implicitly abandon the totalized view of the city without giving up on the possibility of any kind of knowledge constructed out of the city's semiotic noise" (1998: 367). It is, perhaps, in the work of Elmore Leonard that we find the earliest examples of such multiple narratives, while Richard Price provides a more recent example. But I focus on just one modern crime writer who uses such tactics, the British crime writer John Harvey, one of whose novels I briefly discuss here.

Easy Meat (1996) is the eighth in Harvey's Charlie Resnick series, all of which are set in and around the city of Nottingham. Harvey employs similar tactics to Leonard in swiftly cross-cutting between scenes and points of view, but his fiction works more clearly as socio-political commentary than does that of the American author. The novel begins with the point of view of Norma Snape, a middle-aged single mother just about holding together her family of three teenage children in their too-small terrace house in the Radford area of the city. Her backstory – an under-age pregnancy with the baby adopted; an early relationship with Patrick, "part-Irish, part-Scottish, part-wild . . . a gentle hippy with the most violent of tempers" (8) who physically abuses both her and their baby, Shane; another partner (now left), another two babies, and periods of failing to cope with all the consequent pressures – prepares us for the wrong turnings, petty (and not-so-petty) criminalities, frustrations, and violent eruptions of her own children's lives. Harvey paints a grim picture of life on the margins, and the failure of adequate social support systems to help in any positive way. Indeed, quite the opposite is true: for it turns out that Shane, seventeen as the novel starts, who (we discover) is both drawn to homosexuals but also harbors a homophobic rage that ends up in the death of a gay police officer, had himself been abused in the children's home he spent time in when he became too much for his mother to handle.

Harvey tells his story by alternating narratives. Starting with Norma's perspective, the book concludes with that of her daughter, Sheena – whose life in the course of the novel has slid ever further down the pan. (This ending, and the long odds it gives against escaping the consequences of detrimental environmental circumstances, is among the bleakest of any crime novel I have read.) But, between these bookends, we follow a variety of other perspectives. That of Harvey's main protagonist, Detective Inspector Resnick, is (as we would expect) the most dominant. But we also see events through the eyes of Bill Aston, Mark Divine, Lynn Kellog, Graham Millington, Kevin Naylor, and others – all police officers on or connected to Resnick's police team. Divine's point of view is particularly interesting in that the novel tackles themes (among others) of racism and homophobia, and Divine's attitudes to both are not that far removed from those whom we would have little problem here as labeling society's dregs, with right-wing and anti-gay activist and thug Frank Miller being the novel's prime example. Harvey's urban world is no black and white one when it comes to such matters.

One other important narrative and point of view represented in the book is that of secondary school English teacher Hannah Campbell. Hannah is the teacher of Nicky Snape – the schoolboy and petty criminal who becomes uncontrollably violent when himself physically attacked by Eric Netherfield, the elderly man into whose house he has broken; and who, once apprehended, commits suicide after suffering sexual intimidation and abuse at the children's home where he is being held. Hannah – seen by Resnick in connection with Snape's house-breaking and consequent actions – becomes romantically involved with the detective. Her literary and filmic tastes, occupation, and middle-class background make her into a strong foil for Resnick (and his official police role), and one who questions his views on criminality ("[I]n your book, are criminals born and not made? Nature or nurture, Charlie, which are you?") and the point and effectiveness of imprisonment as a punishment for crime (117–118).

Harvey, then, gives us a variety of perspectives on the Nottingham world he represents. (Assuming a particular character's point of view is not the only way to do this, though it is one of the most effective and convincing. The use of dialogue and reported information, both also parts – as it happens – of Harvey's formal armory, can provide other routes to the same end.) And the intersecting life-narratives we get here are symbiotically linked to the geography of the city through which each character or group of characters pass. For Nottingham (or any city) – following the implications of my argument so far – cannot be known as a panoptic whole. Instead we have fragmentary knowledge – separate and different sets of tracks through, and views of, the urban world. Harvey maps the movements of his protagonists and, as he does so, provides us with symbolic signposts to their social and cultural priorities and positions, evidence of the multiple routines and practices that compose both the city's and the story's whole.

So we have Nicky Snape busying about, selling the credit cards from Hannah Campbell's purse, stolen on one of his rare appearances in school:

> At the back of a pub edging onto the wholesale fruit and veg market he had sold one of [her] two credit cards for twenty pounds; less than thirty minutes later, in the pleasant surroundings of St Mary's rest garden, her cheque-book and cheque guarantee card had changed hands for double that. Cutting through the Victoria Centre towards the Mansfield Road, he had chanced to bump into Sally Purdy. . . . Purdy sent Nicky back inside to Tesco's to buy a six-pack of Tennents, two of which she shared with him on one of the benches opposite Peachey Street. (33)

Conversely, Resnick is described in terms of his professional vision but he is also described by way of his private life, with routines, and their meanings (as we would expect), very different from Nicky's. His two lives (private and professional) cannot, unsurprisingly, be held entirely distinct, as suggested when the view of the city from his Mapperley Park home back garden is described: "Between the railway station and Sneinton Windmill, the floodlights of the two soccer grounds showed up clearly. . . . Along the canal, warehouses with peeling fronts . . . stood beside architect-designed office buildings and the new marina." His professional knowledge of the city is at stake here, and what he cannot see is just as significant as what he can: "[He] could not see the night shelters, the needles discarded below the old railway arch, the benches . . . where the homeless slept, but he knew that they were there" (56–57).

If Resnick's role as a detective allows him access to, and knowledge of, some of the spaces the Snape brothers and other criminals inhabit (as well as to those inhabited by others on the margins of society), and if his investigative processes can map some of the movements of these groups, such a process must always be partial, even haphazard. And if (to draw an analogy with Resnick's knowledge of the city's addicts and down-and-outs) he knew crime was there, he cannot access, see directly into, every one of its locations. If "Notts . . . [has the] [b]est detection figures in the country. . . . Clear-up rate per officer of fourteen cases a year," the amount of crime is proportionately high ("148 crimes per 1000 of the population, the second highest after Humberside," 25). We assume, accordingly, that the earlier (apparently unmotivated) murder of Resnick's colleague, Dipak Patel, is far from being the only crime that remains a mystery and unsolved. The panoptic eye of the law is highly limited in such respects.

And, as Harvey charts Resnick's day-to-day experiences of city space, we see very different trajectories, and ways of seeing and thinking, than those of Nicky Snape. Resnick, too, walks in the Victoria Centre (one of the two main shopping centers in the city), but not as a cut-through; rather – for he is of Polish origin – to buy the ethnic and other (specialty) food that makes up his diet:

> Resnick entered the market past the corner music stall where the Tremeloes' Greatest Hits were always playing. . . . [He] was heading for the Polish deli. . . . He made his purchases – several of the salamis sliced thin, a loaf of crusty rye bread with caraway, sour cream – and carried them over to the Italian coffee stall. (112–113)

Resnick's recognition of the music gives some insight into both his age and musical history (though his main love is jazz). And he and Hannah, as they get closer, introduce each other to new places, routines, and cultural habits: for her the Polish Club; for him the Broadway cinema on Broad Street and the highbrow film they see there (*Vanya on 42nd Street*). Their walk, too, to a shared picnic in the Arboretum (281–285) is a world away from (attack victim) Declan Harris' late-night and secretive foray over the fence into the park near Hannah's house, his visit to the toilet there ("ripe with the stink of stale urine," 329), his quest – though he will not admit it – for consensual homosexual sex, and the rape that follows (331–336).

The Nottingham that Hannah knows – her short shopping trip from her Volkswagen in the Victoria Centre underground car park to the supermarket Tesco; "her usually healthy purchases" there, "compromised . . . with a Sarah Lee ready-baked Pecan Nut Danish pastry" (115); then her short walk on to the market to buy vegetables, cheese, and flowers – is in turn very different from that of Sheena Snape. Sheena's afternoon in town with new mates (and dope and acid users) Diana, Janie, and Dee-Dee involves a trip to Dolcis (where Diana steals some boots), then the gang "walking down through the city centre by Debenham's [department store]" (308), taking advantage of the opportunity for the on-street violent aggression and theft that comes their way. The novel ends with this same group, again on the street but this time outside the bowling alley, eating chips from a burger bar. Again the culture of aggression, violence, and social anomie, fostered (it is implied) by the dead-end quality of the girls' lives, is illustrated as Janie – acting out of all proportion to the provocation given – sticks a broken-off and sharpened screwdriver into the "disgusting fat belly" (420) of the old drunk who has been harassing her. The last words of the book record Sheena's thoughts as she laughs following the stabbing: "[T]ruly awesome. I mean, absolutely fucking brilliant! Brilliant, right?" (420).

It is as we move between such points of view, following the movements through the city of the novel's various and varied protagonists, that we get (to repeat an earlier phrase) a "formal analogue of the multiple stories, overlapping narratives, partial truths, and sheer contingency of city life." To say this is to recognize that there are many other ways to build a crime novel, and that it is ways of representing the city that alone are at stake here. Harvey's, however, is an impressive example of one way of doing this.

I conclude this chapter with brief comments on some recent changes in the representation of detection in crime fiction, and how this affects the depiction and use of urban space. The city – with its particular geography and human and institutional relationships – has been, as I have argued, the primary location for modern crime fiction. And the conventional image of crime-solving is of the detective (usually male) moving through the city streets, by car and on foot, as he seeks out his criminal quarry. All the texts I have referred to above (Chandler, Ellroy, Harvey) basically operate in this way. But recent technological developments have come to stand alongside – and at times replace – such traditional forms of detection. Computer technology, in particular, and its ramifications both in terms of the commission of crime and its solving, has meant that the traditional connection between crime and urban space has been rendered – to some degree at least – obsolete, replaced by what we might call hyperreal immediacy: in Elizabeth Grosz's words, "the replacement of geographical space with the screen interface, the transformation of distance and depth into pure surface, the reduction of space to time, of the face-to-face encounter to the terminal screen" (1995: 110). Differently, but part of a similar technological advance, rapid changes in the field of forensics have tended to move the solving of crime – to at least some degree – away from the streets and into the laboratory, with a consequent increase in, and updating of, what we can call the clue-based mystery of an earlier time.

But it is not just the screen interface and forensic technology that have altered crime and the response to it (and its fictional depiction). For, even in terms of the direct representation of space, the tying of crime to one particular urban space and its geography is becoming increasingly redundant. Crime now is commonly no longer contained within the boundaries of a single city or even a single country. The depiction of space has changed accordingly to reflect this sense of its multi-locational, even global, reach. The (powerful) fictions of Don Winslow with their moves between U. S. and South American locations provide just one example of this.

A final, and quite different, factor we need to take into consideration here is that of gender. Detective fiction traditionally links the male detective to the city streets he travels. And this connection is common too in female crime fiction (in Sue Grafton and Sara Paretsky, for example). But with female detection – and see my final chapter in this part of the book, "Gender Matters" – the sense of physical vulnerability that often affects the male detective is foregrounded to a much greater extent. In consequence, her detective work is often carried out away from the streets, and the reading of its signs, operating in other ways completely.

I will examine some of the developments just sketched out here in my later analysis of individual texts – and with reference to Patricia Cornwell in particular. For the moment, however, I merely signal the fact that, while the relationship between urban space and detection remains crucial to the majority of modern crime fiction, the genre is not a static one. There are (and increasingly) other ways of reading crime – in the city, beyond its limits, and in quite other contexts – than those I sketch here.

Crime and the Body

Crime fiction, more often than not, focuses on harm done to the human body – and especially the female body. There are plenty of male corpses in the history of the genre, too, but it is rare to find the same type of emphasis on physical mutilation, and especially of a sexual nature, as when the victim is a woman. The male body found at the beginning of Ellroy's *The Big Nowhere*, and referred to in the last chapter, with its eyes removed and bite marks between navel and rib-cage ("shredded flesh outlines the perimeters, entrails coated with congealed blood extruding from them," 1988: 6), is an exception here to a general rule – though this rule may now be starting to lose at least some of its ground. (See, for instance, Elizabeth George's 2005 novel *With No One as Witness*, where Kimmo Thorne's fifteen-year-old male body is found sliced "open from sternum to waist" and with the navel "chopped right off," 21, 29.)

But it is the victimized female body, often graphically described, that remains the genre's most typically depicted sight, and site for investigation. So Ellroy's earlier *Black Dahlia* (1987) describes the discovery of Elizabeth Short's nude dismembered corpse in horrific detail: body sliced in half, breasts stippled with burns from cigarettes, "nose crushed deep into the facial cavity, the mouth cut ear to ear" in a leering smile (77). There is a good cultural reason for the excessive violence Ellroy introduces in the evidence it indicates of a "viciously inverted fantasy" – the would-be Hollywood star subject not to the admiring male gaze but to murderous male rage, her own agency diminished by her role as a "victimized object of urban power" (Cohen 1997: 175, and see my reading of the novel in Part 3). This, though, fails to make the description of the horribly disfigured corpse any less shocking or disturbing.

The Crime Fiction Handbook, First Edition. Peter Messent.
© 2013 John Wiley & Sons, Ltd. Published 2013 by John Wiley & Sons, Ltd.

Similar representations are common in contemporary crime fiction. And, if this fascination with such excessive and usually bloody violence dates back to the earliest days of crime writing (see Part 1), it has certainly taken on increased frequency and explicitness in the last thirty years or so, and certainly with a greater emphasis on the female body as crime target. Thomas Harris' *Red Dragon* is, arguably, one of the key texts in this process. Dolarhyde's first victims described in detail in the novel are the Leeds family – the father with his throat cut "as he lay asleep beside his wife" (1983: 12) and each of their three children simply killed by "a single gunshot wound in the head" (13). Mrs. Leeds is a different matter, however. Shot, and later strangled, her body is "bitten and torn" (17), with pieces of the mirrors Dolarhyde smashes in the family house "wedged in the labia," the mouth, and the eyes (21). These mirror fragments are "set so he can see himself" (66) reflected back from his victim's damaged features, her death the sign of his own transformation into a figure of authority and power: into the "majesty of [his] Becoming" (96).

There are countless other examples of such harm done to the female body and it is not my intention to give any more than is necessary for my immediate critical purposes. But I would point too, for example, to the serial killer who appears in a number of Patricia Cornwell's novels, the "French wolfman," Jean-Baptiste Chandonne, who sees his calling as to "destroy beautiful females . . . rip women apart" (2003: 48). In an impressionistic passage in *Blow Fly* (2003), with Chardonne now on death row in a Texas prison, he slips into a future-/present-tense recall of his past murders, as he looks "to find his next chosen one and rip away her flawed sight and beat her brains into forgetfulness. . . . Her blood is fine red wine, whichever vintage he craves . . . making his teeth ache with joy" (50). And, when Denise Babbit is murdered in Michael Connelly's *The Scarecrow* (2010), the "[a]utopsy would show that she had been repeatedly raped with a foreign object. Minute splinters found in the vagina and anus indicated this object was possibly a wooden broom or tool handle" (71). Tami Hoag's *Deeper than the Dead* (2009) starts with the buried body of a dead woman but with her head "entirely above ground, propped up on a stone the size of a loaf of bread." The body is "staged for maximum shock value," and with mouth and eyes "glued shut" (2010: 21–22). As we move into the perpetrator's consciousness, we learn the reason for this last detail, for it "rendered her blind and mute, making her the perfect woman. Beautiful. Seen and not heard. Obedient. . . . [S]he was nothing and he was God" (1–2). In Jo Nesbø 's *The Leopard* (2009), the novel starts within the consciousness of the first victim, Borgny Stem-Myhre, an implement called a Leopold's Apple forced into her mouth. When activated (as she does in an attempt to relieve her situation), this metal ball shoots out seven-centimeter-long needles: "Four burst through her cheeks on each side. . . . Two needles pierced the windpipe and one the right eye, one the left. Because the metal ball impeded movement, she was unable to spit out the blood pouring from the wounds into her mouth"; she thus drowns in her own blood (2010: 7).

There are patterns apparent in these descriptions to which I will return. The high level of bodily violence so painstakingly represented here may be in part a product of the increasing gothicization of crime fiction – its moves toward the type of excess previously associated with the horror genre. But there is more to it than this – or rather, the reasons for such a move are deeply embedded in the contemporary consciousness. I have suggested one explanation of crime fiction's long-standing fascination with the slashed body in my introduction (see Part 1). I give alternative and additional reasons for its present-day prevalence here. I then connect my discussion of the violently damaged bodies of the victims of crime with the noticeable increase in interest in the inspection and deciphering of such bodies in recent examples of forensic detective fiction – or what Kathy Reichs, one of its practitioners, calls "science-driven mysteries" (Stanford 2006: n.p.). For, as the success of Reichs, Cornwell, Iris Johansen, and others suggests, such a focus on dead bodies, their dissection, and the detective work related to such activity also holds major interest for today's crime fiction audience.

The constant diet of bodily mutilation, and especially of women, in contemporary crime fiction can, then, be explained. The simplest way of thinking about this is in terms of standard gender stereotypes. Attitudes to women in twentieth- and twenty-first-century Western societies have persistently been expressed through the medium of their physical bodies, the two (women and their bodies) often seen as synonymous in a cultural imagination partly produced, and certainly dominated, by men. Such an objectification of women can go hand in hand with deep-rooted misogyny and male anger, but it is more often associated with a general, rather free-floating, sense of gender anxiety, usually unexpressed at any fully conscious level. It acts accordingly – in its various manifestations – as a way of asserting linguistic, psychological, and physical authority and control over women in a gender context where traditional patterns of dominance and submission (the male as the physically and vocally powerful head of the household; the woman in the weaker, quieter, nurturing role) no longer hold.

Many men (and most women) would no longer defend such traditional gender stereotypes – challenged and largely reconstructed by 1970s (and subsequent) feminism and its long-term social impact. But they are so deeply imbued in the cultural imaginary that their influence remains persistent – with male anger and/or anxiety about such gender matters often finding symbolic release in the disfigured female corpse. This can happen at a conscious or unconscious level. So, in *Red Dragon*, for example, Harris links the callous everyday treatment of women as bodily objects to its psychopathic and exceptional criminal counterpart. Accordingly, just prior to Will Graham's nightmare in which he imagines the "bitten and torn" body of Mrs. Leeds lying in his own bed in the Atlanta hotel at which he is staying as he investigates her case, he overhears two men attending a convention in the same hotel (and drunk, it is implied) in conversation, as he takes the elevator to his room:

> They held to the rail and looked over the lobby as they ascended.
> "Looka yonder by the desk – that's Wilma . . . just now coming in," the larger one said. "God damn, I'd love to tear off a piece of that."
> "Fuck her till her nose bleeds," the other one said.
> Fear and rut, and anger at the fear.
> "Say, you know why a woman has legs?"
> "Why?"
> "So she won't leave a trail like a snail." (16)

Harris makes his point in an unsubtle, even unconvincing, manner here. But the connection he suggests between the (supposed) verbal banter of the conventioneers and the murderous actions of Dolarhyde is valid nonetheless. In reducing Wilma to her nose, torso, and vagina, figuratively "tear[ing] . . . a piece" off her and imagining her legless, the two men in Harris' novel deny her individual identity. Their fantasy vision of her bleeding and slimy bodily orifices (the nose and, presumably, the vagina) is, in its mindset, not far removed from Dolarhyde and his physical attack on Mrs. Leeds, and her mutilated eyes and violated labia. It is similarly linked to the repeated attention to bleeding, penetrated, and disfigured mouths, noses, eyes, vaginas, and anuses in the other passages about the bodies of female murder victims earlier quoted.

Paying attention to these particular bodily parts helps to suggest a deeper level of cultural analysis that we can bring to such depictions of violated bodies in the genre, and of female bodies in particular. I take my cue here from recent film criticism and its concern with what has become known as "body-horror" – horror based on gory images of the human body being torn apart or transformed in unexpected and "monstrous" ways. (Well-known body-horror movies include such films as *An American Werewolf in London*, *Black Swan*, *The Exorcist*, *Inside*, *Night of the Living Dead*, *Scanners*, *Suspiria*, and *The Texas Chainsaw Massacre*.) I focus particularly on a 1995 article on the horror genre by Barbara Creed, where she draws on feminist theoretician Julia Kristeva (1941–) and her work on the *abject* (my emphasis) to explain the changing depiction and symbolic significance of the human body in this popular form of film.

The abject is defined by Creed as "[e]verything that threatens the subject's identity as human" (1995: 149). Blood, torn flesh, spilling entrails, and dismemberments are seen as part of this threat, transgressing the boundary between the human and the non-human, violating the body's integrity, dismantling it in a "fragmented, grotesque, gruesome" way (Horsley and Horsley 2011: 5). Selfhood, Creed argues, is "intimately bound up with the constitution of a sense of stable subjectivity, coherent speech, and the clean and proper body" (1995: 149). Our identity as human subjects, then, is put in jeopardy when the borders of the body are ruptured, and as such fragmentations, penetrations, and blood-lettings occur. The abject is associated particularly with those points that "link the inside to the outside of the body," the places where bodily wastes ("faeces, blood, tears, urine, vomit") are expelled. So the "mouth, eyes, vagina, womb, skin, and blood" (and I would add the anus) have special status (150). It is in such places that the precarious nature of our subjectivity is most evident, where our (imagined) self-sufficient intactness is most likely to be symbolically exposed for the wishful thinking it is. "The ultimate in abjection," Creed explains, "is the corpse" (149). For here the body is reduced to the status of an object and nothing more, all that makes it living and human evacuated.

To apply what Creed says about body-horror and the abject to crime fiction is to see the genre's shared interest in bodily violation in a number of different ways. (I am not suggesting that the horror and crime fiction genres are one and the same, but there is some overlap between them in this particular respect.) Most straightforwardly, Creed identifies such abjection (she quotes Pete Boss' description, "the body in profuse disarray," 128) as "displace[d] anxiety" (143) about the status of the subject in the contemporary period: symptomatic of "an increasing sense of individual helplessness" (129) and of fears of a loss of individual authority and control in our contemporary (and post-modern) world. In one of the best-known essays on post-modernism, Fredric Jameson argues that "the alienation of the subject" of high modernism – that sense of "solitude and social fragmentation and isolation" so prevalent in its art – has been "displaced by the fragmentation of the subject" (1984: 61–63), the dissolution of our sense of centered subjectivity in a commodity-driven, image-saturated, and depthless contemporary culture. In body-horror (and its crime fiction equivalent), this idea of "fragmentation" takes on a more literal meaning, but indicating a similar deep-seated concern about both identity and agency. For, as Creed writes, 'Images of the bleeding body . . . point symbolically to the fragile nature of the self, its lack of secure boundaries, the ease with which it might lose definition, fall apart, or bleed into nothingness' (1995: 144). We can then go on to argue that such violations of the clean and proper body, and denial of "the sanctity of life" (132), can also imply a larger challenge to traditional ordering structures and values – the family, the normative routines of community life – for, if our identity as individual subjects is insecure, so too the successful functioning of the contemporary social system as a whole is put in question.

Creed, then, associates the representation of the torn and damaged body in horror films with abjection and the fragile nature of subjectivity. But such a representation has a specifically gendered charge, and it is accordingly no coincidence that in crime fiction it is the woman's body on which attention is focused. Creed argues that this aligns with a whole pattern of thinking in Western culture where "the body is linked to the feminine . . . whereas man is usually positioned on the side of logic and rationality" (127). This statement maps easily on to the crime fiction genre, where (traditionally) the male detective is associated with exactly those latter qualities, charged with investigating the harm done to slashed and bloodied, silenced and powerless female victims.

The patterns of thinking identified here are part and parcel of patriarchy – the dominant Western social model based on the father as the head of the family and on the male members of the larger community as its governing authorities. In this system (to expand the gender binary above), maleness is synonymous with "law, rationality, logic, truth" and with "the whole and proper body" (Creed 1995: 136–137): a hard physical intactness rather than its abject female opposite (with the womb, parturition, and menstrual blood its primary signs). The scream, the sound that in both horror and in crime narratives issues from the female victim, stands as one further sign of this opposition between masculine authority and order and its (feminine) collapse, signaling the loss of language (exactly that on which the rule of patriarchal law depends) and representing "terror at its most abject." This female scream is usually accompanied by a loss of bodily control – the woman's body "thrash[ing] frantically in the dark" – and so represents not just the loss of the female victim's "powers of coherent speech" but also her very "sense of her 'self' as a coherent whole" (144).

In crime fiction (as in the horror genre), then, it is the feminine to which the abject is primarily linked. The increasing emphasis on abjection in the contemporary crime novel – all those bleeding and traumatized bodies that litter its pages – in turn is indicative of a suspicion and a fear that the male patriarchal order, with its assumptions of rationality, authority, and control, has failed. The fact that the male body, too, has to an increasing degree taken on the characteristics of the feminine in contemporary crime fiction – sharing its representational role as bleeding, dismembered victim – figures the increased extent of such a failure: a growing unease (even a sense of crisis) both about the status of the individual subject and the social body of which it is a part. (Contemporary concerns about pedophilia, child abuse, and the fracturing of traditional family ties may well start to explain the particular prevalence of murder stories about young boys.) So much human waste – ragged flesh, jagged bones, torn sinew, bleeding mouths, damaged eyes, and the like – indicates the fragility of our present sense of selfhood, our sense that the social order that contains and supports it may, too, be ineffective.

But, as Creed also points out, there is more than one way to read such violent slashings and dismemberments. I am reminded here of the ambivalences noted by David Stewart earlier, as, in a similar type of discussion but (appropriate to the period of which he writes) in a rather lower key, he identifies two different positions the reader can take in reading of bloody urban crime. S/he can respond anxiously to it, as fears are triggered about her or his own vulnerability in an environment where bloody violence lies ready to erupt not far beneath the everyday social world. Or, s/he can relish the depiction of such excess as quite separate from, and bringing a voyeuristic sense of exhilaration to, the lack of excitement and the regimentation of that same everyday life. Creed suggests a similar type of interpretive doubleness in a contemporary audience. So – once more to apply what she says to the crime novel – violent harm done to the victim's body can act as a reminder not just of our own physical vulnerability but "of the fragile nature of all limits and boundaries" (1995: 157), fearfully shaking our own sense of secure identity, autonomy, and firm social belonging. But, on the other, it can allow us to reconstruct a sense of our own body as "clean, whole, impregnable, living, inviolate" as we distance ourselves as spectators from the vulnerabilities and mayhem of the represented world about which we read, and reaffirm thereby a confidence in our own autonomy and agency: "a comforting but illusory sense of a unified, coherent, authentic body and self" (156–157). It may be, indeed, that it is the very indeterminacy in our reading of the bloody excess in crime novels – secure in our distance from the fictional text we read but drawn into its world as reflecting a certain sense of our own lives – that accounts both for its power and popularity.

As a coda to this chapter, I consider a different, but related, kind of crime fiction (and one that has become immensely popular in the last few decades) – that featuring female forensic detectives working on the bodies of the dead, and dissecting those bodies as a crucial part of their detective work. Patricia Cornwell, the most successful author working in this territory, indirectly recognizes the interest of her own audience of readers in the abject, the depiction of violent death and bodily violation, when in *Unnatural Exposure* (1997) she describes onlookers at a crime scene "gawking" at the victim, a "decapitated" woman, with "arms and legs severed." "Looking," her protagonist Kay Scarpetta comments, "was too much of a temptation for most people to resist. The more gruesome the case, the more this was true" (21–24). Her words here implicate the reader, also figuratively "gawking" at the spectacle of this headless and limbless corpse, and looking on as Scarpetta defleshes and degreases bones (58). Similarly, in *Cause of Death* (1996), she conducts autopsies on other murder victims in her charge – removing a breastplate, inserting "a scalpel blade between two ribs," cutting up sections of a lifeless heart, watching her colleague pulling loosened face skin "forward over the eyes to expose [a] skull" (44, 41, 51, 54).

The description of such dissected bodies generally fits the analysis in the earlier part of this chapter. But there is something different here in terms of the normal relationship between detective and corpse in crime fiction. The victims Scarpetta examines have – in a good number of cases – passed over into a state of complete non-being, sometimes (as in *The Body Farm*, 1994) exhumed, with all immediate signs of ebbed life – blood and other bodily fluids – no longer present. Away from the murder scene, the forensic detective then clinically reduces the body to its component parts. Several things accordingly happen. We recognize, first of all, a certain uncomfortable doubling between the actions of the criminal and those of the medical expert/forensic pathologist, both of whom deal in dead bodies, both cutting and severing them in various ways. In *The Body Farm*, Scarpetta visits the University of Tennessee's research facility known informally by that title, and describes the corpses on display there – on open ground, in cars, woodland, a shed, and in "plastic-lined pits where bodies tethered to cinder blocks were submerged in water" (269–270). The purpose of such activity (if this is the right word) is to study the process of decomposition, in the various conditions in which it might occur, as an aid to detection in future criminal cases. Though the intentions behind the work are entirely laudable, this patch of land littered with the bodies of the dead has remarkable similarities to a crime scene – or, rather, to a crime scene as re-imagined by Hieronymous Bosch, with its series of tableaux featuring bodies in various states of decay. (We remember, in turn, Michael Connelly's detective protagonist Harry Bosch, named – as the author writes on his website – to indicate the "metaphoric possibilities of juxtaposing contemporary Los Angeles [and its "hellish landscape"] with some of the Bosch paintings," Connelly, n.d.)

Scarpetta's own role as a pathologist can be interpreted similarly, as rather too close to her criminal counterpart for comfort. Sabine Vanecker (1997) may overstate the case in describing her as "a woman hero [who] is a dealer in death, who aggressively 'manhandles' the corpses of victims and gruesomely thrives off decaying and decomposing bodies." But her description of

Scarpetta as "a Dr Frankenstein in reverse, unpicking what used to be a living body into its component parts" (66) is apposite in identifying Scarpetta's profession and actions with transgressive activity. Another aspect of such transgression is the use, in this type of fiction, of a protagonist dealing with dead (and sometimes long-dead) bodies, and, to at least some degree, cut off from the world of the living by the unofficial taboo associated with such intimate contact.

Katherine and Lee Horsley (2011) describe this uncomfortable sense of "gothic doubling and boundaries violated" (3) found in Cornwell's representation of Scarpetta – and in Kathy Reichs' Temple Brennan forensic detective series too. They write that "[d]issection," the business of both protagonists, does not "just suggest an act of delicately separating the body's structures; it also refers to a violent act of partition, to a brutal reduction or dismemberment. 'Anatomy,' similarly, carries destructive suggestions" (4). "The sheer violence of the procedures" carried out on the autopsy table, they suggest, "link them with the criminal act – the autoptic dismemberment a further, brutal reduction of the body into constituent parts" (16). So, in *The Body Farm*, Scarpetta has the dead body of eleven-year-old Emily Steiner exhumed in the course of the investigation of her murder to make sure all the bodily evidence possible has been garnered from it, conducting her consequent examination with Dr. Jenrette (who had done the original autopsy). The type of "brutal reduction" the Horsleys speak of becomes very clear as the two doctors "removed eye caps beneath eyelids and took out sutures . . . quickly lifted . . . out . . . [o]rgans . . . from the chest cavity," and as Scarpetta then "wedge[s] a long thin chisel between molars to open the mouth" (1994: 112).

In Cornwell's first novel, *Post-Mortem* (1990), Scarpetta remarks – as the Lori Petersen murder investigation begins – that "[t]he dead are defenceless, and the violation of this woman . . . had only begun" (7). Bodily violation then, as in Emily's case too, runs in a related sequence from the murderer's criminal actions to Scarpetta's professional activity. I explore the implications of such parallels further in the reading of *Unnatural Exposure* in Part 3. There is, of course, a fundamental difference in kind between the deliberate bodily harm wrought by a murderer and the professional dissections of the pathologist (whatever the unsettling connections between them). But the graphic descriptions of physical violations their activities have in common are noteworthy – and certainly continue (in the cases of Cornwell and Reichs) the interest in, and emphasis on, abjection I have previously discussed.

Gender role, though, takes on a qualitative difference in such texts. I have (mostly) focused on the female victim in my analysis to this point. In Cornwell's and Reichs' work, murder victims are of both sexes but the lead protagonist is female. This undermines the neat opposition between rational male mind and passive female body previously drawn. This is not to deny that the female body is a particularly resonant site of abjection (as previously discussed). But it is to argue that the traditional gender oppositions of earlier crime fiction have – as one would expect – become more complex in many recent crime novels. Here, the woman forensic detective takes center stage and is given the authority and agency conventionally associated with the male detective, but in a narrative whose overall representations of gender are more complicated than this statement might suggest. Something of this will emerge in the general comments on women's crime writing in my next chapter. And, again, in my reading of *Unnatural Exposure* in Part 3, I show the fractured nature of Scarpetta's identity as she moves between the living and the dead, between her dedication to her professional role and personal quest for romantic fulfillment. Cornwell's anxieties about her heroine, and the complicated relationship between genre and gender that results, become clear in such an exploration.

Gender Matters

> "[I]n detective fiction gender is genre and genre is male."
>
> Roth (1995: xiv)

> "Not only masculinity but also whiteness and heterosexuality are fundamental elements of . . . the hard boiled genre. . . . [It] seems clear that racism (and sexism and heterosexism) is a necessary element of hard-boiled detective fiction and is in fact a cornerstone of that fiction's ideological orientation."
>
> Reddy (2003b: 7, 27)

The two quotes above should generate no great surprise. Most people, if asked to identify the key figures in the history of detective fiction, would think first of Sherlock Holmes, Hercule Poirot, Sam Spade, and Philip Marlowe, in a tradition dominated by heroic (white) male protagonists. Moreover, the woman most likely to figure in that list, Christie's Miss Marple, hardly confronts gender stereotypes in any fundamental way. While "her characterization . . . [as] an astute, shrewd, and knowledgeable woman" may "quietly challeng[e] and rewrit[e] the expectations of women of a certain age who are unmarried and live alone" (Makinen 2010: 422), her status as a genteel and elderly spinster investigating crimes that take place in a small local community implies only a minimal disturbance to accepted gender roles and assumptions.

The link between genre and gender has much to do with such assumptions. For Western culture – as I suggested in the previous chapter – is deeply patriarchal, its ways of thinking and its structures rooted in male/female difference. So, in crime fiction, as Lee Horsley argues,

> However marginal his position, simply by virtue of his maleness the traditional detective is counted as a member of the male power structure. In restoring order

The Crime Fiction Handbook, First Edition. Peter Messent.
© 2013 John Wiley & Sons, Ltd. Published 2013 by John Wiley & Sons, Ltd.

within the narrative, he is acting to confirm the rightness and authority of this patriarchal stasis, the male-dominated status quo. (2005: 246)

The detective's "masculine" identity is, accordingly, associated with a set of specific gender traits. Reason and analysis are opposed to the stereotypical "feminine" qualities of intuition and emotion, with the latter normally seen as a barrier to the detachment necessary for the firm decision-making, judgment, and coolness of mind that are so essential both to successful detective work and to larger systems of authority and power. We see something of such gender opposition and division at work in Arthur Conan Doyle's *The Sign of Four*, with Sherlock Holmes' disappointment on the news of Watson's engagement to be married. As Holmes explains:

> I think she is one of the most charming young ladies I ever met. . . . But love is an emotional thing, and whatever is emotional is opposed to that true cold reason which I place above all things. I shall never marry myself, lest I bias my judgment. (2001: 117)

The male detective is, traditionally, a free agent, self-sufficient, and autonomous, and (in the hard-boiled variant of the form) tough-talking, physically active, and – where necessary – violent: Reddy, indeed, speaks of an equation in the genre between "violence and manliness" (2003a: 198). Sabine Vanecker comments on the independence and self-sufficiency so commonly associated with such a protagonist: "It is precisely because he stands alone and needs no help or support that he is a hero, a unified subject on whom incomplete and frustrated others depend" (1997: 71). The quest for knowledge and truth on which the detective hero embarks also connects him to larger structures of male power, as Vanecker again notes:

> [A] phallocentric western culture . . . has tended to associate masculinity with the search for knowledge, and femininity with the object of this search. The mythological hero, Prometheus, is the main paradigm for this association, the tireless and transgressing seeker who discovered the sacred and divine knowledge of fire. The male heroes of the crime novel . . . are latter-day incarnations of this epistemological subject, individuals who traverse the mean streets to reach understanding as they "read" the conspiracy behind the incomplete clues available. Typically, and traditionally, the genre's *femme fatale* has been associated with this mystery, one of the signs to be read. (78–79)

Women tend traditionally to play two main roles in crime fiction – victim or femme fatale. A third possible role, however, is as the detective hero's assistant or helper (for example, Effie Perrine in Hammett's *The Maltese Falcon*). I have explored the way male and female difference is generally represented within the genre in the previous chapter. To continue here: the role of victim – associated, then, with the "feminine" – is contrasted with "masculine" agency in two ways. The stilled (and often mutilated) woman's body is, most frequently, the end result of violent male criminality: "the Woman is the body in the library on whom the criminal writes his narrative of murder" (Horsley 2005: 247). That same silenced female corpse also provides the investigative ground for the (apparently) intensely masculine figure of the hard-boiled private eye – independent, active, and autonomous. Horsley reads such patterns in terms of "male ascendancy" and "female debasement": the former seen as "clean, whole, rational and possessed of effective agency"; the latter as a "reduction to the abject, the grotesque body, the corpse" (Horsley 2005: 282).

But not all women victims in crime fiction texts start off (or necessarily finish off) dead. They can be alive, though still silenced in various ways: bound and gagged, imprisoned, entombed in a cellar or darkened and often underground space; awaiting rescue – sometimes successfully, sometimes not – by the typically strong and heroic male protagonist. Such stereotyping has been subject to considerable modification since around the 1960s, but still remains common. Police detective Patrik Hedström in Camilla Läckberg's *The Preacher* (2004), set in the small fishing village of Fjällbacka in the author's native Sweden, is very different from Chandler's self-sufficient Marlowe (whom Joyce Carol Oates calls "the very essence of virility," 1995: 34). But his role, and that of the blond, seventeen-year-old Jenny Möller (the last victim abducted by murderer Jacob Hult), both fit the described model. Jenny is kept by her captor in an old bomb shelter in the woods near his family house, a nightmarish and totally dark space, no more "than two meters across" and barely head-height, claustrophobic, and padlocked from above (Läckberg 2010: 363). Tortured by Jacob (who is possessed by a form of religious mania), she dies shortly before Patrik and his team solve the case and find this hiding place. Our last view of her is lying on the ground, the sight of her damaged body intensified by "her nakedness . . . so vulnerable, so degrading" (405). One of Patrik's colleagues takes off his shirt to cover her, and Patrik "knelt down and spontaneously took Jenny's cold hand in his. She had died alone, but she would not have to wait alone" (405–406): small comfort, one might think, to the victim, but very much in line with the traditional gender stereotype of the vulnerable female protected (even in death) by the male detective hero.

The role of the femme fatale – the other type of woman that conventionally figures in the genre – is similarly stereotyped in terms of gender. Female transgressors are conventionally portrayed as "dangerous, seductive villains . . . repeatedly position[ed] . . . as the dangerous Other that must be contained and controlled." Those women who support the detective in his task play the contrasting role of "nurturing but essentially insignificant helpmates" (Reddy 2003a: 193–194).

But I return briefly here to the question of male agency. I have mainly focused so far (following Oates and Reddy) on the hard-boiled crime novel as representing a hard and tough masculinity that conditions our overall gender assumptions of the form. As I have suggested earlier – and as I show in some of my readings of individual texts – the representation of masculinity in such crime fictions is in fact often far more fragile than it may at first appear. There is, too, another tradition – the Golden Age classic detective novels of Agatha Christie (and others) – that presents a very different version of masculinity than we find in the likes of Hammett and Chandler. I use Christie's most renowned detective protagonist, the Belgian Hercule Poirot, as an illustration. Our first introduction to Poirot is in *The Mysterious Affair at Styles*, where he is described prior to his actual appearance by Hastings (the man who will act as his assistant and documenter) as "a funny little man, a great dandy, but wonderfully clever" (2007: 19). His "cherub-like face" (55), immaculate turnout, and nervous mannerisms, and even the "tiny Russian cigarettes" he occasionally smokes (120), all indicate "feminine" rather than "masculine" characteristics (in terms of normative gender constructions). Similarly, he is not defined by physical toughness, relying on observation and analysis, the brain not the body, to solve the mysteries that confront him. The fact that Poirot is presented in this way may, as Alison Light suggests, be in indirect response to the historical situation in which Christie writes, for:

> [i]n his own small way, Agatha Christie's Poirot was part of the quest for a bearable masculinity which would make what had previously seemed even effeminate preferable to the bulldog virtues of 1914. Christie, like [Dorothy] Sayers, recognized the impossibility of creating a confident, British middle-class hero in the old mould. (1991: 43)

But it is the representation of women in crime fiction and the limited roles they have been given that is my main subject here. Given all I say above, how, we may ask, have women writers (through their female detective protagonists) found space within the genre for their voices to be heard and their gender interests to be served? For there is, indeed, a long history of women crime writers, stretching back to gothic and sensation fiction of the late eighteenth and nineteenth centuries (see Knight 2004, in particular). Agatha Christie, Patricia Highsmith, Dorothy L. Sayers, and the variously authored Nancy Drew stories of the 1930s and 1940s are the some of the best-known names and texts in the twentieth-century historical field, though other writers (of the same period and earlier) such as Anna Katherine Green, Gladys Mitchell, Catherine L. Pirkis, Mary Roberts Rinehart, Metta Fuller Victor, and Patricia Wentworth are also significant.

It is since the 1960s, though, that there has been an explosion of woman-centered texts and that the issue of gender role has been more assertively addressed, with a series of feisty, tough-minded, and (often) tough-bodied female protagonists. This upsurge, undoubtedly linked to the impact of post-1960s feminism, is usually dated back to Amanda Cross' Kate Fansler series (the first, *In the Last Analysis*, came out in 1964) and P. D. James' 1972 novel *An Unsuitable Job for a Woman*. Walton and Jones estimate that the number of women detectives/investigators rose from thirteen in the late 1970s to more than 360 by the mid-1990s (1999: 28–30). It is this period and the time following it that I focus on to suggest (briefly) how traditional gender oppositions in the genre have been undermined and restructured, and to assess some larger implications of that process. This commentary will be buttressed by my reading of the Patricia Cornwell novel *Unnatural Exposure* in Part 3.

Recent woman-centered crime fiction responds to the male tradition, claiming equal status for its female protagonists to that of male detectives. Writers such as Sue Grafton and Sara Paretsky – probably, alongside Cornwell, the best-known of present-day women crime writers – appropriate the first-person voice of Chandler's Philip Marlowe and other male hard-boiled P. I.s. And, in doing so, they achieve a similar end: signaling authority and self-confidence on the part of the narrating female subject as she negotiates a dangerous surrounding world. The voicelessness of the traditional female victim and the slippery and untrustworthy use of language of the typical femme fatale are replaced – in the case of both Grafton's and Paretsky's central protagonists – by the wisecrack, one-liner, or astute comment that signals a refusal to be second-bested by anyone, whatever their gender or position. Such modes of speech (typical, as we have seen, of all forms of hard-boiled detective writing) serve as "a stylised demonstration of knowledge, . . . an assertion of autonomy, a defiant refusal to be brow-beaten" and "an irreverence toward . . . institutional power" (Willett 1992: 8–9) entirely suiting the needs of the doubly marginalized (by gender as well as by profession) female private detective.

So, when V. I. Warshawski is physically barred by his assistant Trish from entering Jasper Heccomb's office in Paretsky's *Tunnel Vision* (1993), she uses her wit to mock such prohibitory action, and implicitly to undermine any sense of status difference or assumed gender inequality between the two:

"What's he doing in there?" I asked mildly. "Holding an orgy?"
Her face flooded with color. "How can you say things like that?" (182)

Similarly, the narrative voice introduced at the start of Sue Grafton's first Kinsey Millhone novel, *A is for Alibi* (1982), foregrounds the no-nonsense attitude and consciousness and the confident self-sufficiency of her series heroine:

> My name is Kinsey Millhone. I'm a private investigator, licensed by the State of California. I'm thirty-two years old, twice divorced, no kids. The day before yesterday I killed someone and the fact weighs heavily on my mind. My apartment is small but I like living in a crammed space . . . one room, a "bachelorette." I don't have pets. I don't have houseplants. I spend a lot of time on the road and I don't like leaving things behind. (1)

Interestingly, the only note of self-doubt in this initial statement is in regard to Kinsey's own violent actions, revealing an awareness of possible moral culpability unusual in the majority of her male predecessors.

This, indeed, echoes an ambivalent attitude to violence found in many women's detective novels, suggesting something of the way they shape the genre to their own gender values and way of seeing the world. The necessary self-protection, anger, and (often) fear felt by their detective protagonists does commonly spill out in violent action. But, however immediately justified, the nature of such a response generally sits uncomfortably with a feminist ideology that views aggression and rage as damaging "masculine" traits, normally countered by women's more nurturing and accommodating virtues. This can lead to a certain sense of self-division on the part of such protagonists. So, for instance, Kay Scarpetta's violent anger is triggered at the end of *Post Mortem* when the murderer invades her most personal space (her bedroom), potentially to add her to his list of female victims. But as, holding a gun, she confronts him ("'*You son of a bitch! You goddam son of a bitch!*' The gun was bobbing up and down as I screamed"), she qualifies her feeling of murderous outrage with a phrase that implies a complete sense of disassociation from her normal state of being: "my terror, my rage exploding in profanities *that seemed to be coming from someone else*" (313, my final emphasis). A similar sense of double consciousness occurs in Sara Paretsky's *Killing Orders* (1985) when a furious Warshawski shoots a gangster in the leg and then (trying to get information) threatens to destroy his kneecap with a second shot. Immediately after, however, she describes "[n]ausea at the depths of my own rage. How like a mobster I had behaved – torture, threats. I don't believe the end justifies the means. I'd just been plain raving angry" (1986: 201).

Recent women's crime writing looks, then, to write back against a male-coded tradition, redirecting the crime novel, as Vanecker puts it, "to represent a feminist ideology and reconceiv[e] [it] with a woman hero at its centre" (1997: 62). What this has generally meant has been the taking of the most admirable traits of the established male detective protagonist and adjusting them to values and attitudes that are less assertively "masculine," bending the tradition in a more woman-centered direction. This can, though, lead to the type of ambivalence indicated above. Vanecker is useful in pointing out some of the avenues such re-workings have taken. But I recognize here that we cannot reduce female crime writing to a single model and that, for instance, Cornwell's police procedurals are very different from Grafton's and Paretsky's P. I. novels. The comments that follow, then, are not meant to be all-encompassing.

Grafton and Paretsky's protagonists certainly follow the tough-talking and self-assertive pattern identified above, their directness of speech countering any "conventional 'female' qualities of tact, diplomacy, politeness and the like" (Vanecker 1997: 65). But they are also aware of their physical vulnerability and explicitly recognize such feelings. This is perhaps even more true of Cornwell's Kay Scarpetta, who, as (for example) she retraces the steps of the child victim of *The Body Farm* around a deserted Lake Tomahawk (in Black Mountain, North Carolina), becomes increasingly fearful, taking on the mindset of a potential victim: "[f]urtively," she reports, "I glanced around, listening to every sound. The noise of my feet crashing through leaves seemed horrendously loud." By the end of what she calls "this awful journey," she is "trembling" with fear and anxiety (1994: 97–98). Warshawski, in Paretsky's *Killing Orders*, justifiably anxious after an unsuccessful attempt by an unknown assailant to throw acid in her eyes, recognizes her limits and looks for male protection, asking some-time lover Murray Ryerson for his help, with the words "I'm kind of embarrassed to ask this, but the truth is, I'm not up to a night alone. Can I crash with you?" (1986: 94).

Perhaps the most obvious thing to note about Paretsky and Grafton's heroines is that they both live alone and both are divorced (Millhone with two marriages behind her, Warshawski with one). (Different relationship patterns in Cornwell's books will be discussed in the reading of *Unnatural Exposure* in Part 3.) This signals the failure of traditional gender roles to foster the independence and self-fulfillment each woman needs in her life. So, Paretsky's website describes V. I. as follows:

> V I was married once as a young woman. The marriage lasted about eighteen months, when she found her husband only admired independent women from a distance. These days, she's a serial monagamist [sic]. She lives alone, but shares two dogs with her neighbor, Mr. Contreras, a retired machinist whose main hobby is V I herself.
>
> (Paretsky n.d.: n.p.)

Grafton is more reticent about Kinsey Millhone's marital past, saying only that Kinsey, a "rebellious type," "had two brief marriages. Almost nothing is known about the first except that Kinsey left him. The second husband left Kinsey unexpectedly, but shows up years later in one of the novels" (Grafton n.d.: n.p.; and see too *E is for Evidence* and *O is for Outlaw*).

Grafton's work is particularly focused on broken and dysfunctional families, with Kinsey herself orphaned in a car crash at the age of five, brought up by her Aunt Gin (a single woman), and estranged (like Kinsey's mother) from the larger family (Kinsey herself does re-make contact with her mother's larger family, but the set of relationships remains strained):

> Ill-equipped to inherit a daughter, [Aunt Gin] did her best to raise Kinsey. She was a no-nonsense kind of person who instilled in Kinsey a strong sense of independence and self-sufficiency, both of which would serve Kinsey well throughout her life. Other traits received or reinforced by Aunt Gin were an aversion to cooking, a lack of interest in fashion, and an affinity for books.
>
> (Grafton n.d.: n.p.)

Grafton's novel *U is for Undertow* (2009) has more than its fair share of dysfunctional families, and the novel's one deliberate murderer, novelist Jon Corso, is in many ways a psychological victim of his mother's death (while his father was away, pursuing an affair) and of his father's second marriage to a woman who hates him.

Both Millhone and V. I. are financially independent professional women – a fact of crucial importance (see especially Grafton 1990: 102). Both too "are free from the frustrations and limitations that characterize the traditional patriarchal family" (Vanecker 1997: 71), with parents dead (though V. I.'s mother is particularly missed) and husbands gone. Both women have built an alternative and looser support network of considerable importance to them. V. I. is particularly reliant on female friends, of whom Dr. Lotty Herschel is by far the most important. These friendships are part and parcel of V. I.'s political identity: heavily engaged in the 1960s, "fighting the straights – the prowar, antiabortion, racist world," "feminism was [her] most important [cause]," absolutely "central" to her own life and those of her friends (Paretsky 1986: 78). Though Kinsey Millhone's friendship with tavern-owner Rosie plays a supportive role in her life too, there is not the same immediate commitment here to female sisterhood and nurturance. But, when it comes to the cases she takes on and the way she lives her life, "female solidarity" does play its – important – part (Vanecker 1997: 75). Both women have close and platonic relationships with much older men: Henry Pitts in Kinsey Millhone's case and Mr. Contreras in V. I.'s. As Vanecker perceptively comments:

Both men . . . offe[r] an ideal of an active, alert, sexy old age that holds no demands of practical care for the detective. . . . Both men . . . have taken on female roles, which removes them . . . from the traditional, powerful father. . . . Sentimental but ultimately safe, fussing around and "mothering" the women detective, these are examples of idealised father–daughter relationships. Warshawski and Millhone can have their family cake [both men cook and Pitts is a not-quite-retired baker] and eat it. (72–73)

There is more to be said here about the way that these detectives combine and move between traditional gender traits, both "feminine" and "masculine" (see Vanecker 1997: 69–70). In the case of Cornwell's Scarpetta, this leads to jarring effects – her nurturing love of good food preparation and cooking sometimes disturbingly juxtaposed with her professional interests (Cornwell 1997: 72–73) and her own cutting and weighing on the autopsy slab (194). More, too, can be made of the "powerful search for knowledge and information" traditionally associated with the male detective (and with masculinity more generally) and the way that this search is appropriated – with a difference – in women's crime fiction. For, in female detection we see an alteration in this process, "a subjective, involved, empathetic type of knowing" rather than the "objective, distanced knowledge" of its male counterpart (Vanecker 1997: 79).

This is relatively straightforward so far. We see, then, a series of women detective writers looking to re-fashion the genre and re-gender it "female." This has, however, led to a number of difficulties and contradictions: to women protagonists who are, to varying degrees, self-divided – treasuring their independence and autonomy but looking for some kind of sustaining group solidarity; tough (at times violently so), and thus veering toward the type of "machismo" behavior incompatible with a feminist consciousness, but aware too of their own vulnerability and physical powerlessness; looking to combine gender traits conventionally seen as "masculine" with the "feminine," but sometimes caught uncomfortably between the two. And, for some feminist critics, female P. I.s such as Millhone and Warshawski, however they adjust their role to accommodate more "feminine" traits, come worryingly close at times to merely mimicking the style and actions of their male equivalents. But this perhaps is unavoidable as their creators look to break down the traditional gender paradigms of the genre's past.

There is, though, a larger point. And it is here that we should remember the way that crime fiction so often pulls in contradictory directions, "is coded to both resist and re-inscribe the dominant cultural discourses" (Pepper 2003: 211). So, detectives such as Millhone and Warshawski may carry their feminist credentials and challenge (now mostly outmoded, one hopes) ways of thinking that see women as the passive opposite of strong male agency, as "biologically" better suited to a domestic role than a public and professional one. But in the final analysis they do what (almost) every other fictional detective does: they serve (to quote Pepper again) as "a crucial part of the machinery by which social control is maintained and existing hierarchies policed" (2003: 211). Despite their opposition to a patriarchal social order, in other words, their actions do little to shift its power or to change its structures.

We can see this by looking briefly at two novels, one from Grafton and one from Paretsky. (I leave Cornwell to one side for the moment because of what I see, despite her strong female protagonist, as deep-rooted conservative values.) Grafton's *U is for Undertow* is typical of her work in its relative lack of concern for larger social structures and institutions. Her interest lies in her main protagonist: Millhone's professional abilities ("like a little terrier . . . flushing out rats," 2010: 13), persistence, tough independence (paralleled by her difficulties with close relationships and especially with her new-found larger family), and willingness to resort to violence where necessary (she is involved in a brief stand-off at the end of the novel, which she resolves by swiftly shooting her opponent in his gun hand). At a larger level, it is the failures in family relationships generally (and not just her own) that drive the book. There is also a concern over class division and the way it distorts social relationships. So Millhone, with her "blue-collar roots" (4), reacts against the local private Climping Academy and the various other privileges money and social position brings (47–48), and describes, finally, the way Jon Corso's wealth will delay, and possibly frustrate, his prosecution (481). But Millhone's self-assertive feminist values exist, basically, below the institutional parapet as it were, having little effect on, and paying little regard to, the larger structures of the society through which she moves.

Paretsky is different in that her novelistic concerns are explicitly political and institutional. In *Killing Orders*, Warshawski takes on the Chicago police force – primarily in the shape of her father's friend, Bobby Mallory, who "thinks Tony Warshawski's daughter should be making a better world by producing happy healthy babies, not by catching desperadoes" (1986: 75). If her resistance and lack of co-operation in this instance are in many ways personal (a hangover from her relationship with her father), her various interactions with the F.B.I., the Church, and the Mafia carry more political weight. The central crime in the novel is the attempted laundering of stolen Vatican money (through the acquisition of a Chicago insurance company) by Panamanian Archbishop and Vatican functionary Xavier O'Faolin, a rogue Catholic. He gains the support of Corpus Christi (loosely modeled on Opus Dei), a secretive and conservative Catholic lay organization that "supported right-wing Governments with close Church ties" (106), in the undercover and illegal attempt to acquire this company – though that religious body is ignorant of his criminal purposes. As part of O'Faolin's machinations, Augustine Pelly, the procurator of a local Chicago Priory, has stolen valuable share certificates from his order and replaced them with forgeries. He has been assisted in this by Walter Novick, a gangster who also works for local Mafia boss Don Pascale – also involved to some (unknown) extent in aiding this part of Pelly and O'Faolin's scheme. Warshawski finds out that the F.B.I. did not follow up on the share-certificate forgery due to the powerful interests involved – friendships between Jerome Farber (the Cardinal Arch-bishop of Chicago), O'Faolin, and Mrs. Paciorek, a wealthy Corpus Christi member heavily under O'Faolin's influence and centrally involved in the insurance company buyout. For this group, as Pelly reveals, "have a lot of influence in Chicago" (229).

All this makes for a very complicated plot. But the crux of the matter is that Warshawski finds her way through its various strands, stands up to the (mostly male) authority figures who would seek to prevent her doing so, and manages even to prompt Don Pascale into action against O'Faolin (even while the former carefully avoids any admission of involvement in the crimes that have occurred). Punishment mainly occurs outside the court system, with O'Faolin bumped off by Pascale, and Paciorek (and her innocent husband) dead by their own hands. If the immediate crime is solved, however, the patriarchal structures that have fostered it remain unchanged. The Church (and its Pope) retain their power and ability to work to conservative social ends through Corpus Christi. The Mafia, with its pow-erful and frightening boss, remains finally unaffected. And the police, brokerage firms, F.B.I., and press (as each is represented in the novel) remain bastions of male power.

Despite this, however, feminist detective fictions of this type are not altogether politically neutered. For society is gradually changing, women's opportunities have advanced, and fictions such as these do play a part in that process. Warshawski, in particular, continues to resist gender prejudice, and does meet men in positions of power (in *Killing Orders*, Prior Father Carroll in particular) who accord her the full professional respect she deserves. There is a double movement here as these protagonists oppose any form of patriarchal oppression at an immediate level yet finally protect larger (patriarchal) structures in their restoration of the status quo. But perhaps that is all that can be expected. Novels are not revolutionary documents and a chipping-away at ground level at the gender assumptions of the past helps to further that social evolution in which we are all engaged.

Representations of Race

Much of what I say about women's crime fiction applies, though in a different form, to writing by African American crime fiction authors, and to others writing from a non-white racial background. I focus on the American tradition for illustration throughout most of this chapter, though would recognize the historical and cultural differences that give crime writing by both women and black (to use the term as a convenient shorthand) writers from Britain and other European countries (and beyond) a different trajectory. If to be a woman in Western culture is to be marginalized in certain ways, subject (to varying extents) to male hegemony, to be black is to be even more so – but subject to the hegemonic power of whiteness. For there is no doubt that in both America and the United Kingdom race has greater weight than gender in determining social and political position and power (or, rather, its lack). And, in the particular case of crime fiction, "the tough masculine persona of the hard-boiled protagonist has almost invariably been white" (Horsley 2005: 202). Blackness – almost inevitably – comes accordingly to stand in contrast: for criminality, "otherness," and an unfamiliar, unknown, and threatening social world. So, as Alan Branson (2010) asserts, "[c]urrent images of African-Americans as drug dealers, junkies, thugs, street hoodlums, and predatory violent males abound" (n.p.) in all forms of popular culture.

Such stereotypes abound in crime fiction. James Lee Burke – in his Hurricane Katrina novel *The Tin Roof Blowdown* (2007) – does much to counter what Dave Robicheaux, his detective protagonist, calls "the latent racism in our culture" that "rear[ed] its head" at the time of the disaster (83). And he consistently challenges racist thinking in his other novels. Nonetheless, he commences the book with black criminality, as the Melancon

The Crime Fiction Handbook, First Edition. Peter Messent.
© 2013 John Wiley & Sons, Ltd. Published 2013 by John Wiley & Sons, Ltd.

brothers – armed robbers and rapists – loot the abandoned homes of the flood victims: "Eddy and Bertrand saw the storm as a gift from God. White people in New Orleans had been making money on the black man's back for three hundred years. It was time for some payback" (58). Similarly, in Richard Price's *Lush Life* (2008), the crime around which the book is focused – a street holdup and a "murder" that is in fact mostly a result of sheer panic – is committed by a Puerto Rican/African American teenage pairing. Eric Cash, who was with the dead man when the holdup occurred, is asked to describe the killer and his accomplice, and replies: "I don't know. Black. Hispanic. I'm not trying to be racist, but in my mind? I close my eyes and see wolves" (44). Both authors introduce such stereotypes only to later undermine much of their cultural freight. But, despite this, they also help to perpetuate their prevalence.

James Ellroy does something similar, though perhaps more successfully, in his novels. Using the first-person perspective of his white cop protagonists, he captures their persistent, casual, but extreme racism: "Leotis Dineen . . . was a bad jigaboo to fuck with"; "crazy [Dudley Smith] circa '38 – brass-knuckling a nigger hophead half to death for drooling on [his] cashmere overcoat" (1988: 104, 184). But, in magnifying "the Africanist presence . . . through the demonological lens of [his] protagonists" and "[r]epresenting blackness in terms of rampaging deviants whose propensity for violence is essentialised in their pathology" (Pepper 2000: 43–44), Ellroy both recaptures something of the mindset of an earlier period in West Coast American history and also – as he shows the rottenness and the bigotry of white power structures and the use of racial politics as a tool in its continuation – exposes the falsity, and explodes the legitimacy, on which such racist stereotype is based.

To go back to an earlier period of writing is to find a more one-dimensional representation of racial difference. So Liam Kennedy uses Raymond Chandler as his example when he defines crime fiction as a "white genre" – seeing "hard-boiled fiction's most distinctive narrative codes, conventions, and characterisations" as "traditionally . . . structured around the consciousness of a white subject" (1997: 42). When Chandler, Kennedy suggests, moves the site of his fiction from white to African American urban space, he finds violence, degeneracy, and anarchy there, "discover[s] an excessive (passionate, violent) difference in blackness" (45). So, at the start of *Farewell, My Lovely* (1940), when Moose Malloy causes violent havoc in a black club, Marlowe describes his throwing of a young African American man from the bar: "It landed on its hands and knees and made a high keening noise like a cornered rat. . . . It was a thin, narrow-shouldered brown youth in a lilac-coloured suit and a carnation. It had slick black hair" (Chandler

1949: 8). We see here Marlowe's distance from the alien racial territory he enters, the absolute difference he assumes in terms of his own human value from this black world. His pronoun use dehumanizes the black youth to the status of a thing or an animal, presumably a near relative of the rat whose sound he mimics. (The lilac suit may also suggest that homophobia as well as racism is involved here.)

Black Mask magazine – crucial to the development of hard-boiled crime fiction, and where Chandler's work first appeared – published, throughout the 1920s, "stories in which the presence of the African American . . . connotes pathological violence, sexual license, lack of civilisation, and absence of morality" (Kennedy 1997: 44). Chandler does not spend much textual time on African Americans but nonetheless does – through Marlowe – consign them to complete "otherness." So, in *Farewell, My Lovely* he refers to "the dead alien silence of another race" (1949: 10) and, in his writing as a whole, describes African Americans variously and casually as "smokes, shines, bucks, dark meat, niggers . . . [who] live in darktown" (Widdicombe 1981: 33).

Kennedy suggests how contemporary African American crime writer Walter Mosley subverts Chandler's racial politics at the start of his first published Easy Rawlins novel, *Devil in a Blue Dress* (1990). Here Mosley takes the alien space, the black bar of *Farewell, My Lovely*, and – in what serves as a type of statement of intent – more or less reverses the meaning of Chandler's scene. Here whiteness, not blackness, is other and alien. The intrusive all-white presence of DeWitt *Albright* (my emphasis) – a white man wearing "an off-white linen suit and shirt . . . and bone shoes over flashing white silk socks" (1992: 9) – brings fear and anxiety to Joppy's: "a small bar on the second floor of a butcher's warehouse" on 103rd Street (near Central Avenue in Watts) catering mainly for the "Negro butchers" who work there (11). The scene is viewed from an African American perspective, that of Mosley's detective protagonist, Easy Rawlins, and it is he who leads us through the action, assuming the role Marlowe plays in Chandler's work. Easy is part of the richly textured local Watts community, and reacts to the white intruder Albright with distaste. So his description of their handshake, and of Albright's "grip . . . strong but slithery, like a snake coiling around my hand" (10), implies a reptilian, perhaps venomous, presence. The metaphor, though, also suggests Albright's power – which the black youth in Chandler, cornered like a rat, lacks. The black world represented here (which, by and large, is that in which Rawlins moves and engages throughout the series) is one where whiteness does not belong, and is over-conspicuous by its presence: "I can't go into those places [Watts' clubs and bars] looking for her," Albright says of his quest for Daphne Monet, "because I'm not the right persuasion" (26). Mosley – to use Henry Louis Gates' term – "signifies" on Chandler, a father figure of the white hard-boiled tradition here, "repeat [ing] the dominant white American story with a black difference" (Gruesser 1999: 240).

While Mosley does this, however, the notion of a clear – and segregated – borderline between black and white worlds, of different racialized spaces where belonging, or a failure to belong, depends on the color of one's skin, remains. This is pretty much a given in all African American crime fiction. So, in Chester Himes' earlier, and crucially important, series of "Harlem domestic" novels, the black community is confined within more-or-less absolute racial boundaries. In *The Real Cool Killers* (1959), Grave Digger Jones – one of Himes' central pair of black detective protagonists – roughs up a witness in front of a white man. When the latter protests his action, Grave Digger responds: 'I'm just a cop. . . . If you white people insist on coming up to Harlem where you force colored people to live in vice-and-crime-ridden slums, it's my job to see that you are safe" (1988: 65). Skin color demarcates slum from non-slum, Harlem from the rest of Manhattan, protected white subject from casually abused black one. If the abutting district, Spanish Harlem, is even more run down, there is a crucial difference there, for – as Coffin Ed Johnson (Jones' partner) notes – a Puerto Rican can gain acceptance as white if his skin is light enough, "but no matter how white a spook might become he's still a nigger" (1974: 69).

As Grave Digger's words (above) suggest, Himes' black detectives are in a complete double bind. Upholding the law in a Harlem segregated from the rest of Manhattan along racial lines (a situation that can be read as paradigmatic for the larger American social world to which it points) is necessarily to protect the interests of the white majority and, ultimately, the law. But to do so is to endorse a status quo that merely validates and continues the immiseration of the city's African American population. The anger and violence of Jones and Johnson's attitudes and actions throughout Himes series of novels signals an inner rage: a product of these characters' fundamental impotence in the face of an apparently unalterable racial, and thus social, status quo. Thus, the localized crimes the two detectives are expected to solve are – at every point – "contained," distorted, and reduced to a type of comically grotesque and violent sideshow by the larger (but entirely legal) "crime" of the systematic white suppression of African American opportunity, potential, sense of equality, and national belonging. This explains the deep irony of Himes' Harlem "domestic" label. For, as Himes writes in *Cotton Comes to Harlem* (through the perspective of his two black detective protagonists), "Harlem is a city of the homeless." So the families defrauded by Deke O'Malley's Back-to-Africa scam in that novel had, we are told, left the South "because it could never be considered their home," only (equally) to fail to find any "home in the North." This, in turn, explained their then looking "across the sea to Africa." As the passage finally comments, "Everyone has to believe in something; and the white people of America had left them nothing to believe in" (1974: 34–35).

But Himes' work is not that of unmitigated defeat and determinism. There is plenty of energy in the Harlem he represents, plenty of comedy in the (often surrealistic) mayhem enacted there. Gravedigger and Coffin Ed, too, look to act as best they can for the Harlem people even within the white power structure that regulates their official roles. And, in the political movements and ideas circulating at the time (and within Himes' texts) – Black Power, the Black Muslim movement, and militant African American Christianity are just some of these – there is at least a sense of some possible liberatory alternative to the present status quo. If such possibilities are treated ironically by and large by Himes, they are nonetheless projected as (on the Harlemites part) worth the investment, whatever the self-interests involved and the long odds on their succeeding; better than just knuckling under to the white economic and political establishment:

> [A]mong the . . . crowd of Harlem citizens . . . there were many serious persons who understood the necessity for a fund for the coming fight. They believed in Black Power. They'd give it a trial anyway. Everything else had failed. . . . What did they have to lose? And they might win. Who knew? The whale swallowed Jonah. Moses split the Red Sea. Christ rose from the dead. Lincoln freed the slaves. Hitler killed six million Jews. . . . The Americans and the Russians have shot the moon. . . . Anything is possible.
>
> (Himes 1986: 51)

The shift of rhetorical gear here (from Lincoln to Hitler and the moon shots) suggests Himes' own wry cynicism about the possibility of such change. Moreover, the African American liberation movements in his novels are, more often than not, locked in a self-destructive battle for ascendancy. The very fact that they are represented in his texts does, though, provide at least some sense of possible escape from present alienation.

In Himes' later novels, however even this (faint) promise tends to evaporate. Indeed, the crime fiction form itself – dependent as it is on the righting of present wrongs, the authority of a law that has at least some pretence to social justice – implodes. In *Blind Man with a Pistol* (1969), Himes' last complete crime novel, any idea of the formal resolution we would normally expect from the genre – the solving of a particular crime and the re-establishing of the status quo – is abandoned. The detective work of Jones and Johnson is similarly rendered both pointless and irrelevant in the novel's ending. This focuses first on the city's demolition of a condemned building and the dispossession this brought with it ("no matter if these homes were slum flats that had been condemned as unfit for human dwelling. They had been forced to live there, in all the filth and degradation, until their lives had been warped to fit, and now they were being thrown out," 1986: 191). The anger that results, though, then gives way to apathy as the crowd just stands and watches as the building is destroyed.

Coffin Ed and Grave Digger are sidelined here, reduced to bystanders themselves, their role curtailed to the pointless shooting of the rats running from the wrecked housing. Any part they might play as the representatives of the law and restorers of the (supposed) social compact is then further dimini-shed when random violence and "pandemonium" (190) breaks out. This literally bursts from underground (the subway), first with a situation of confused and misdirected interracial conflict and then with the emergence of the blind man of the title, "the nigger with the pistol," who randomly shoots a white cop dead (he is aiming elsewhere, "at [a] big white man" who has slapped him in – another very confused – subway dispute, 194). The novel ends with the blind man's death (at the hands of white police) and a consequent riot. When Coffin Ed and Gravedigger's white superior, Lieutenant Anderson, asks what caused the riot, Grave Digger replies with the sequence that ends the novel: "A blind man with a pistol." Anderson continues the dialogue:

"What's that?"
"You heard me, boss."
"That don't make any sense."
"Sure don't." (195)

The novel ends, then, with things not making sense. The social order is finally in meltdown, riven by racial conflict and marked by random and misdirected acts of violence and general mayhem. And, if some of the dominant ideas on which the detective novel form is based have to do with vision, supervision, and control, they are here replaced by blindness, randomness, and riot. Himes' sense of an America fractured by racial difference and inequality gives his crime fiction nowhere to go. Further escalation of this type of apocalyptic racial violence in Himes' final book, *Plan B*, left him at a complete dead end, his artistic creativity compromised, his book necessarily unfinished.

Himes published *Blind Man with a Pistol* in 1969, the year that the Supreme Court ordered the end of public school segregation in the United States "now and hereafter" (a striking advance on the 1955 Brown v. Board of Education ruling that segregation should proceed with "all deliberate speed"). But this was also a year of continued racial violence in the United States, with the shooting of Black Panther leaders Fred Hampton and Mark Clark by the Chicago police in a raid on December 4 on Hampton's apartment. Walter Mosley's first Easy Rawlins novel, *Devil in a Blue Dress*, came out in 1990, some two decades later and at a time when many of the gains of the Civil Rights Movement had been consolidated. We should not, accordingly, be surprised that his fiction is "gentler, less polemical" than Himes', "the product of a more conciliatory era" (Pepper 2003: 217). Mosley's widespread popularity as a writer (named as one of Bill Clinton's favorite authors) – certainly in an entirely different league than Himes' – was undoubtedly in good part a result of this political and social climate change.

In his novels, Mosley gently undermines notions of essential racial difference, most simply by showing the lack of fit between skin color and racial identity. "Black" and "white" become – in this sense – meaningless terms. In *Devil in a Blue Dress*, Italian American Benny Giacomo is Easy's boss at his Santa Monica workplace (a fictional version of the Douglas Aircraft Factory) and treats Easy and his fellow African American workers in a racially defined manner. But, as Easy reports, Benny's own "skin color was darker than many mulattos I'd known" (1992: 71). Similarly, Hattie Parsons, the African American woman who acts as gatekeeper to John's illegal nightclub, is hardly "black" at all – her skin "the color of light sand" (33). Daphne Monet, on the other hand, the "French girl" (95) and novel's femme fatale, appears to be, and is treated as, a "pretty young white woman" (25) for most of the book. At its denouement, though, she turns out to be mulatta, (officially) "colored" (211). Borderlines between "black" and "white" disappear into nothingness here.

Further turning traditional stereotype on its head, it is whiteness in Mosley that is often given unpleasant connotations. Casper Langdon in *A Little Yellow Dog* (1996) "had no nose to speak of and hardly any lips. He . . . resembled a great albino turtle in overalls" (68), while Conrad Hopkins is "an older man, more washed out than white" (70). Breaking down standard black–white binaries, Mosley insists on the variety of shades of color and of race and ethnic type that compose American identity. In *A Little Yellow Dog*, the first corpse discovered is that of Roman Gasteau: "I didn't think he was a white man; his skin was dark olive and his nose was wider than most Caucasians'. I wasn't claiming him for a Negro either. His racial roots could have been from at least four continents, or a thousand islands around the world" (35). And, in representing Rawlins' own adopted family in terms of ties of the heart not of blood – his daughter Feather is biracial, his son Jesus is Mexican, his sometime girlfriend Bonnie Shay is from French Guyana but was raised in New Jersey – Mosley gestures in the direction of a larger American ideal family shorn of its obsession with race and color difference.

Having said this, Mosley fully recognizes the continuing power of American racism in the period about which he writes. And his novels trace an (alternative) history of Los Angeles – that is, from a black perspective – from 1948 (the time of *Devil in a Blue Dress*) to 1967 (*Blonde Faith*, seemingly the last in the Easy Rawlins series). They allude – in various ways, and among other subjects – to African American migration from the South, the Watts riots, Kennedy's assassination, and Vietnam and the counter-culture. Mosley gestures toward an American world of increased racial fairness and equality (and in the 2005 *Cinnamon Kiss*, for instance, illustrates some of the positive changes that have occurred). Easy Rawlins, nonetheless, continues to live in a divided racial world, where he and his fellow African Americans are treated, without so much as a second thought, as second-class citizens and criminals.

So, in *A Little Yellow Dog* (which I use as my example here), Rawlins notes the complete lack of racial trust and honest interaction in his world: "[w]hite people like to keep their eyes peeled on blacks, and vice versa. We lie to each other so much that often the only hope is to see some look or gesture that betrays the truth" (1996: 23–24). Easy habitually lives, in W. E. B DuBois' words, "behind the veil" (1999: 10), his worth and real identity invisible to the vast majority of the whites with whom he comes into contact, and he in return masks both his feelings and intelligence from them. When a white cop says to Easy, as he takes part in a (rigged) identity parade, "What're you lookin' up for, boy?" Easy reacts instinctively:

> I was back, suddenly, in the deep south. All feeling drained out of my body and my face went lax. My eyes felt nothing, my mouth had no words or expression. I was empty of all past doings. I had no future. I stood up straight and presented my face toward the wall, but still, it wasn't me standing there. Easy had gone undercover and there was no bringing him out. (152)

And when Bonnie, born in French Guyana, says to Easy (on hearing of his involvement with the murder cases at the novel's center), "If you didn't do anything there's nothing to worry about," he responds: "I knew right then that she wasn't a fully American Negro. A black man or woman in America, with American parents, knew that innocence was a term for white people. We were born in sin" (198).

Such dominant racial patterns necessarily reflect back on the crime fiction form Mosley uses. Easy is a type of private detective, who can function as such in the African American community because of the natural disguise that his race, social position, and way of speaking give him. But, if he works to solve crime, he distrusts the law (and the white establishment for which it stands), its operating inequalities, and its unfairness, and their effects both on himself and his community. Looking to better himself in the conventional (white) American way – through astute business dealings (in his case in real estate), home-ownership, and family – he constantly finds himself pulled back into the violence and criminality of the Watts street world of which he is also a part. For, as he says, "I had spent most of my adult years hanging on by a shoestring among gangsters and gamblers, prostitutes and killers" (20). This street world, however, as Mosley insists, has its valuable adjunct in the rich black culture and sense of community that exists alongside, and overlapping, it.

Rawlins then is constantly off balance, caught between his best friend Mouse's violent masculinity and an altogether more thoughtful nurturing and caring side, between the establishing of a settled life and a sense of impermanence and vulnerability, between illegal action and a concern for justice. All this means that, while he solves the individual cases in which he gets caught up, the justice that is served occurs in highly "unofficial" ways, and with a primary recognition of the need to protect the interests of Easy himself and his immediate family and African American community. So, in *A Little Yellow Dog*, Easy works out that it is Bonnie who has in fact murdered Holland Gasteau, after Holland has raped her. But the case is officially closed in a different way, with the police believing (or being left with no alternative but to accept) that both Gasteau brothers died as a result of their criminal activities and "a falling-out among thieves" (296). As Rawlins reaches the end of the case, he himself goes blood-crazy and murders Sallie Monroe (a gangster who booby-traps him and Mouse, and has apparently killed the latter). He also destroys the large heroin consignment at the center of the case. He ends up, too, accepting a good deal of money from Philly Setz, the powerful white criminal who runs the local Numbers business, and whose underlings have reneged on the deal Rawlings has made with him. So, a very messy, complicated, and compromising ending is covered up by the simple official version that, while it leaves most of the major criminals in the case untouched, does restore some version of the social and racial status quo.

We see here (again) the central problem for the African American crime writer: how to find his (or her) way between presenting the detective in a conventional role (protecting a status quo geared toward the interests of the dominant white world) and acting according to his racial positioning, subject to racial discrimination and a denial of both a full social identity and justice by that same white world. In Himes' case, this tension led to a racial dissonance that found expression in the explosive and apocalyptic violence of his final books, and the consequent collapse of the generic form. In Mosley's case, the subject of race tends constantly to distort and highjack (though in nothing like as extreme a way) his detective plots. Thus, in *Devil in a Blue*

Dress, for example, the final emphasis on a narrative of "passing" – that the "white" Daphne Monet is in reality the "black" Ruby Hanks – knocks askew any prior focus on the crimes previously committed and their solution.

It may be, too, that the tensions apparent in Mosley's depiction of Easy Rawlins' life and work – where, too often, Easy is ignorant of, or has little control over, the larger circumstances that shape the world through which he moves, and where racial oppression, violence, and shape-shifting are the unavoidable and too-constant conditions of his life – has limited his use of the detective fiction form and where it can take him as a writer. So, while the Easy Rawlins series was evidently initially intended to take us up to the present day, it seems to have stalled with the 1967 setting of *Blonde Faith*. And, though Mosley has gone on to start another series of detective novels (the Leonid McGill Mysteries, set in New York), there are signs that he has, for some time, been looking for alternative forms that will better suit his needs as an African American (and Jewish) writer. The Socrates Fortlow series (types of Platonic dialogue conducted in the street language of present day Watts), a number of non-fiction and "serious" novels, and even science fiction books all testify to this ongoing quest.

Clearly, my treatment of gender and of race has been highly selective here, and I have focused particularly on the best-known American writing in the field. My intention is that my commentary will ease the way for analysis, and stimulate critical discussion, of the many, many other writers I have not mentioned. As far as gender goes, I have rather taken for granted the tough masculinity of the white male detective protagonist: in my chapters on Hammett and Chandler in Part 3 I return to this subject to suggest that all is not necessarily quite what it seems – that anxieties about masculine self-sufficiency and authority are present not far below the surface of these texts.

My coverage has also (necessarily) been limited both in terms of the many different types of women's crime writing now published and in terms of other crime writing that comes from what we might call a "subaltern" position (in terms of gender, ethnicity, and/or race). There is, for example, a thriving tradition of lesbian detective fiction, which has been used (at least in some cases) to challenge and rework traditional gender constructions and other of the genre's normative conventions. So Christopher Gair, for example, shows how, in Barbara Wilson's *Gaudí Afternoon* (1990), the "unstable gender identity" of her detective protagonist, Cassandra Reilly, and her move from America to Europe, are used for radical purpose: to indicate the new ways of seeing that can result from such boundary crossings (Gair 1997: 117). Approaching gender and sexuality in a very different way, Megan Abbott, in *Queen Pin* (2009) and her other novels, revisits the type of noir crime fiction associated with James M. Cain and Jim Thompson, but rewrites it from the point of view of a tough woman protagonist learning to live, survive, and thrive without qualm in the world of violent criminality, sexual predation, and financial opportunity in which she finds herself.

To focus solely on Himes and Mosley is, too, to give a very limited indication of the range of crime fiction written from a perspective other than that of the dominant "white" Western world. Barbara Neely explores the conjunction of racial and gender subordination in America in her Blanche White novels. Paula Woods, writing in *Inner City Blue* (1999) about race in Los Angeles in the aftermath of the Rodney King beating, uses the police novel form to explore this important cultural moment in American life. James Sallis, a white writer (or rather, as he also calls himself, a "nonblack" one), uses a black private eye, Lew Griffin, in another (very interesting) challenge to the conventions of the crime fiction form. Sallis completely disrupts the usual certainties on which the genre rests: the authority, self-sufficiency, and stable sense of identity of the investigator himself; his ability to remain separate from the world of violent criminality in which he finds himself; the existence of rational explanations for the disruptive events that occur; and even the sense of any logic (bar that of unadulterated power) or value to the larger social system that criminal action (apparently) disrupts. Thus, "the incidents that Griffin is called upon to investigate, the people who have gone missing or been killed, are not disruptions to the status quo but rather are the status quo" (Pepper 2003: 221). Sallis' powerful fictions are an accomplished and controlled post-modern update of Himes, his black protagonist surviving (just) in a world existentially and socio-politically loaded against both himself and the race to which he belongs.

But I have only been talking of African American writing here. And "black" crime fiction cannot of course be limited to just this country or racial group. So, for instance, British writer Mike Phillips bases his fiction on much different circumstances, that of the black Caribbean diasporic experience. Post-colonial crime fiction (that written by native authors of previously colonized countries) – much of which focuses on race and ethnic difference – is another whole area that I can do no more than mention (though see Christian 2010). There is also a growing tradition of Latina/o and Asian American crime writing in the United States itself. This is a rich and fascinating subject area and much more work still waits to be done on it.

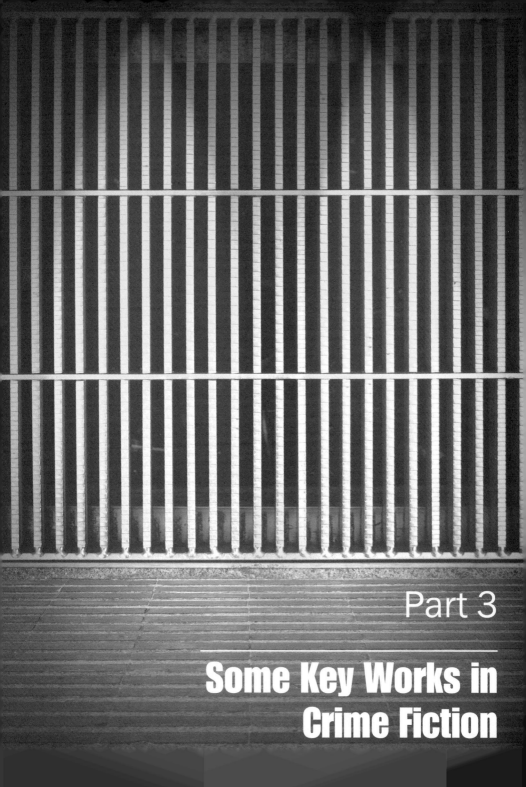

Part 3

Some Key Works in Crime Fiction

Edgar Allan Poe: "The Murders in the Rue Morgue" (1841)

"The Murders in the Rue Morgue" contains a reference to Eugène Vidocq, Head of the Paris Sûreté Nationale until his 1827 retirement. Monsieur C. Auguste Dupin, Poe's detective-protagonist, describes Vidocq as a detective who, despite his talents, "impaired his vision by holding the object too close," who "lost sight of the [investigative] matter as a whole" (Poe 2000: 545) in his focus on selective detail. We are given a suggestion here of a pre-history to Poe's crime fiction, in the *Mémoires* (1828–1829) Vidocq wrote with the help of a ghost-writer and which moved into increasingly imaginative territory as they progressed (see Knight 2004: 23), and in the stage dramas produced in their wake. Despite this, and other early forerunners of the genre (most especially William Godwin's *Caleb Williams*, 1794), it is Poe who is usually credited with being "the father of detective fiction" (Thoms 2002: 133), with inventing the genre of analytic detective fiction (Irwin 1994: 1). And, if we look at "The Murders in the Rue Morgue" ("Rue Morgue" henceforth, for convenience), we can see why. For the narrative works, in what would become the best tradition of the classical detective story, from violent crime to its solution. It focuses on the steps in this process as the brilliant-minded detective reconstructs the events leading up to, and including, the crime that has occurred and, in doing so, arrives at its solution.

One problem, however, is immediately evident here. The murders Dupin investigates are violent and gory. Mother and daughter, Madame and Madamoiselle L'Espanaye, have been brutally killed – the one strangled

The Crime Fiction Handbook, First Edition. Peter Messent.
© 2013 John Wiley & Sons, Ltd. Published 2013 by John Wiley & Sons, Ltd.

and then stuffed forcibly, head downward, up a narrow chimney; the other with her head severed from her body with a razor. But, as Dupin reveals, no "crime" has taken place (at least in these acts), no "murder" has been committed. For we discover that it is an orangutan that has wreaked this havoc. At first glance this might seem another of Poe's hoaxes (and in part it is), a con at the reader's expense, engaging her or his interest and attention only to solve the puzzle that has been set up in a far-fetched, elaborate, and artificial way. It may accordingly seem ironic that what has been held up as the model for a whole genre is a narrative with no real crime to solve, since an animal cannot be legally or morally responsible for its actions. Poe, though, is a very clever and interesting writer indeed, and (as I show) his story fully deserves the attention it has been paid.

Poe undoubtedly works at the level of "high art" (Irwin 1994: 1). Pertinent references within "Rue Morgue" to classical mythology (the Greek Achilles and the Roman goddess Laverna) and to a series of French intellectuals and artists (poet and playwright Prosper Jolyot de Crébillon; naturalist Georges Cuvier; philosopher and novelist Jean-Jacques Rousseau) confirm this. But such references – together with the emphasis on Dupin's rational intelligence and the high "analytical power" (Poe 2000: 530) he possesses – run along-side the type of gothic excess we associate with popular culture and its appeal: the "thick tresses" of grey hair torn from the mother's head, "[t]heir roots (a hideous sight!) . . . clotted with fragments of the flesh of the scalp," and the general "butchery" of the most extreme kind done on both bodies (557–558). If this seems odd, even schizophrenic, we see later that it has its purpose. And, if the three detective stories Poe wrote that feature Dupin are foundational narratives in the crime fiction genre, they have also proved of enormous fascination to philosophers and psychoanalysts, especially in France (a country that, as far as we know, he never in fact visited) – and to Jacques Derrida and Jacques Lacan in particular (see Lacan 1991 and Johnson 1991).

Shawn Rosenheim explains some of the reasons for such interest – though he refers to "Rue Morgue," while it is "The Purloined Letter" on which Derrida and Lacan (and, later, the American psychoanalytic critic Barbara Johnson) focus. For this story, Rosenheim says, "seems to gloss the analytic process itself" (1995: 168). Dupin prompts the sailor to narrate (and so repeat) what he has seen when he glimpsed through the window just behind the L'Espanaye bed-head, as "the beast [which he owns] . . . flew upon the body" (Poe 2000: 567) of the night-gowned daughter. In this sequence, Rosenheim argues, Dupin "stand[s] in for the analyst, the sailor that of analysand, and the orangutan as the figure for the remembered primal scene." "Dupin, one might say," he continues, "enters into an alliance with the sailor in order that he might 'subdue certain parts of his id,' [the words are Freud's] unmistakably represented by the ape" (1995: 169). Moreover, not just this story but all detective narratives of this type have much in common with the Freudian analytic method: with clues gradually uncovered to reveal a buried truth; an incomplete narrative reconstructed through such a recovery and repetition of past events; and with past trauma resolved in that process. "Freudian readers," Rosenheim notes, "have long been attracted to detective fiction just because the genre's structure and themes so often echo central psychological scenarios" (1995: 168). But my interests here are not in the psychoanalytic, so I leave Rosenheim's powerful argument at this point. I do, though, make other use of his critical work as I proceed.

Poe's narrative starts (as outlined earlier in this book) with a section describing "the higher powers of the reflective intellect," "the host of observations and inferences" made by the "truly imaginative" mind, and the pleasures to be gained from this exercise and the "deductions" that follow on from it. This rather abstract prelude to the main narrative – then described as "a commentary on the propositions just advanced" – prepares us for the apparently "praeternatural" (528–531) powers of the master detective: not just Dupin, but all the other analytic detectives to follow in his wake (and especially Sherlock Holmes). This commentary, though, also introduces us to one of the main oppositions that structure the text – that between head and body. For the conceptual section heading the tale works in contrast to the body of its narrative action, just as the analytic powers of the detective there discussed contrast with the presence in the main story of the sunburned and "muscular-looking" sailor and the "huge oaken cudgel" he carries, and the physical power of the brutally violent animal he has captured on his recent Borneo voyage. Thus, at each extreme, the "powers of the ratiocinative mind" are contrasted with the "mindless acts of [the] orangutan" (Rosenheim 1995: 154), a contrast that affects the structure of the narrative as well as it theme.

This motif of head and body and the separation between the two is literalized in the central horror of the narrative – the head of Mme. D'Espanaye slashed from her body using a razor. But the motif is also continued with the contrast between what can be described as the master–slave relationship (Dupin and the sailor, the sailor and the ape) and that further contrast – already noted – between high art and culture and gothic excess. It is also encoded in one of the crucial clues in the narrative: the nail that appears to hold the window sealed but that in actuality is faulty, its head sheered from most of its shank (or body). I am suggesting an extreme narrative sophistication underpinning this tale of death and mayhem. The pun contained in the last-named clue – for "nail" in French, as Irwin points out (1994: 196), is *clou* – is a further example of this.

If the gap between head and body forms a key area of signification in the narrative, it connects strongly with a related theme – the possession and use of language and its lack. Language is the site of difference between human and animal, and Poe's plot, indeed, turns on language. Aural witnesses of the "crime" have heard a harsh or shrill voice – there is no agreement on which – variously interpreted (in each case by those who have no understanding of the language they identify) as speaking in French, German, Italian, and so on. However, in every instance, "no syllabification could be detected" (Poe 2000: 555). Dupin "unriddle[s]" (553) this mystery – deducing that what witnesses have taken for words are in fact "the fiendish jabberings of [a] brute" (568). The name "orangutan" in Malay means "the wild man of the forest" (Irwin 1994: 65) but for Dupin this is no man but pure beast. The story then traces an arc from the linguistic sophistication of Dupin and the narrator (both are readers of rare books and have knowledge of Latin and the ancient Greeks) to pure animal noise.

"Rue Morgue" combines two characteristics of later detective fiction. First, it is set in the city. Dupin and the narrator, indeed, are types of flâneur, exploring and observing urban public spaces. Second, and more crucially, it is also the first locked-room mystery. So Dupin explains through his analytic intelligence the seemingly inexplicable: the presence of a razor-wielding wild beast in this cosmopolitan Parisian space, and just how it entered and exited a room that appears completely impenetrable, locked from within, with windows nailed shut. So far, then, so good: the figure of the master detective solves an apparently insoluble crime and in doing so confirms and re-establishes a set of normative boundaries between reason and instinct, head and body, human and beast, morality and both criminal action and mindless animal act that were previously disturbed.

Careful reading, however, shows these oppositions starting to falter (just as the opposition between high literature and gothic sensation is collapsed in the aesthetic range and shaping of the narrative). Poe starts to question commonly held judgments and assumptions about the perceived gap between the above-named poles. Dupin is – as Holmes will be – a detective endowed with strong supervisory power, and the vision to see what others do not see and accordingly to penetrate where others cannot go: "He boasted to me, with a low chuckling laugh, that most men, in respect to himself, wore windows in their bosoms" (Poe 2000: 533). But the authority and command this gives him is not depicted as morally neutral; it has negative as well as positive connotations and is associated with a form of power that is not disinterested – for Dupin revels in it, takes pleasure in the edge it gives him in competition with the official police investigators. Dupin exercises control over the sailor, getting him to tell him all he knows about the two deaths via a mixture of kindness, knowledge, and reassurance ("You have done nothing . . . which renders you culpable," 564), but also by the threat of force ("Dupin . . . drew a pistol from his bosom and placed it . . . upon the table," 563). His maneuvers in some ways parallel the actions of the ape in the display of physical power over its victim(s), for their effects, though not mortal, mimic that state: "The sailor . . . fell back into his seat, trembling violently, and with the countenance of death itself" (563). The detective's relationship to the sailor, what is more, is in some ways analogous to the sailor's to the ape. His manipulation of, and control over, the sailor, and the wiping away of his "boldness of bearing" (564), bears at least some similarity to the sailor's capture and imprisonment of the ape, and his keeping it in check (until its escape) not with a pistol but by "the use of a whip" (565). This whip, as Thoms notes, "highlight[s] the connection between power and violence" (2002: 139) – a connection that links ape, sailor, and Dupin himself, the last-named not as secluded from the larger world, its interests, and the way it works as he would at first appear to be.

In putting all responsibility for the L'Espanaye killings onto the orangutan (and declaring the sailor not "culpable" for the deaths), Dupin keeps the lines clear between human and animal, and the social compact and its criminal rupture, in what is, in fact, a fraudulent way. For the sailor's own "criminal negligence" (Irwin 1994: 66) is covered up in this process. Similarly, simply to associate Dupin with the mind and the ape with the physical body and the brute is to ignore the emphasis on the sailor's own physique; to ignore too the way Dupin himself acts, disentangling animal hair (presumably with some effort) from "the rigidly clutched fingers of Madame L'Esplanaye" (Poe 2000: 558); having the narrator (in many ways his double) attempt to mimic the actions of the ape in closing his fingers around a modeled version of the throat of the strangled victim. Everything Poe does here puts into question the apparently firm oppositions by which the story works, and suggests that the borders between both mind and body and human and animal are not nearly as secure as we would imagine or hope, and that the master detective, Dupin himself, is not as far removed from the latter terms in these pairings as his initial representation might imply. The fact that the narrator describes the peculiar routines of his and Dupin's Paris lives as, seen from the outside, similar to those of "madmen" (but "of a harmless nature," 532) is strangely reprised later in the text when that same narrator considers all the details of the violent acts being investigated, concluding: "A madman . . . has done this deed – some raving maniac, escaped from a neighboring *Maison de Santé*" (558). The two men's alienation from the day-today social world, then, has at least something in common with the violent response of the ape to a city and its inhabitants where it does not belong. Again, Poe muddies the conceptions of absolute difference on which the narrative first seems to be based.

The slippages I have identified (and noted variously by the critics to whom I have referred) take on additional meaning if we look to put this story into a socio-historical context. The ape's imitating his master and "flourishing the razor about [Mmme. D'Espanaye's] face, in imitation of the motions of a barber" (566), reminds me of Babo in "Benito Cereno," Melville's great 1855 story about slavery, holding an open razor at Benito Cereno's neck. Babo – in fact leading a slave rebellion on board Cereno's ship – plays the part of attentive servant before the unknowing Captain Delano, even as he represents for Cereno (once his captain, now his slave) menace in its most extreme form. This might seem, at first glance, an extreme textual leap to take, but there are other connections here. For we can see Poe's narrative as about slavery too (so see, for instance, Peterson 2010), though specifically in the context of the American South.

Slavery and the fears, anxieties and doubts about that "peculiar institution" were always to the forefront of Poe's mind, though usually, as in *The Narrative of Arthur Gordon Pym* (1838), represented in indirect form. Descriptions of blacks as ape-like, lower in the evolutionary scale than whites, and with a greater propensity for violence (recall the brutal violence of the black cook of *Arthur Gordon Pym* and his description as a "perfect demon," 84) were common in the eighteenth and nineteenth centuries. So Thomas Jefferson in *Notes on the State of Virginia* (1784), for instance, spoke of "the preference of the orangutan for the black women over those of his own species" – implying a form of natural connection between inferior race (as he suspected blacks to be) and animal-kind. He also held, in a sentence that connects up with the patterns I have been thus far tracing, that "[i]n general [the] existence [of blacks] appears to participate more of sensation than reflection" (Jefferson 2006: n.p.).

What, then, is the connection here with Poe's narrative? If orangutans were seen by some – though not by Dupin – as almost human ("wild men of the forest") then African American slaves were seen by many southerners almost as apes. Unlike apes, slaves were syllabic but were restricted in their language development, commonly forbidden the opportunity to learn to read or write. At the time Poe wrote "Rue Morgue," there was considerable anxiety in the South over the threat of slave rebellion (Nat Turner's revolt had taken place a decade earlier, in 1831). Such concerns seem to be figured in this story. We can read in the "fulvous" (Poe 2000: 559), or brownish-yellow, orangutan a type of figurative stand-in for the African American slave – captured from its homeland by a (white) intruder, kept closeted by its master in his home, quieted by the use of the whip, breaking from confinement to wreak a form of bloody vengeance on white womanhood (black male sexuality and miscegenation were high on the list of the South's racial fears), before being recaptured and sold on by its owner. An odd parable of American race relations, then, appears to underpin this Parisian story.

Poe's racial politics here (as in *Arthur Gordon Pym*) seem complex, even confused. The narrative seems to encode a critique of slavery and of the violence that underpinned its practice and continuation. The move from orangutan to its slave equivalent carries with it a number of clashing interpretive possibilities, all of which play on those same human/animal, head/body borderlines. An ape is an animal, instinctual and without reason; a slave was not. Thus, to look to possess and confine the latter, and treat him in a brutal and brutish manner (wielding that whip), is unsurprisingly to court a violent (and justifiable) payback. But the very analogy made, the equation of the animal with the human, cuts in a different direction. For it suggests that the ape/black slave are, indeed, both of a similar animal nature, pure body and lacking mind, using the tools of civilization in a purely imitative manner and to a barbaric end. Implicit in the narrative, then, lies a deep anxiety about slavery, a fear of the violence threatened by the muscular black body (we remember the inhabitants of Tsalal, completely "other" to the white sailors, treacherous, "jet black," and with "muscular and brawny frame," Poe 1980 [1838]: 189) and of the overturning of the established sexual and social order that any uprising or rebellion might bring.

The oppositions in the text here can either be read as firmly constructed or subject to slippage, depending on the reading one takes. With its body stuffed up a chimney, decapitation, and ape on the rampage, this unsettling story works as a first-rate narrative of detection, but as much more besides. It blends gothic device and rational analysis to highly effective and provocative ends.

Arthur Conan Doyle: The Sign of Four (1890)

There is little doubt that Conan Doyle was heavily influenced by Poe in his creation of the figure of Sherlock Holmes. So Doyle, too, like Poe in "The Murders in the Rue Morgue," starts his book with a section on the detective's analytic power, here renamed "the Science of Deduction" (Doyle 2001: 5). He rewrites Dupin's "it is not our part, as reasoners, to reject [a conclusion] on account of apparent impossibilities. It is only left for us to prove that these apparent 'impossibilities' are, in reality, not such" (Poe 2000: 551) as the more punchy "How often have I said to you [Watson] that when you have eliminated the impossible, whatever remains, *however improbable*, must be the truth?" (42). So he, too, nods in the direction of a French detective (here, the fictional François le Villard) while at the same time detailing his rival's shortcomings (7–8).

Holmes pronounces himself "the only unofficial consulting detective . . . in the world" and "the last and highest court of appeal in detection" (6), words that would not have sounded out of place on Dupin's lips. Both men, too, are marked by their unconventional departures from the norms of bourgeois living and their schizophrenic swings of mood: in Holmes' case between "nervous exaltation" and "black depression" (80). Holmes, though, is associated more strongly with *scientific* detection than Dupin: the monographs he has written ("Upon the Distinction between the Ashes of the Various Tobaccos" and others) are evidence of his "extraordinary genius for minutiae" (8). Holmes, too, is generally more active than the generally "passive, academic figure" (Knight 1994: 369) of his French predecessor. Both detectives, crucially, are assisted by less perceptive companions

The Crime Fiction Handbook, First Edition. Peter Messent.
© 2013 John Wiley & Sons, Ltd. Published 2013 by John Wiley & Sons, Ltd.

who take on the task of narrating the stories in which each great detective features – though Watson's voice and character are much more developed than his (unnamed) counterpart in Poe.

It is Sherlock Holmes, however, who has dominated the Western cultural imagination more thoroughly than Dupin – or any other detective hero. Doyle fleshed out his protagonists over the course of four novels and fifty-six short stories, developing characterizations and the type of intertextual connections that would provide a model for so many later serial detective narratives. His Holmes stories were enormously popular in their period and have remained so ever since. The reasons for this must, to some extent, be speculative. It is in part, though, due to the sophisticated interaction between the brilliant Holmes and the stolid Watson, and the way in which the characters of, and relationship between, both men are portrayed and developed during the series. As I have mentioned previously, the way Holmes (first in print and later in the stage and film versions of Doyle's stories) is associated with particular, and iconographic, detail is also crucially important here. So, in *The Sign of Four* we have references to Holmes' Baker Street lodgings, to his "clear-cut, hawk-like features" (14) and boxing skills (35), to his use of "a powerful convex lens" (10, 38) and fondness for his "old brier-root pipe" (7) (the last two quickly transformed in illustration and stage version to the magnifying glass with handle and distinctive calabash pipe respectively), and to his cocaine-taking (5–6, 118), violin-playing (69), and scientific experiments (73, 81). All these, then repeated, helped to form the highly distinctive Holmes persona.

But there is more to Holmes' appeal than this. Very much a product of his time and place, Doyle's hero spoke, too, to ongoing Victorian social anxieties and concerns. Holmes' eccentric genius stood as a significant counter to public fears of growing standardization and anonymity in a mass urban culture – and continued to strike such a responsive chord in later times. Moreover, in a rapidly modernizing city environment, Holmes' confident authority and ability (using his delegated agents, where necessary) to penetrate this labyrinthine space, and restore order to it, are highly reassuring. So, in *The Sign of Four*, Holmes' "unofficial force – the Baker Street irregulars" (in fact "a dozen dirty and ragged little Street Arabs") – give Holmes the kind of supervisory powers over the city unavailable even to the police: for "[t]hey can go everywhere, see everything, overhear everyone" (67). The scientific reason driving Holmes' detective work also stands in high and attractive relief to the gothic horrors still inhabiting that urban world. So, in this novel, Holmes is faced by, and finally kills, an "unhallowed dwarf," a "savage, distorted creature . . . all bestiality and cruelty" (86), a cannibal presence and sign of all that a rational and civilized late-nineteenth-century world might think it had conquered and repressed, here let loose on London's streets and waterways.

One final reason, perhaps, for the success of the Sherlock Holmes series, both when Doyle was writing it and since, lies in Holmes' sheer narrative ability. For these stories succeed in such terms even more than a century after they were produced. The moves in *The Sign of Four* between Watson's narrative, his and Holmes' actions, Holmes' own explanatory words and account (to Watson) of his motivations, and Jonathan Small's final story of the pre-history of his crime, are highly effective; similarly the moves, overlaps, and tension between genres (detection, adventure, and romance). The narrative clarity of the book, too – the clean and direct lines of Doyle's style as action is described and his skilful use of dialogue – mean that these stories have not dated to anything like the degree of comparable texts of their period, and have retained both their freshness and their force.

In terms of content, too, Doyle's narratives retain their interest and their power, and *The Sign of Four* is very much a case in point. (I am influenced in the reading that follows by a number of critics but would especially mention Haynsworth 2000 and McLaughlin 2001.) I start by recalling my prior comments on Franco Moretti and his reading of Sherlock Holmes as a defender of the status quo, "interested only in *perpetuating* the existing order"; as the "great doctor" of his historical period, convincing his late Victorian readers "that society is still a great *organism*: a unitary and knowable body" (1983: 140, 145). Given that *The Sign of Four* starts with Holmes – against the advice of his own doctor – injecting his own body with cocaine, and continues with the figures of Jonathan Small and the "black cannibal" (Doyle 2001: 115) Tonga infecting the British social body as they unleash violence upon the (supposed) stillness and peace of the (Upper Norwood) Surrey landscape (see 98), Moretti's metaphor seems particularly pertinent to this text – but its use is also (as I will describe) not without its complications.

It seems perfectly possible, though, to read the narrative according to Moretti's larger formula. I would do this on three levels. First, Holmes acts as a figure of supervisory power in the novel, able to pursue criminality through the complex urban labyrinth and so to banish its infection of the social body. The crimes he investigates are the murder of Bartholomew Sholto and the theft of the treasure in Sholto's possession. As Holmes and Watson make their way, via Bartholomew's brother Thaddeus' house, toward Bartholomew's Upper Norwood residence (this before the latter's murder is discovered), the size and growth of the "giant city" is emphasized, with the "monster tentacles which [it] was throwing out into the country" (23). There is strong emphasis, too, on the "labyrinth of streets" and "tortuous by-streets" they pass through, and the consequent possibility of spatial dislocation: as Watson comments, "I lost my bearings and knew nothing save that we seemed to be going a very long way" (22–23). Once the crime is discovered, Holmes and Watson set out in delayed chase of the perpetrators, initially using "a specially trained hound" to follow the track (for one of the criminals has stepped in creosote). That Holmes himself is himself referred to here as "silent, and furtive" in his movements, "like . . . a trained bloodhound" (44), links man and animal in the relentlessness of pursuit and its likelihood of success.

It is worth noting, as the dog follows the traces of its quarry back into the Vauxhall area of the city and to the termination of the trail at the banks of the Thames, the emphasis placed on the working-class nature of the area: "continuous streets, where labourers and dockmen were already astir, and slatternly women were taking down shutters. . . . [P]ublic house business was just beginning, and rough-looking men were emerging, rubbing their sleeves across their beards after their morning wet" (59). The criminals have now taken to the river, in a hired steam launch, but the chase is no easier here, with "a perfect labyrinth of landing-places for miles" (64) where the launch might hide. It is at this point that Holmes calls in his "irregulars." Even their panoptic range fails, however, so well is the boat hidden, and Holmes has to use other tactics, disguising himself in "seaman's rig" (82) to enquire about the vessel (to which he assumes the criminals will return) at boat-builders and repair yards. This tactic works and prepares the reader for the final "mad, flying man-hunt down the Thames" (86) with Holmes, Watson, and police detective Mr. Athelney Jones pursuing the criminals in a fast police launch. Civil order is restored with the death of the tiny cannibal who has murdered Bartholomew – gunned down by Holmes and/or Watson as he shoots a poisoned dart at them through his blow-pipe during the chase. Jonathan Small, too, is arrested and faced with long imprisonment at the story's end. An improved version of the existing order is restored at this point, with the more moral-minded of the two Sholto brothers (we assume) taking possession of Pondicherry Lodge, the Upper Norwood house, and with Miss Mary Morstan, the other interested party in the case, in love with – and engaged to marry – Watson. The stolen treasure has been lost in the Thames but, as we will see, this is necessary to an unproblematic resolution to the Morstan–Watson romance.

I focus briefly on that romance now as part and parcel (if an unintentional one) of Holmes' social doctoring. Holmes' detective work starts off as a type of locked room mystery – as in "Rue Morgue," the corpse is discovered in a room locked on the inside. The narrative soon develops, though, into a tale of adventure, with the strenuous search for the criminals and the Thames boat chase. Meanwhile Watson, in a move that goes against the grain of Holmes' own self-interests, tells not just the tale of the latter's detections but another and different story of romance (Haynsworth argues that "Holmes and Watson repeatedly enact an explicit, dialectic engagement between logic and affect," 2001: 461). But that romance, as Watson falls in love with Mary and announces their engagement, also helps to repair and seal the social compact, and is brought about by Holmes' work. Both men, in Mary's eyes, are "knight-errants to the rescue" in the story of "[a]n injured lady" (71). There is in fact little direct threat to Mary's physical self in the story, for she stands rather to one side of the main narrative. But, as a result of the quest for (and loss of) her treasure, Mary's status changes from governess to married woman. And, if one ending to the novel consists of Holmes listening first to Small's story and then to Watson's (to Holmes, unfortunate) engagement news, the other consists of Watson's proposal and Mary's acceptance of him, and his discovery of a different kind of treasure than he expected but one that, in his eyes, is of much greater worth: "Whoever had lost a treasure, I knew that night that I had gained one" (94).

In a novel where gender relations seem strangely out of joint (of which more later), heterosexual union finally triumphs. Such union, what is more, undergirds the English social order. Watson turns from the "wild, dark business" at Pondicherry Lodge to take Mary to her current home, then looks back to see her with her employer (and friend). He comments retrospectively, "I still seem to see that little group on the step – the two graceful, clinging figures, the half-opened door, the hall-light shining through stained glass, the barometer, and the bright stair-rods," describing the experience as "a passing glimpse of a tranquil English home" (51). It is just that tranquility and settled domesticity – as it will now be lived by Watson and his soon-to-be wife – that is called into being at the novel's close.

The final way Holmes doctors the social body relates to issues both of class and empire. The central crime portrayed in the narrative is the murder of Bartholemew Sholto, and the taking of the jewel chest that at this point "belongs" to him and his brother, and "by rights" (of at least a certain kind) to Mary too (the quote marks here are mine). The murder has been committed by Tonga, an Andaman Islander. (The Andamans, off the east coast of India, were part of the British Empire, with a penal colony established there in 1858.) Tonga is, as I previously suggested, and in a representation that bears little relation to historical reality, depicted as a savage "other" – a monstrous and murderous cannibal now on the loose in England. As McLaughlin comments: "At one level, *The Sign of Four* is a prophetic nightmare of decolonization imagined as reverse colonization and savage vengeance by the vanquished" (2000: 67). Tonga, then, stands as a nightmare figure in the national imaginary, the meant-to-be-submissive native out of all control and invading the very home of empire to highly disturbing effect with his savage and (in one case) death-dealing tools: a crude stone-headed hammer and a blow-pipe. On a metaphorical level, as Tonga is linked to the poisoned thorns that kill Bartholemew (and endanger Holmes and Watson too), he stands in sharp opposition to Mary, the figure of appealing domesticity, with her "refined and sensitive nature" (13) and "angelic" qualities (50) – the very epitome of the thornless English rose.

As Tonga's poison pierces Sholto's body and kills him, so metaphorically he threatens serious (even terminal) infection to the national body. His cannibalism is a sign that this "hell-hound" and "little devil" (89) has turned figuratively to eat not just the (holy?) hand that feeds him but potentially the whole body of his national host. The Indian "great mutiny" (98) of 1857–1859 anticipates this sign of the cannibal's invasive threat, but on colonial rather than home ground. For here "black devils" (98), "drunk with opium and with bhang" (101), turn the British weaponry they have been trained to use back on their masters. (We remember that Holmes remains in control of the bodily-invasive substances he takes, restricting his cocaine to a "seven-per-cent solution," 6, and retaining the self-discipline these Indian "black fiends" lack, 99.) It is these same Indian rebels who set the house of indigo-planter Abel White (the name is clearly allegorical) ablaze, cutting the body of the white wife of his employee "into ribbons" and leaving it to be to be "half eaten by jackals and native dogs" (98–99). So they enact en masse on a distant frontier what Tonga threatens in (metonymic) miniature on home soil.

Tonga, though, is devoted to his master, Jonathan Small, as race (to a certain degree) combines with class to threatening effect. We have already seen the distaste with which Watson describes working-class men and women, and Small is among the dregs of this latter group, the black sheep of a Worcestershire farming family. An accessory to murder in India as well as in England (in Bartholemew's case), and a convict, his "much sunburned" face (47) and "mahogany features" (89) link him to foreign "otherness." He, too, is seen as a dreadful threat: his "bearded, hairy face, with [on occasion] wild, cruel eyes" (29) and "heavy brows and aggressive chin" give him "a terrible expression when moved to anger" (89). Small's representation is complex, though. For, if he is associated clearly both with savagery and with class threat, the fact that he is an Englishman and white works ultimately to differentiate him from his cannibal friend. Thus, Watson presents Small in a rather sympathetic light (89) as he starts to tell his final story.

It is Holmes, though, who restores the British national body to health (if we take Sholto's murder as having figurative resonance). The threat from the working class and colonial other is obliterated, with Tonga dead and Small to be imprisoned. With the bones of Tonga, this "strange visitor to our shores," now left lying "[s]omewhere in the dark ooze at the bottom of the Thames" (87), Holmes (as McLaughlin says) "capture[s] and contain[s]" the cannibal. He continues: "[I]n order to preserve the safety, purity, and integrity of both individual Londoners and the national body . . . [Holmes] symbolically restores the unassimilated primitive visitor to his 'true home' amid the undifferentiated primal muck and evolutionary ooze" (67, 69; I replace McLaughlin's "Doyle" with my "Holmes" here). We can, then, read this novel through a Moretti-inflected lens, with Holmes as protector and defender of the status quo, concerned with preserving the health of the larger social body.

Any astute reader, however, will raise objections to my reading so far as over-simplistic. For inherent in this text are a whole series of questions and anxieties about British culture at the century's end and the directions in which it is heading. Such complications, however (and this ties in with my earlier argument about the difference between the classical and hard-boiled forms), become apparent only on delving below the surface of the text, and are at no point explicitly thematized. They do, however, make the novel into a much less single-visioned whole than I have thus far suggested, and suggest that Moretti does Holmes something of a disservice in the clear lines he cuts through his work.

So, for instance, McLaughlin points out that, though Tonga is dead at the end of the text and his bones lie in "undifferentiated primal muck," nonetheless "this muck is a quintessentially English muck; it is the foundation of the Thames, that most symbolically of English rivers" (69). The river is also, though – as Conrad made so clear in *Heart of Darkness*, published just two years later – a primary physical and economic link between England's capital hub and far-flung Empire, "a waterway leading to the uttermost ends of the earth" (Conrad 1989: 28). And Doyle's narrative, too, suggests how Britain and its empire have become interconnected; how any talk of home and foreign "other," of secure domesticity and outside threat, no longer quite makes sense. There are many signs in this text of the interpenetration of the two worlds, British and colonial, as the one irrevocably affects the other. Thus, India is recollected and in part reconstructed in London's suburbia with Pondicherry Lodge, a house "full of Indian curiosities" (Doyle 2001: 46), named after the Indian city governed by the French (though fought for by the British too). The powerful image of the Lodge's "desolate grounds" with its "great rubbish-heaps" (35–36) where the Sholto brothers have searched for the missing treasure (their father has died before revealing where he has hidden it) provides an image of waste and desolation surprisingly contrasted with the more ordered activity in the colonies ("digging and ditching and yam-planting," 109), and a metaphorical mile away from the British "house and garden" domestic ideal that the text conjures up elsewhere.

Describing the "great [Indian] mutiny," Jonathan Small tells of how "[o]ne month India lay as still and peaceful, to all appearance, as Surrey or Kent; the next there were two hundred thousand black devils let loose, and the country was a perfect hell" (98). But it is in Surrey, too, here, that not only is any idea of the rural picturesque exploded (in that ruined garden) but where, also, "something devilish" (38) takes place – though now with just Small and his one black "devil" (89) accomplice responsible. When Small makes his deal with the three Punjabis at the Agra fort to steal the treasure (from its Indian rajah owner), one of the latter group comments on the trust existing between them: for "the Sikh knows the Englishman and the Englishman knows the Sikh" (102). All these examples provide strong images of interdependency and similarity, and not of separate difference. Empire, it is implied, breaks down any sense of isolated cultural identity of any of its parts, collapses distinctions between center and peripheral other, and inevitably compromises nostalgic notions of national self-sufficiency and belonging. The fact that Small exhibits Tonga as an exotic curiosity in England ("[h]e would eat raw meat and dance his war-dance," 115) indicates how commerce, too, embraces the foreign, translating it into just another part of the home country's consumer spectacle and experience (and see McLaughlin on the move from scientific racism to commodity racism in the period, 2000: 74–78).

The relationship between colony and imperial center is, then, made more complex here, a product of mutual interaction and interconnection. Similarly, straightforward associations between the British establishment and its threatening other, crime and its identification with particular racial and working-class groups, are undermined in the book. Murder and theft may be committed by Small and Tonga, but it is the desire to recover the Agra treasure that prompts their actions. And this treasure has been "stolen" from Small and his three Indian confederates by Major Sholto – who, in turn, has double-crossed his army compatriot and "bosom frien[d]" (110), Captain Morstan, in the process. It turns out, then, that any quest to recover the treasure on Mary's behalf, or – accordingly – to link moral superiority to the established British order, is highly questionable. But the ownership of the treasure is even more complicated than this and rights of ownership are confused. In theory, the treasure is – following the Indian mutiny – up for grabs, confiscated from its outlawed former owner (110); but that does not give Small and his gang ownership rights. For (whatever the treasure's legal status at the time) the act of murder by which they first gained it remains an illegal and punishable offence – thus Small's Andaman confinement.

There would appear, here, to be an implicit critique of Indian colonialism and the grasping acquisitiveness that (for some) underpinned it. But, as in the case of much in the book, that depends on our taking the part for the whole: Sholto and Morstan for the British establishment; Small for their, and its, unscrupulous agent. And – quite apart from Doyle's own imperialist politics – there are good reasons to argue against such a reading. But the textual details on which I focus do complicate the very notion of theft and what it means in an Indian context, both in terms of the Rebellion situation and even before it. The original (real?) owner of the treasure is a "rajah in the northern provinces" (102), and we have no idea where he (and his father, also mentioned) made their money. It is quite possible that the treasure is tainted at source, perhaps taken legally, but ultimately by hierarchical force, from the people and resources of the region over which that rajah ruled. Both the definition of theft, then, and the point in the historical and ideological chain where it becomes, as a descriptor, legally and/or morally applicable, are problematized here.

If the surface move of the narrative has Sherlock Holmes doctoring and healing the British social body, then, a more complex story lies beneath – and one that reveals certain anxieties and doubts over that body's original state of health. The same is true of the depiction of British masculinity and gender roles in this text, the final subject I address. One could argue that, as a tale of mystery and adventure, we would not expect a fully rounded depiction of gender, and with this I agree. There is, nonetheless, something decidedly odd in the representation of British masculinity in the text, and especially in the representation of Thaddeus Solto and of Holmes himself.

Solto is a type of late-nineteenth-century aesthete – modeled some say on Oscar Wilde. He has created his house as "[a]n oasis of art in the howling desert of South London" (24), and has found his inspiration not in India but the Orient, with deeply sensuous amber and black carpeting, "Oriental vase," "huge hookah," and the like (24). In retreat from the workaday business world, Thaddeus' masculine force has been replaced by a type of nervous debility: he has writhing hands and "features . . . in a perpetual jerk" (24), hypochondria, and "weak, watery blue eyes" (25); he talks incessantly; and he is described as "half blubbering with fear" (37) when faced with the strange events at his brother's house. This debility is explained as "a natural shrinking from all forms of rough materialism" (26), a retreat to the world of art (with his Corot and his Bouguereau) signaling a profound rejection of the normal bourgeois routines of the time.

Holmes, too, though very different from Sholto, finds his male identity deeply compromised by the everyday Victorian world. The novels starts and ends with his cocaine-taking, and his first injection (with "white, nervous fingers" adjusting "the delicate needle," 5) has, as McLaughlin suggests, "clearly erotic overtones" (2000: 53). Holmes, too, has something of the neurasthenic about him, and like Sholto has channeled his energies away from heterosexuality and marriage into either narcissistic pleasure or his detective work. He fails to notice Mary's beauty since, for him, she is just "a mere unit, a factor in a problem" (Doyle 2001: 17), while his disappointment with Watson's engagement stems from the latter's emotional commitment, one "opposed to that true cold reason which I place above all things" (117).

It is Holmes' detective work that primarily sustains him. But a distinction is made between this work and conventional labor. Both Sholto and Holmes, we might suggest, are in retreat from the routine forms of late-nineteenth-century capitalism and its effects on the bodies and minds of its workforce: the body supervised and controlled, regulated (as Michel Foucault would see it) by the various systems of power (and forms of discourse) by which a modern bourgeois system disciplines its subjects; the mind similarly shackled. Holmes revels in work and the satisfactions to be gained from fulfilling activity: "Give me problems, give me work, give me the most abstruse cryptogram, or the most intricate analysis, and I am in my own proper atmosphere. I can dispense then with artificial stimulants" (6). But he is completely alienated from the dull and dulling routines increasingly apparent in the period, with the worker relegated to the efficient functioning of the economic and industrial machine that he or she serves; caught up in the material with the higher faculties accordingly muted. This explains Holmes' words to Watson:

> I abhor the dull routine of existence. . . . I cannot live without brainwork. What else is there to live for? Stand at the window here. Was ever such a dreary, dismal, unprofitable world? See how the yellow fog swirls down the street and drifts across the dun-coloured houses. What could be more hopelessly prosaic and material? . . . Crime is commonplace, existence is commonplace, and no qualities save those which are commonplace have any function upon earth. (6, 12)

This is an extraordinary passage, and suggests that, even while Holmes doctors the social body, he is fundamentally alienated from it. It is Watson, rather, who provides an acceptance of contented bourgeois living in the text, a willingness to engage in the routines of everyday life and the heterosexual relationships that conventionally sustain them. But in the representations of Holmes and Sholto we see deep anxieties about Victorian masculinity and how it might relate to a fulfilling individual and social existence.

On one level, then, it is perfectly possible to read this novel as ideologically conservative. Holmes, accordingly, uses his genius to repair the rent that has been made in the social fabric, to counter the outside threat to the authority of Empire, to preserve the status quo. Indeed, this seems to be the overt message of the narrative. But there are also a whole raft of questions and anxieties implicit in the various details, and turns, of this complex narrative that suggest a more critical stance toward British life, values, and imperialist practice. It is this complexity and ambivalence that helps to suggest just why the Sherlock Holmes stories hold such a deep and lasting grip on the Western cultural imagination.

Agatha Christie:
The Murder of Roger Ackroyd (1926)

I turn now to a classic Golden Age detective story by Agatha Christie – who stands alongside Conan Doyle in terms of best-known British crime writing. "Golden Age" refers, by and large, to the period between the two world wars, and to British crime fiction in particular – though a good number of American authors (S. S. Van Dine, for example) wrote in a similar mode. If the term can serve to conceal the different types and varieties of detective novels being produced in the period, it is nonetheless useful. Introducing, typically, a multiple cast of suspects, it uses "the clue-puzzle" as its "central mechanism" (Knight 2003: 77). It is set generally in an enclosed space, and especially the English country house: in the case of *The Murder of Roger Ackroyd*, "Fernly Park" (Christie 2002: 17), "une belle propriété" (133) – the words are Poirot's and translate as "a handsome property" – with formal flower beds, yew hedges, and a wooded slope offering "a splendid view over the countryside" (134). The use of such closeted settings goes together with a general avoidance of larger social and historical issues. Charles Rzepka is not alone in seeing a conservative and nostalgic impetus at work in Christie and her like, a recall of a more stable and settled pre-war world of "sprawling country estates, tidy villages, and [when the setting is urban] townhouses populated by comfortable eccentrics":

> Here was a world embodying the virtues of the vanishing gentry class and prominently featuring members of the four most ancient and honourable professions: retired military officers, local clergy, lawyers and doctors. . . .
> With its reliable evocation of order out of disorder [and] its respect for the rule of law in defence of life and property . . . the new genre of detection seemed

The Crime Fiction Handbook, First Edition. Peter Messent.
© 2013 John Wiley & Sons, Ltd. Published 2013 by John Wiley & Sons, Ltd.

tailor-made to alleviate the anxieties that lingered below the superficial complacency of British middle-class life.

(Rzepka 2005: 153)

As Rzepka's words suggest, Golden Age crime fiction was socially as well as spatially enclosed, representing a hierarchically ordered world and focusing especially on the upper middle classes. There are few professional criminals here and few members of the working class (though see below). This is a world of wealth and property – of those who have it and those who are their dependents (but who hope to share it). This is a world, too, of masters or mistresses, their households and their servants, though the latter normally play a relatively minor role in the action. Murder – for the first time "an essential part of the detective story" (Horsley 2005: 37) – is the most common crime here (most of the Sherlock Holmes stories are about theft and fraud): a crime committed for personal and private motives. Thus, on the surface at least, there is little suggestion of any fault line in the larger social system that might cause such rupture; little indication that crime might be the result of any social inequality or injustice in need of address.

To see such Golden Age fiction just as a cosy and conservative affirmation of a high-bourgeois status quo is, however, one-sided. For the very disturbances that occur, and the presence of those "anxieties" to which Rzepka refers, suggest a certain fragility to the apparently generally well-ordered social world portrayed. Gill Plain suggests that the prevalence of murder in Christie's novels works as a veiled form of socio-historical comment, a reference and response to the slaughter of war years: "in [Christie's] construction of the grievable body she offers a talisman against death's fragmentation and dissolution, a sacrifice to ameliorate the wounds of war" (2001: 53). Not everyone will be convinced by this, but undoubtedly the representation of the particular social world Christie presents, and the forms of disruption that occur, do suggest deep and ongoing anxieties about the problems and instabilities lying beneath its apparently stable surface. Thus Horsley (following Alison Light) writes that:

> Instead of giving her readers a reassuring, defensive fiction or nostalgia for the aristocracy, Christie creates plots that are symptomatic of instability. She focuses on the disruptions of family life from within, reworking Victorian transgression in plots that turn on masks [and] mistaken identity. . . . She portrays a society of *strangers* in which all social exchange is theatrical and she structures her narratives to reveal sources of menace that seem inextricably bound up with the traditional social hierarchies she represents. In this reading, "containment" of crime is double edged: it allows reassuring closure but also implies that the class represented is preying on itself, and that it contains the seeds of its own destruction.

(Horsley 2005: 40)

This double-edged quality is (as we have seen) not unusual in crime fiction, where a conservative politics and a critique of, and anxieties about, the current social order often run hand in glove. Undoubtedly, as R. A. York writes, "[t]hat the detective story tends to accept a conservative society is undeniable, with reference to Christie at least" (2007: 7). As I explore perhaps her most famous novel, I will show how such conservatism is, though, implicitly undermined by the anxieties about the portrayed social formations and relationships evident within the text.

Christie's work has been and is (especially in its TV versions) incredibly popular, almost certainly overshadowing that of all other crime novelists, with over two billion worldwide sales (Makinen 2010: 416). This is, in part, due to Christie's skill with the "clue-puzzle" form: her ability to keep the reader engaged as she marshals her cast of characters and presents the motives that might have led some or all of them to commit the central crime. It is due, too, to the way she has her detective, Hercule Poirot in this case, draw attention to the various clues to the case – so seeming to offer the reader equal chance to first-guess the solution (though never really doing so).

As with so much such Golden Age fiction, Christie makes playful allusion to the artificiality of the form she uses. So, in this novel the maps of the ground floor and nearby grounds of the Ackroyd dwelling (74) and of the room in which the murder occurred (110) serve, too, as reminders that this is a purely imaginary landscape. The lists of the house's inhabitants and their where-abouts, and who can vouch for them at the time of the crime (125–126), serve a similar function, nodding in the direction of a scrupulous realism that we know does not exist. There are, moreover, repeated self-reflexive references to detective fiction and its devices – murder by way of rare poisons (26–27); the kind of exotic rewards ("rubies and pearls and emeralds from grateful Royal clients") a fictional "super-detective" might expect (171). If the latter allusion is to Sherlock Holmes (see, for instance, Doyle 1981b: 34), Christie's model then becomes explicit as Dr. Sheppard, the narrator, tells how, for the first part of the investigation, "I was at Poirot's elbow the whole time. I saw what he saw. . . . [M]y narrative might have been that of Poirot himself. I played Watson to his Sherlock" (203–204).

This leads us straight to the cleverness of this novel (or, for some, its deceit), in Christie's putting control of the narrative in the murderer's hand. As I commented earlier, this goes against all the rules of classical detective fiction. It also indicates Christie's own games-playing with the genre, as she tried – as on a number of other occasions too – to stretch the form beyond normally accepted limits. We have here two overlapping narratives based on entirely opposite premises and written for completely different ends. Dr. Sheppard acts as Watson to Poirot's Holmes and takes on, too, Hastings' previously role in the series. As such, he stands at Poirot's elbow, reporting all that the detective says and does, part of the investigation, "keep[ing] a written record of . . . [his] impressions of the case as [he] went along" (326–327) – and completing that record as the final chapter ends. He acts as a type of amanuensis for Poirot, reporting on the progress of the case and on the clues the detective thinks important (but given no access to the conclusions Poirot reaches as a result). As Sheppard says – and note the prolepsis as he alludes to knowledge that lies in the future – "Though Poirot showed me all his discoveries . . . he held back the vital and yet logical impressions he formed. As I came to know later, this secrecy was characteristic of him. He would throw out hints and suggestions, but beyond that he would not go" (203).

As the murderer, however, Sheppard's role is central in a different narrative, but one that he – in large part – conceals: how and why he committed the crime, and what he is consequently thinking and feeling as Poirot goes about his business. In playing the role of detective's assistant and recorder, he covers over the story of his own guilt and attempt to evade discovery – a story only Poirot himself will finally reveal (Sheppard himself never says why he blackmails Mrs. Ferrars: we rely here only on Poirot's interpretation of his possible motives). Christie's play with the telling of a narrative, and the perspectives that inform it, is subtle, and cleverly undermines the assumptions of the reader, "the seductive power of the perspectives we take for granted" (York 2007: 23). Thus, right at the end of the novel, Christie (through Sheppard) draws our attention to the gaps in his previous story, asks us – in fact – to re-read the book from a completely different angle and replace our assumption of narrative reliability with its opposite. Or rather, she asks us to see how, while a narrative may be – in one sense – reliable (for Sheppard tells no lie here), all that it omits in the interest of self-concealment renders it worthless as a record of the fullest truth. Sheppard repeats an earlier section of the narrative describing the last moments he spent with Ackroyd. This time, though, he emphasizes his past fraud:

> I am rather pleased with myself as a writer. What could be neater, for instance, than the following:
>
> "The letters were brought in at twenty minutes to nine. It was just on ten minutes to nine when I left him, the letter still unread. I hesitated with my hand on the door handle, looking back and wondering if there was anything I had left undone."
> All true, you see. But suppose I had put a row of stars after the first sentence! Would somebody then have wondered what exactly happened in that blank ten minutes? (366–367)

In fact, this interlude is when he kills Ackroyd and sets up the dictaphone to provide his alibi. Christie may break the rule of trustworthy narration here but creates a tricksy and interesting novel as a result.

I turn now to Christie's conservative social vision and the countering tendencies and anxieties that (to a certain degree) undermine it. The social order Christie represents here is almost unbelievably old-fashioned. The "tiny village" (36) of King's Abbott is traditional England almost to a T. The action of the novel centers on Fernly Park, where Roger Ackroyd's murder occurs. The cast of characters is a limited one, and confined by and large to stereotype – for Christie's interest is in the puzzle, clues, and the detection process, rather than in character and social context. Ackroyd is "more impossibly like a country squire than any country squire could really be" (17) and "hand in glove with the vicar" at the center of local community life (18). And, even though his status results from his money rather than a long-established social position (he has made his fortune as a manufacturer), it is significant that what he makes – Sheppard thinks it is "wagon wheels" (18) – belongs to a rural order that (by 1926, the date of the novel's publication) was already fast disappearing.

Indeed, there is more than a hint of fustiness about the village society Christie describes. There are the doctor and his inquisitive and gossipy sister Caroline. The latter is, perhaps, an early try-out for Miss Marple, though Poirot's description of her "wonderful psychological insight into human nature" (173) is rather cancelled out by the silliness of her guesses and suggestions at the novel's end (304). And there are Ackroyd, his relatives, and his household – including the spend-thrift and weak-willed son-in-law, Ralph (staying, when the novel starts, in a local hotel or pub), and his house-guest, the plain-speaking though taciturn "big-game man," Major Hector Blunt, who – it is said – "has shot more wild animals in unlikely places than any man living" (51). In addition, there are the local "servants and the tradesmen," the cook, milkman, farm boy, barmaids, and "the Boots at the Three Boars" (216–217), some of whom form the "Intelligence Corps" (10) on which Caroline relies for her insights into village life. Both the Sheppard and Ackroyd households have their servants, too – seven in the latter's case, the women all dressed in "caps and aprons" (211). Ackroyd also has a secretary, Geoffrey Raymond. This cast list is both formulaic and one that speaks of a rapidly vanishing, if not vanished, English social world. Set against Lawrence's *Women in Love* (published in 1921), James Joyce's *Ulysses* (1922), and Dos Passos' *Manhattan Transfer* (1925), both the tone and the content of Christie's novel seem way behind their times.

I write this, though, with the benefit of historical and literary hindsight, and it is, perhaps, unfair to compare a detective novel of this type with canonic literary texts. And one cannot deny the novel's popular appeal, to which this retreat to a near-feudal version of British life may have con-tributed. The whole movement of the novel, too, is to restore a version of this vanishing world. Sheppard's criminal act is personal, and has little to do with any obvious flaw in the social system. His sister knows that he is "weak as water" (259). But it is Poirot, speaking in the abstract (for Sheppard does not yet know he is under suspicion), who pinpoints the reasons for his black-mailing Mrs. Ferrars: the first link in the chain that leads to Ackroyd's murder. Poirot links the "weakness" of the criminal to the greed that results when the "chance of money . . . open[s] at his feet" like a "gold mine" (261–262). Sheppard has earlier compared his sister's indecision as to what she chooses to tell him about a conversation with Ackroyd (before the murder) to "a roulette ball . . . coyly hover[ing] between two numbers" (39). This, together with his failed speculations in "a gold mine in Western Australia" (35), suggests an attraction to risk, gambling, and money (and see the repetition of "gold mine" here) that undermines his own self-representation as a rather stolid "old fogey" (98), the respectable and slightly old-fashioned representative of English village life.

It is Poirot who sees through this mask, and who restores the established order. He allows Sheppard to commit suicide, the effect of which is that the doctor's good reputation will remain (it seems) intact – so, too, no shadow will be cast on the normative patterns and assumptions of the community's life. The Ackroyd fortune goes to its proper heir (Ralph), whose personal weakness will be shored up by his bride-to-be, Ursula, a member of the "Irish gentlefolk," brought low by poverty but unafraid to earn her living by determination and hard work (315–316) as a maid in the Ackroyd house-hold. Flora Ackroyd (Roger's niece), a young girl of some vivacity, wit, and beauty, is freed of her financial worries, freed too to marry Blunt, the man she really loves. Village life will presumably now return to its normal rounds and routines, and England once more to its peaceful and unspoiled rural beauty (134).

But a good number of questions about this life, about its social roles and its limitations, inhabit this text, whatever their lack of explicit development. Though I describe the social system represented as near-feudal, real feudal-ism is in fact dead here, however much its patterns may be replicated. For it is money, not inherited social position, that drives this social world. Even the otherwise-admirable Flora steals from Ackroyd, due to her material desires ("[w]anting things") and the financial pressures under which she conse-quently finds herself (283). Similar pressures also affect her mother, who consequently rifles Ackroyd's desk to see what she can expect in his will, her "testamentary expectations" key to her ability to borrow money (209–210). Ackroyd himself is an honest and, in many ways, admirable man (58), who extends a generally benevolent influence over the village, with his "genial patronage to the lower orders" (37). But he uses his money as a weapon of power over his niece and stepson. Ackroyd's butler, Parker, has a record of blackmail (249–250). His son-in-law Ralph is "self-indulgent and extravagant" (42) and in debt. Money makes the world of this novel go around. Flora's "twenty thousand beautiful pounds" (138), her legacy from Ackroyd, gives her the freedom to choose her own direction in life and marry the partner of *her* choice. But a society built on mere money and the desire for its acquisition is, so the whole text suggests, deeply flawed. Christie here seems to be raising her own doubts about the fundaments (and laissez-faire economics) of post-war English life. But those doubts, and the vision that lies behind them, seem to imply a preference for an earlier social order, nearer to the feudal model – one based on fixed class relations and mutual responsibilities, and where the market was not, at least in theory, the measure of the man.

Certainly, however, the novel does present the social order it represents as flawed, with almost every member of that society playing a part, performing a misleading version of the self. Mrs. Ferrars, until her suicide, is high in the village social hierarchy (she owns one of its two important houses) but is – unsuspected – a murderess and blackmail victim. The doctor speaks as the voice of the village (see 17 and 19, for instance) but harms, not cures, its social body as blackmailer and murderer. Ackroyd's housekeeper, "a redoubtable lady called Miss Russell" (20), keeps the existence of her illegitimate and cocaine-addicted son secret, knowing that her "so very respectable" (300) reputation, and her job, will otherwise be lost. Ursula Bourne is "masquerading as a parlourmaid" (315), when in fact she belongs to a different class, her marriage to Ralph kept secret. Mrs. Ackroyd's wall of obfuscatory language hides both her own abuse of Ackroyd's hospitality and her daughter's theft (as Sheppard remarks, "words, ingeniously used, will serve to mask the ugliness of native facts," 210). Indeed, language itself, the basis of social interaction, is treated with suspicion throughout the book. So Blunt's deliberate, simple, and staccato way of speaking is contrasted with the artificial and deceptive world of "manners" that he now has to navigate, where he can "never remember the things one's expected to say" (137).

Christie then demolishes the basis of the social order she represents even as she gives us no alternative to it, and as she uses Poirot to set it once more to apparent rights at the book's end. But even here there are hidden doubts about its value, about what happens next. The fact that it is the charming but feckless Ralph who will now take on his uncle's role as the nearest thing the village has to a "country squire" is not encouraging for the future (even despite the new supportive presence of Ursula). All this, though, remains unsaid, implicit rather than explicit. And it is Christie's conservative vision that (to my mind) prevails overall, the sense of a falling-off from a simpler and more admirable time, and a utopian desire for its recovery rather than any type of real engagement with the conditions of modernity.

The one area in which Christie does seem to make such an engagement is in terms of gender roles. Ackroyd, the center of village life, is undoubtedly something of an autocrat, and a type of vacuum of authority occurs with his death. In many ways it is Poirot who temporarily fills it as he investigates, moving with certainty and taking center stage in the events that then occur. And Poirot, too, can be autocratic, with his "merciless analysis, and the ruthless power of [his] vision" (263). It is, however, his "feminine" qualities that are most noticeable as Christie implicitly questions a previous tradition of action and adventure and (to repeat from earlier) its "confident, British middle-class hero in the old [pre-war and bull-dog] mould" (Light 1991: 43). Sheppard initially takes Poirot for a "retired hairdresser" (Christie 2002: 31), using his "two immense moustaches" (32) for evidence. He represents Poirot as a somewhat comic figure with his lack of height, his "egg-shaped head, partially covered with suspiciously black hair" (32), and the "puffed-out . . . chest" that makes him look "ridiculously full of his own importance" (123). His "finicking habits" and narcissism (144–145) also help to feminize him, as does the way he focuses on the domestic details of the case as he looks to solve it: a chair pushed out of place, "a scrap of stiff white cambric" (131) that he recognizes, due to its ironed state, as from a maid's apron. Sharing something of the intuition of Sheppard's sister Caroline, Poirot depends, too, on his knowledge of "the psychology of a crime" (124) rather than any active physical pursuit of its perpetrator for his success.

Christie here replaces (and suggests the limitations of) the stereotypical construction of male heroism, emphasizing instead the value of qualities that are traditionally feminine-coded – and usually, accordingly, denigrated rather than admired. She also, though, considers what it means to be a "lady," and lady-like, in this social world. Mrs. Ackroyd's words – spurred by her feelings about Ursula Bourne – "You can't tell who are ladies and who aren't nowadays" (212) are significant here. For, traditionally, to be a lady is – the novel implies – to be dependent on patriarchy for one's living and economic support. The authorial sympathies in this text, however, clearly go to Flora and Ursula, the young women who face the future with the most bravery, confidence, and vim. Despite Flora's crime, she is represented as otherwise honest, loyal, and capable of a freedom of expression unseen elsewhere, and finally gains both financial independence and a male partner who both appreciates and complements her. Similarly, Ursula is seen as perceptive and intelligent, much braver than Ralph, and someone who has taken a no-nonsense and hard-working response to her economic needs.

There is an incipient feminist consciousness at work in this novel, even if it may be thinly developed.

It is hard, despite all I have said, to see why Christie's fiction has been quite so enormously popular, given its thinness of characterization, its relative lack of psychological insight and socio-historical depth, and a style that continually trembles on the edge of cliché: see its descriptions of pleasant young fellows (45), of sharp beady eyes (24), and of fat, smug, oily faces (64), its pointing of dramatic forefingers (341), and the like. Perhaps Christie's popularity is due to the undoubted success with which she handles the main "jig-saw puzzle" (204) of clues and their solution that make up her detective stories, and her skill in adapting the form to achieve a series of innovative (and sometimes quite startling) effects. And it may be that the nostalgic and conservative quality of her fiction – the conjuring up in this novel, for instance, of apparently simpler and more stable times in a typically English rural setting – provides readerly reassurance and satisfaction, even despite the social anxieties and challenges her novels also implicitly pose. Whatever the reasons, though, Christie's fiction is a force to be very seriously reckoned with in any consideration of the genre.

Dashiell Hammett: The Maltese Falcon (1930)

I have already commented extensively on *Red Harvest* in Part 2. Here I discuss aspects of *The Maltese Falcon*, the book William Marling calls "probably America's greatest detective novel" (Marling n.d.: n.p.). I approach this novel first in terms of its difference from the British Golden Age crime novel by Agatha Christie discussed above. In Hammett's novel, as in Christie's, the reasons for the various crimes in the novel are personal: here, the desire to get hold of the black enameled statue of a bird that conceals a "glorious golden falcon encrusted . . . with the finest jewels" (Hammett 1953: 519). This falcon was made in the sixteenth century – in Hammett's elaborate backstory – by the Order of the Hospital of St. John of Jerusalem as tribute for Emperor Charles V, Holy Roman Emperor and King of Spain, and has now, in the present day, gone missing after its earlier theft. The scope of the crime in this novel, though, is far greater than in Christie's *Roger Ackroyd*, directly involving in one way or another almost every character in the novel, of international rather than local dimension, and involving (primarily) not just one weak-willed man's desire for the easy money to be made from blackmail (and the murder that then follows) but a whole gang of criminals led by Casper Gutman (who has dedicated his life to hunting down the bird), ready to murder in their quest for the desired object.

In Hammett's novel, any notion of normative everyday life and social connection (we recall the fabric and routines of village life that provide the backdrop to *Roger Ackroyd*) is blown apart. The action takes place, typically for a hard-boiled text, in a city (San Francisco). And this environment, at least as Hammett depicts it, lacks any sense of shared group identity, except

The Crime Fiction Handbook, First Edition. Peter Messent.
© 2013 John Wiley & Sons, Ltd. Published 2013 by John Wiley & Sons, Ltd.

in the ongoing quest of Gutman and his entourage to find the jeweled bird; is a place of affectless modernity, intrusive violence, and sudden death. This violence is depicted in more detail, and is more prevalent, than in Christie's more genteel world, with Jacobi – for instance – staggering into Spade's office with "liquid bubbling . . . in his throat" and "a little blood . . . spurt[ing] out" of his open mouth before he dies of gunshot wounds (545–546).

The novel starts in the office of Sam Spade, Hammett's private detective protagonist, and then moves through the city's streets and alleys, cigar stores and restaurants, hotel rooms and lobbies, rental apartment houses and office buildings. The one (apparently) domestic space that features is Spade's small apartment. This functions, though, less as a domestic space than as one where the action of the novel – Spade's various dealings with his client Brigid O'Shaughnessy, with Gutman and his associates, and with the police – can continue. Spade does use his bedroom (where he sleeps with his client!), but the intimacy usually associated with that space is reduced by its doubling as a living room, the bed normally folded up into the wall (470). Human relationships here are conducted warily, alliances between the characters shift, and the concept of trust is by-and-large untenable. This is a world with little sense of the domesticity and sustainable community on which Christie's novel is based.

Christie recognizes the financial circumstances that affect the actions of almost all of her characters, but she also focuses on romance (and thus, implicitly, ongoing family life) and in part constructs her novel around it. In Hammett the greed for wealth taints almost all of the relationship represented. He shows how both sexuality (an absent term in Christie) and traditional family values have been displaced by material desire in the capitalist world he depicts. The displacement of family values is most obvious when Gutman (smiling "benignly," 576) agrees to allow the "gunsel" (509) Wilmer to be given up to the police as he negotiates with Spade over the falcon: "Well, Wilmer, I'm sorry indeed to lose you . . . *I couldn't be any fonder of you if you were my own son*; but – well, by Gad! – if you lose a son it's possible to get another – and there's only one Maltese falcon" (576; my emphasis). (The word "gunsel" has two meanings: a gun-carrying gangster and "'a catamite'; specifically 'a young male kept as a sexual companion,'" Harper n.d.: n.p.) The displacement of sexuality, meanwhile, is illustrated in the most acute moment of passion in the novel (at least as it is represented though language) when Gutman, and those around him, finally get their hands on the falcon:

The girl's lower lip was between her teeth. She and Cairo, like Gutman, and like Spade and the boy, were breathing heavily. . . . Gutman turned the bird upside-down and scraped an edge of its base with his knife. . . . [His] breath hissed between his teeth. His face became turgid with hot blood. (583)

The representation of material desire and the passion it provokes (in the shape of an object – the falcon – rather than a person) lies right at the center of the novel, replacing the far more circumspect and oblique treatment of such drives in Christie's book.

Brigid O'Shaughnessy (aka Miss Wonderley), too, is a much tougher cookie than any female protagonist in *Roger Ackroyd* and sets the template for the femme fatale – the beautiful but deadly female lure at the center of so much hard-boiled crime fiction. Described by way of her physical features ("brightly red . . . full lips," blue eyes and dark red hair, long legs and high breasts, 425), the initial impression she gives of trembling vulnerability is a total fraud – but one that completely suckers in Spade's partner, Miles Archer. Spade quickly realizes that Brigid is not to be trusted, recognizing the gap between the language she uses and the reality beneath. So she emotes: "Help me, Mr. Spade. Help me because I need help so badly. . . . I've no right to ask you to help me blindly, but I do ask you. Be generous, Mr. Spade. You can help me. Help me." He, though, recognizing the quality of what is finally just a performance, replies: "You won't need much of anybody's help. You're good. You're very good. It's chiefly your eyes, I think, and that throb you get into your voice when you say things like 'Be generous, Mr. Spade.'" (450). Brigid uses her sexuality to achieve her ends (to retrieve and retain the falcon for herself). She double-crosses her supposed partners over the falcon without a second thought – murdering Spade's partner, "in cold blood, just like swatting a fly" (592). Spade finally refuses to "play the sap" for her, telling her he does "maybe" love her (592), but that "if you get a good break you'll be out of San Quentin in twenty years and you can come back to me then" (590). He puts temptation behind him, ensuring that Brigid's threat (as is common in the case of the femme fatale) is finally neutered and dismissed.

There is more to say about Brigid and Spade's relationship. But I approach this via an analysis of Spade and the vast difference between Christie's and Hammett's detective heroes (if we can use that last term to describe Spade). If Poirot is small, fussy, even slightly comical, and a man of intellect (he recurrently refers to the importance of using the "little grey cells," Christie 2002: 350), Spade is a physically impressive six-footer (425) and a man of action. Caught up in a complicated plot, employed by an untrustworthy client, and dealing with a group of dangerous criminals, he is immersed in danger and violence in a Darwinian San Francisco urban world where "[m]ost things . . . can be bought, or taken" (465). The narration is third- and not first-person, so the reader never knows quite what Spade is thinking or what his intentions are; whether – as is constantly suggested – he may indeed be operating solely on his own behalf, looking to get whatever he can gain financially (and sexually) from the situation in which he finds himself,

Dashiell Hammett: The Maltese Falcon (1930)

whatever the ethics of the case or the interests of his client. So, when Gutman asks Spade whether he is representing Brigid O'Shaughnessy or Joel Cairo (another player in this deadly game), Spade says, "It depends." And, when Gutman presses him on who else besides these two he might be acting for, Spade points "his cigar at his own chest" and says, "There's me" (506). Further, when he and Gutman are negotiating as to how they might "give the police a fall-guy" (562) for the three murders that have occurred, Spade professes himself happy to put his client Brigid into the mix: "As for Miss Shaughnessy . . . if you think she can be rigged for the part I'm perfectly willing to discuss it with you" (567).

But Spade's motives and thought processes remain unknown. The police – mostly presented as incompetent and off-track in their investigative efforts – think he is criminally mixed up in the whole business. And the law, it is implied, is ready to take short cuts as long as the crime can officially be solved (565). It is Spade who juggles the various aspects of the case. He does not solve it, though, by standing back and analyzing the various bits of evidence he finds, and then putting the jigsaw puzzle that composes its various parts back together again. Rather – like the Op in *Red Harvest* – he mixes things up, plunges into the action, knowing that as a reaction occurs, so his knowledge will advance: "My way of learning is to heave a wild and unpredictable monkey-wrench into the machinery" (490). (Remember here the words of Race Williams, the detective protagonist created by Caroll John Daly, another *Black Mask* writer: "You can't make a hamburger without grinding up a little meat," The Thrilling Detective Web Site n.d.: n.p.). In acting in such a way, he puts his own physical safety on the line; he is threatened, held at gun point, drugged, and beaten at various points in the narrative. Like Poirot, he does use his "grey cells" to work out who has committed the various murders and for what reasons, but it is action not analysis with which he is primarily identified.

If Christie uses Poirot as the reflective center of her text, he is pretty well detached from the social world he investigates, and with little attention paid to his fuller professional or emotional life. Here, though, it is Spade, alongside Brigid, Gutman, Cairo, and Wilmer, who is held up for the reader's close inspection. Hammett called Spade "a hard and shifty fellow, able to take care of himself in any situation, able to get the best of anybody he comes in contact with" (*Augusta Chronicle* 2005: n.p.). This suggests both Spade's ready adaptability to the situation in hand and his lack of trust in any sustaining external social structure or support (as suggested, too, in his "Flitcraft" story).

To all appearances – and appearances are almost all we get – Spade is pretty much self-contained, negotiating the world that surrounds him both to gratify his own physical needs and to succeed in his professional role as private detective. He is sleeping with the wife of his partner, Archer, and takes an unemotional and matter-of-fact view of Archer's murder: "He knew what he was doing. They're the chances we take" (449). Indeed, he considers himself better off without his partner (455). It could be argued that this is just part of the hard-boiled and cynical stance that typifies the protagonist of this type of fictional world, but there are very few signs here (as there often are in Chandler) of any softer center. Spade sleeps with Brigid, his client, partly, we assume from what he says at the end of the novel, from real sexual attraction, but also so he can steal the key to her apartment and search it while she still lies sleeping in his bed. (This is one of the few points in the text where there is an indication of emotion stirring beneath Spade's surface, though the meaning of that sign remains opaque. His eyes, we are told, "burned yellowly" as he holds Brigid close to him here, 493.) Spade strips away all masks and pretences to get to the raw truth but in doing so he demolishes any chance of sustaining human relationships. When Gutman claims that Brigid has stolen a thousand-dollar bill (part of a proposed deal with Spade), Spade literally strips her bare, asks her to remove her clothes so he can be sure of her innocence (in fact Gutman himself has palmed the missing note). Brigid recognizes the emotional damage that is done here ("Can't you see that if you make me you'll – you'll be killing something?" 578) but that has no influence on Spade's actions.

Spade is a shape-shifter, adjusting his identity to the situation at hand as he looks to get to the truth of the situation and unmask the killers. But there are real questions asked here about what lies behind the masquerade self he projects. He shows his basic integrity at the novel's end when he returns the money he has been given by Gutman and gives Brigid up to the police. But in doing so he puts any emotion he feels for the latter to one side, retreating into his hard self-sufficiency ("I won't play the sap for you"). He explains himself to Brigid: "Listen. When a man's partner is killed he's supposed to do something about it." He gives, too, a whole series of other reasons for giving her up to the police, again making it clear that his professional role is at stake here: "I'm a detective and expecting me to run criminals down and then let them go free is like asking a dog to catch a rabbit and let it go. It can be done . . . but it's not the natural thing." He then puts the counter-argument – "Now on the other side . . . [a]ll we've got is the fact that maybe you love me and maybe I love you" – but only to finally (and with some emotion) insist that "I won't [let you go free] because all of me wants to – . . . and because – God damn you – you've counted on that with me the same as you counted on that with the others" (593–594). John Whitley is astute in pointing out some of the implications of this powerful sequence in terms of the representation of Spade in the larger book:

[T]here is surely a terrible irony in vesting your identity in a job which cannot allow you to reveal a true identity but only a series of bogus identities; which cannot allow you any authentic relations with people or nature or ideas. . . . [The strength of] Hammett's detectives . . . resides . . . in the ability to change like a chameleon to meet the needs of a fluctuating world. . . . They operate not from the base of a recognizable interior self but from a deliberately created void. They cannot be seriously damaged because there is nothing there to damage. (1980: 454)

I would only differ in suggesting that there are *some* signs of interiority on Spade's part, while acknowledging that they are always veiled, never revealed to the reader in anything but very partial, and often enigmatic, form.

I end this chapter by discussing the politics of Hammett's novel. Hammett represents the city of San Francisco (or, at least, the part of its world he depicts) as the locus of violence, murder, and criminality, with a largely ineffectual police force and a district attorney whose rhetoric may be impressive but who is completely off the ball in his understanding of the case. And it would be easy to read the novel as accepting, rather than challenging, that current – if flawed – social order. Such a reading would emphasize that we are given only a partial view of the city, and that the disruption of its normality (a normality that is assumed rather than illustrated) is caused by the Falcon, an exotic and foreign object that – when it is found to be a worthless lead copy – is no longer of any relevance by the narrative's end. Spade, then, despite his poor relations with the police, solves the case and hands Brigid over to the law, while Gutman is dead, killed by Wilmer, also now presumably in police hands. The fissure in the social body is accordingly restored.

Another reading of the novel though – for, like so many crime fictions, it can be interpreted in more than one way – would be in the light of Hammett's known left-wing sympathies (he would join the Communist Party in 1937). I pick up here on a number of revealing phrases in the novel. So, a "businesslike" Cairo speaks of entering "profitable business relations" (461) with Spade; Gutman responds to Spade's directness with his "I like that way of doing business," before confirming that the latter is there "as Miss O'Shaughnessy's representative" (506); Spade tells Gutman – as they discuss the Falcon and the money to be made from it – that "if you won't take the risk just tell me what [the Falcon] is and I'll figure out the profits" (507). That it is the language of business being used here encourages a reading of the novel as a critique of capitalism. The story of Gutman's gang of double-crossing thieves, all pursuing their individual materialist desires (the enormous wealth that the falcon represents) even as they murder to do so, accordingly becomes a parable of all that is wrong with American society, with its economy driven by greed and ruthless competition, its family and sexual relationships perverted by the love of money, and its opportunities for individual gain defeating any lasting sense of group trust and cooperation. The novel then uses criminal behavior as a reverse mirror of the dominant capitalist system and can be read as a bleak comment on American values at the very moment of their collapse (with the stock market crash occurring in 1929, the year before the book's publication).

However one reads it, though, this is a powerful and effective novel. It set the pattern for a good deal of the hard-boiled crime writing that would follow in its representation of its central characters. This is especially true in the depiction of the private eye, Spade, himself – with his independent persona, sexual magnetism, and abrasively tough-talking style ("I'll bury my dead," 438; "People lose teeth talking like that," 496). Hammett introduced, too, the type of vernacular into his novel – "Stay dummied up on him" (499); "You bastard, get up on your feet and go for your heater!" (566) – that may have appeared before in *Black Mask* stories (and in Hammett's own previous novel) but that helped to revolutionize the popular novel form. It is perhaps, though, the 1941 film version of the novel (a previous version had appeared in 1931), with Humphrey Bogart and Sydney Greenstreet, that was responsible finally for stamping *The Maltese Falcon* so indelibly on the public memory. Strangely, Hammett's novel was not the last San Francisco would see of "The Maltese Falcon." For, in 2008, the city would play host to the boat of that same name, a sailing yacht of extraordinary size and value, originally owned by the American Tom Perkins (who made his money in venture capitalism) and the epitome of conspicuous consumerism. Hammett, one suspects, would have appreciated the ironies involved.

Raymond Chandler: *The Big Sleep* (1939)

Raymond Chandler is probably the best known of all American crime writers. Sales of his novels started relatively slowly, but even by 1949 (according to a *Newsweek* report) more than three million copies of his books had been sold (Valerio n.d.: n.p.). He is now acknowledged – alongside Hammett – as the most important figure in the field of hard-boiled crime writing. The literary reputations of both men have been officially recognized and given the critical seal of approval by the appearance of their work in the *Library of America* series – dedicated to "preserv[ing] the nation's cultural heritage by publishing America's best and most significant writing in authoritative editions" (The Library of America n.d.: n.p.). This is a significant marker of what is, in general, a very recent acceptance of the way in which work in a popular form can move beyond its supposedly lowbrow limits. So, back in 1948, W. H. Auden would recognize Chandler's importance even as he, then, would be dismissive of the genre in which he worked, saying: "I think Mr. Chandler is interested in writing, not detective stories, but serious studies of a criminal milieu, the Great Wrong Place [Los Angeles], and his powerful but extremely depressing books should be read and judged, not as escape literature, but as works of art" (n.p.).

Like Hammett, Chandler's writing comes out of the social conditions of his time. So Dennis Porter writes that

> [u]rban blight, corrupt political machines, and de facto disenfranchisement of significant sections of the population through graft and influence-peddling were part of the background in which crime of a new and organized kind was to become endemic. . . . The time was ripe for the emergence in a popular literary

The Crime Fiction Handbook, First Edition. Peter Messent.
© 2013 John Wiley & Sons, Ltd. Published 2013 by John Wiley & Sons, Ltd.

genre of a disabused, anti-authoritarian, muckraking hero, who, instead of fleeing to Europe, like the sophisticates of lost generation fiction, stayed at home to confront crime and corruption on the increasingly unlovely streets of modern urban America. (2003: 96)

Porter's description may be a touch romanticized, and only partly fits the paradigms created in Hammett's and Chandler's fiction, but it does indicate something of the disaffection with the political, economic, and institutional system of America in the Depression period.

The Big Sleep is typical Chandler in terms of the labyrinthine twists and turns of its plot. It starts off as a single criminal investigation by Marlowe on behalf of General Sternwood (an oil millionaire) into the supposed "gambling debts" (Chandler 1979: 12) of his daughter Carmen, and the blackmail he faces as a result. But it quickly detours into the murder of the blackmailer, Arthur Geiger. By the time this murder is solved (half way through the book – Sternwood's chauffeur, Owen Taylor, has murdered Geiger, jealously protecting Carmen's interests), a series other related crimes and issues have impinged on, and highjacked, Marlowe's investigations. From this point on, the plot seems to take a different turn, vaguely organized around Marlowe's interest in Rusty Regan, Sternwood's missing son-in-law, who – it finally turns out – has been murdered by Carmen because he has resisted her sexual advances. Vivian (Sternwood's other daughter) has involved local gangster and gambling-club owner Eddie Mars in a cover-up of her sister's murderous act and has thus laid herself (and her father) open to the blackmail that begins the book (for it turns out that Mars is in fact the figure behind Geiger's threats). This is a condensed and simplified version of a novel that twists and turns in all sorts of ways and that even the most alert reader may struggle to follow. Indeed, when Howard Hawks was making the 1946 film version of the novel, he and Humphrey Bogart (who played Marlowe) were confused as to how exactly the chauffeur, Owen Taylor, dies. They sent Chandler a telegram asking "Who killed the chauffeur?" only to receive the author's reply "Damned if I know!"

This plot complexity is typical of hard-boiled crime fiction, in part the sign of a represented world where crime is not a one-off occurrence but an ongoing and pervasive fact of everyday life. At first glance here, the main crime would appear to be just personal – the actions of a disturbed and sexually predatory young woman. But the fact that this is just one murder in a novel where at least four other murders occur points to a wider sense of social dislocation. Chandler is famous for his atmospherics: his depiction here of the rain-soaked streets of Los Angeles; its insubstantial architecture ("about the only part of a California house you can't put your foot through is the front door," 30); its historic graces now converted to dubious commercial ends (see Eddie Mars' club, 112); and its seedy urban squalor (the Fulwider building, 140–141). The details given provide a backdrop to a city riddled with corruption, where any commitment to the greater social good has been cancelled out by casual greed, the power of money, and criminal influence. So Geiger's dirty-book business runs with the tacit knowledge of the police (94), while Eddie Mars (with his "side lines, like blackmail, bent cars, [and] hideouts for hot boys from the east," 136) has "the local law in [his] pocket" (61). The law here is available only to those with the financial means to access it (107), and the rapid growth of the city has brought "[s]ome very tough people" (61) in its train. Honest cop Captain Gregory's words to Marlowe toward the close of the novel speak of an entire society going down the drain. Describing himself as a "[r]easonably honest . . . copper" who "would like to see the law win" and "the flashy well-dressed mugs like Eddie Mars spoiling their manicures in the rock quarry at Folsom," Gregory recognizes that this is just not going to happen, either in Los Angeles or in towns half its size "in any part of this wide, green and beautiful USA. We just don't run our country that way" (167).

It is when we return to Carmen, however, that we see how, for Chandler, the personal becomes the political. Sean McCann notes the way that blackmail is of key importance in the novel and functions as a form of "predation," the bleeding dry of others (2000: 167–168). This reminds us of General Sternwood at the novel's start, an old man who is close to death seated in the "thick, wet, steamy" air of his greenhouse with "bloodless lips and . . . sunken temples" (Chandler 1979: 8–9). Marlowe feels a certain empathy for Sternwood even as he recognizes that the blood has been drained from his veins (9), partly through age and illness but also (meta-phorically) through the blackmail with which he is threatened, and which he has faced before. But Sternwood himself can be seen as a type of predator too, with the money he has made through the oil business dependent on the labor of others and on a capitalist system that "leech[es] . . . vitality" (McCann 2000: 166) from the body of the nation's workers in the interests of the wealthy few. The fact that Carmen, the degenerate offspring of the General and characterized by her "sharp predatory teeth" (Chandler 1979: 6), murders Rusty Regan, a likeable and hard-living man of action who acts as "the breath of life" (11) to her father, continues the metaphor of predation, even vampirism, that runs through the whole text. So Regan's tough masculinity is sacrificed at the expense of Carmen's continuing corrupt and exploitative life. The novel starts by drawing a link between the luxurious Sternwood mansion up in the Los Angeles foothills and, in distant view below, "the old wooden derricks of the oilfield from which the Stern-woods had made their money" (19). The base and superstructure model suggested here returns at the end of the novel where Rusty Regan's body is revealed to lie in that same oil field, "[a] horrible decayed thing" (187) in "the stagnant, oil-scummed water of an old sump" (178). If Chandler makes his point metaphorically rather than explicitly here, there can be little doubt of his attitudes to wealth and its predatory effects, and to the failings of the political and economic system that supported it.

Marlowe himself stands at the opposite end of the social and economic spectrum to the Sternwoods. His spartan living arrangements and commitment to doing a decent and honest job for a modest financial return (see 48) act as a sign of his democratic and anti-capitalistic credentials. At the end of the novel, though, he becomes complicit with the Sternwoods in allowing Carmen to escape the due punishment of the law, thus effectively accepting the excesses of that economic system the family represents. I discuss this at a later point. First, however, I look at some of the ways in which Marlowe differs from Hammett's detective protagonists to suggest just what it is that makes Chandler's work so distinctive.

Chandler wrote of Hammett that, in terms of his writing style, "[h]e was spare, frugal, hard-boiled. . . . In his hands [the American language] had no overtones, left no echo, evoked no image beyond a distant hill" (Chandler 1962: 12–13). But Marlowe, too, is hard-boiled in his interactions with others, and especially with the Sternwood daughters. So, when he first kisses Vivian (the novel's femme fatale) in a highly passionate embrace, he breaks the erotic intensity of the moment with his hard-edged question, "What has Eddie Mars got on you?" (Chandler 1979: 124). And, when she reacts to his coldness, he continues, "I told you I was a detective. Get it through your lovely head. I work at it, lady" (125). Earlier, when he breaks into Geiger's house to find Geiger murdered and Carmen almost unconscious, naked and drugged, he reports that neither person "paid any attention to the way I came in, although only one of them was dead" (30). Marlowe here comes pretty close to Spade or the Continental Op in his impassive and laconic response to the events in which he finds himself embroiled.

There is, however, a very different side to Marlowe's style, captured by David Smith in a nice phrase: "Marlowe's phraseology is to hard-boiled what baroque is to Jackson Pollock" (1980: 438). Smith has in mind here the figurative embroidery and emotional charge that we find in Marlowe's first-person narration at those points when he departs from that spare frugality noted above. The novel, in fact, opens with a metaphor that suggests Marlowe's underlying deeply romantic sensibility – the "knight in dark armour rescuing a lady who was tied to a tree and didn't have any clothes on but some very long and convenient hair" (Chandler 1979: 5). This describes the stained-glass panel over the Sternwood entrance doors but is clearly self-referential too (see 5, 129, and 171). But the women who need rescuing in the course of the novel, Vivian and Carmen, turn out to be far from lady- or damsel-like, and are rather "perverts and killers" (186); further, in Carmen's case, nakedness is no sign of vulnerability. When she ambushes Marlowe in his bed, her "soft giggling" makes him think of "rats behind a wainscoting in an old house" (127). This, "her face liked scraped bone," and the "hissing noise" (130) that tears from her mouth, imply a verminous/reptilian presence of absolute danger and corruption rather than any type of virgin innocence.

Marlowe's romantic sensibility does, however, find a female subject worth its attention in Silver Wig, a minor character in the novel and (fatally as far as Marlowe's continuing interest goes) married to Eddie Mars. His language changes register completely in her presence, as he describes her delicate breath, blue eyes like "mountain lakes," and "smooth silvery voice" with a "tiny tinkle in it, like bells in a doll's house" (though even Marlowe can't quite let this pass, adding that he judged it "silly as soon as I thought of it") (156–158). The romantic and sentimental yearning we find here is very much more pronounced and explicit than in the developing relationship between the Continental Op and Dinah Brand in *Red Harvest*: a relationship, however, much more sexually charged than that between Marlowe and Silver Wig. The latter couple do, though, manage one (hard and icy) goodbye kiss (162).

But it is in his use of descriptive and (especially) figurative language that Marlowe most fully departs from Hammett's representation of Spade and the Op. Marlowe describes his Los Angeles world, and the events that occur there, in some detail. He is quick to move, though, from plain facts to elaborate and unusual simile. So he describes the General's greenhouse with its wet and steamy air as "larded with the cloying smell of tropical orchids in bloom," then, elaborating further, comments on the forest of plants inside and their "nasty meaty leaves and stalks like the newly washed fingers of dead men" (8). The vocabulary used here and especially his simile are effective in suggesting an atmosphere of claustrophobic over-ripeness, of corruption, decay, and impending mortality surrounding the General; but it is his unusual use of language ("larded," "meaty") and the jarring and unexpected nature of his simile that strike the reader most forcibly. Marlowe's figurative imagination is vividly inventive, almost surreal. So the General speaks slowly to Marlowe, "using his strength as carefully as an out-of-work showgirl uses her last good pair of stockings" (9). So, too, Marlowe describes Geiger's densely textured Chinese rug as one "in which a gopher could have spent a week without showing his nose above the nap" (30).

Marlowe's descriptive style, use of simile and metaphor, and epigrammatic wit ("such a lot of guns about town and so few brains," 66) provide him with a type of verbal weaponry and a sense of authority and control that stand in stark contrast to the facts and forces that in reality constrain and condition his life: the naturalistic urban environment in which powerful interests and pervasive corruption reveal his actions, and the morality that underlies them, to be almost entirely futile. Marlowe's romanticism, his view of himself as a knight meting out justice and operating by a strict code of value and behavior, is part of this same pattern: a desperate attempt to retain some notion of moral worth, integrity, and chivalric standard in a world that refuses them: "where no man can walk down a dark street in safety because law and order are things we talk about but refrain from practising" (Chandler 1962: 14). Marlowe is a man torn apart, attempting to retain his moral authority in an environment where the very concept is meaningless, and trying to control a world through narrative and language despite the knowledge that both his words and his ways of seeing are powerless in the face of a resistant and corrupt social reality that can only bring him moral and personal defeat.

Indeed, this is exactly what happens at the end of *The Big Sleep*. Marlowe ends up protecting his client, General Sternwood, despite his wealth and the social injustice and irresponsibility to which it is linked, and despite the knowledge that in doing so he merely covers up serious crime and restores the status quo more or less as it previously stood. The graft, influence-peddling, and crooked dealings of this world, and the power of wealth to influence the way it works, are scarcely affected by his actions. He does ensure that Carmen's psychotic violence is at least contained ("Will you take her away? Somewhere . . . where they can handle her type . . . ?" 187). But he recognizes that he is thoroughly compromised by his actions even as they protect the personal interests of his client: "I was part of the nastiness now. . . . But the old man didn't have to be. He could lie quiet in his canopied bed . . . And in a little while he too, like Rusty Regan, would be sleeping the big sleep" (189).

It is noteworthy that we move back at this final point from the political to the personal. Those aspects of the novel that draw attention to class and economics, and link Sternwood and his daughters to capitalist irresponsibility and excess, now completely drop away and we are left only with Marlowe's protectiveness of a sympathetic and vulnerable client. This connects with the gender politics of the book, and particularly with Marlowe's homosociality, the sentimental and intense male bonding to which he is so much drawn. This is turn relates to the clearly misogynistic element in his personality. I briefly digress here to suggest a certain anxiety about masculinity and gender performance that both Hammett's *The Maltese Falcon* and this novel share.

To all appearances, Sam Spade in *The Maltese Falcon* is absolutely secure in his masculinity. He is clearly sexually magnetic, able apparently to pick his women at will (Brigid and Iva), and described as looking "rather pleasantly like a blond satan" (Hammett 1953: 425) – an odd combination of words that indicate both allure and danger. But there is something suspect about the depth and sincerity of his heterosexual relationships. He sleeps with Brigid, at least partly, to help him out in his detective work, while he seems not to give two hoots for Iva – seems, as far as we can tell, to merely be taking what is sexually available (even his partner's wife) with no obvious emotional commitment on which to found it.

There is a very odd description of Spade's body in the novel as "like a shaved bear's," with hair-free chest and "childishly soft and pink" skin (432). This seems at odds with the impression of hard, even ruthless, masculinity suggested elsewhere. Spade, too, is homophobic, referring casually to the homosexual Cairo as "[t]he fairy" (496). And he takes a violent dislike to the young "punk" (565) Wilmer: "I don't like him. He makes me nervous. I'll kill him the first time he gets in my way" (510). Such an over-reaction implies some kind of insecurity, and even ambivalence, on Spade's part concerning his own masculinity and sexuality – which is only confirmed by the wonderfully Freudian passage where Spade takes Wilmer's guns from him (517). All this of course can only be speculative, but Spade's homophobia, together with the casual and manipulative nature of his heterosexual liaisons, certainly implies a certain unease about gender performance and sexuality that carries throughout the text. That Spade seems at real ease in women's company only with his secretary Effie, the "lanky . . . girl" with a "boyish face" (425), would seem to endorse this.

Marlowe too is homophobic, though this element of the book is less pronounced than in Hammett's. Geiger, he discovers, is in a homosexual relationship with Joe Brody. And when he enters Geiger's house (for the third time) he briefly describes its various objects and furnishings in terms of their "stealthy nastiness, like a fag party" (Chandler 1979: 54). Later, when Brody hits out at him, he discounts the punch, since "a pansy has no iron in his bones" (83). Marlowe, though, is clearly misogynistic. Living alone, his (small amount of) personal space provides him with a retreat from the sordid and violent world through which he moves professionally: "[T]his was the room I had to live in. It was all I had in the way of a home. In it was everything . . . that took the place of a family. Not much; a few books, pictures, radio, chessmen, old letters, stuff like that. Nothing" (130). When he enters his apartment to find Carmen there, naked in his bed, he quickly says, "I couldn't stand her in that room any longer" (130), and firmly insists that she leave. Once she is gone, looking at "[t]he imprint of . . . her small corrupt body" that remains on his sheets, he tears "the bed to pieces savagely" (131). Though one might argue that it is Carmen's particular presence that causes such a dramatic over-reaction (and see, too, 180–181), there are clear signs of a wider disgust with, or fear of, female sexuality here. For, immediately after the episode he makes the generalized comment, "[w]omen made me sick" (131). And he has earlier described Vivian's teeth as weapons, "glitter[ing] like knives" (115). As in Hammett, a protagonist (Marlowe) who seems the very epitome of maleness shows himself in fact to be something rather different: anxiously protective of his bodily integrity and self-sufficiency and in retreat from full heterosexual involvement. (So Silver Wig, for instance, stands as an impossible dream of pastoral and virginal purity that can only briefly flicker in the tainted urban world through which Marlowe moves.)

This attitude to female sexuality goes together with a pronounced tendency toward sentimental homosocial bonding (I do *not* imply homosexuality here). So Rusty Regan, a man's man with an Irish military background, particularly appeals to Marlowe, as is suggested by Marlowe's description of a photo of Regan's face as "not [that] of a man who could be pushed around much by anybody . . . [T]he face of a man who would move fast and play for keeps" (103). Later, when Harry Jones describes Regan as a man with "long-range eyes" who did not give "a damn about dough" (136), Marlowe again indicates his empathy and approval. Indeed, there is a barely controlled sentimentalism here that spills over to Jones himself (see 138 and 146).

It is exactly such forms of male-to-male bonding and appreciation that mark the relationship with Sternwood, too. In their first interview, Marlowe drinks Sternwood's brandy and smokes, serving as his stand-in in enjoying the pleasures the older man can no longer enjoy, and conducting a conversation based on mutual honesty and respect. And his decision finally not to give Sternwood's daughters up to the police seems primarily the result of his empathetic connection with the father, "to protect what little pride a broken and sick old man has left in his blood" (186). The General's own admission that he has as little "moral sense" as his daughters (13) and his representative position as an exhausted and bloodless representative of a corrupt capitalist order, retaining what life he has through the force and vitality of those (like both Regan and Marlowe) from a lower social order who act as his employees and/or companions, seems quite forgotten here. Chandler's novel is both powerful and effective, as its massive popularity suggests. Its ending, however, rather cuts against the book's social and economic critique as Marlowe's sense of male intimacy nudges him into the massive compromise that he makes with his surrounding world, dulling the moral integrity that up to that point has seemed to be one of his only buoys.

James M. Cain:
Double Indemnity (1936)

I step out of chronological sequence here in the interests of thematic coherence. Hammett and Chandler make a natural pairing, while there is clear logic in connecting Cain and Highsmith (in my next chapter). *Double Indemnity* is a classic fiction of transgression. It tells the story of Walter Huff, an insurance salesman, who murders a Mr. Nirdlinger, one of his clients. He does this so that he and Phyllis, Nirdlinger's wife, can collect on a double indemnity insurance policy (one that includes a double pay-off in the case of accidental death) that the two have arranged, without Nirdlinger's knowledge, on Phyllis' behalf. This story is very loosely based on the 1925 Ruth Snyder murder case, when Snyder and her lover Judd Gray killed Snyder's husband Albert to collect on a fraudulently arranged double indemnity policy. Though Snyder and Judd did manage to murder Albert, unlike Walter and Phyllis they botched pretty much everything else in the commission of their crime. Their case, though, attracted massive press publicity and Snyder would be executed in the electric chair in January 1928 (famously, she was photographed by a journalist at the moment of death).

The novel, as is usually the case in Cain's work, is driven by its plot, by its rapid moves from impulse to action, and by the twists and turns that come to determine the protagonists' fates (I give such plot details as are necessary as I proceed). Like Cain's earlier book *The Postman Always Rings Twice*, this is a first-person narrative told retrospectively by Huff himself. Thomas Leitch, writing on the highly successful Billy Wilder 1944 film version of the novel (starring Fred MacMurray, Edward G. Robinson, and Barbara Stanwyck, and with Chandler helping out on the script), describes the voiceover that performs

The Crime Fiction Handbook, First Edition. Peter Messent.
© 2013 John Wiley & Sons, Ltd. Published 2013 by John Wiley & Sons, Ltd.

this same narrative function. "[T]he Walter who appears on screen," he says, is "a prisoner of his own discourse. Although he undertakes each of his actions as if it were freely chosen, he is trapped in the narrative shaped by his voice, which selects and dramatizes incidents precisely to the extent that they substantiate his confession to murder gone wrong" (2004: 133). Leitch captures well here the double effect that characterizes both book and film, with the impression of agency – Walter's careful plans to commit "[t]he perfect murder" (Cain 2005: 23) – undermined by the heavy sense of determinism that underlies the novel and leads inevitably to Walter's confession and suicide at its conclusion. (Several of the critics I use here write on the film text, rather than the book. I apply their insights only as appropriate.)

This retrospection, the establishing of a sense of direct communication with the reader, and the fact that the story will end in some kind of public discovery and exposure are all signaled as early as the third sentence of the novel: "That was how I came to this House of Death, that you've been reading about in the papers" (1). Part of the cleverness of the novel, though, is how, after a few early reminders that events are happening in retrospect (see, for instance, pages 3 and 39), the reader's attention is focused by-and-large on the immediate sequence of event and action, on Nirdlinger's murder and what then follows, and on Huff's immediate psychological and emotional reactions. It is only after he has confessed to the murder – *not* because his guilty part in it is about to be discovered but to protect Phyllis' daughter Lola, with whom he is now in love and who is under suspicion for the crime – that the retrospective act of narrative construction is once more foregrounded. For, when Keyes, Huff's boss at the Insurance Agency (and the person to whom he makes his confession) demands a written statement of what has occurred, Huff informs the reader: "What you've just read, if you've read it, is the statement" (133). This is not quite the end of the novel, however. Huff continues with his story to take us to his and Phyllis' double suicide. By this point, though, his fate is sealed. He sees no alternative to death, has little control – except through this one final action – over the narrative of his life. The fact that the novel ends with disconnected fragments acts as a formal corollary of that collapse:

> The bleeding has started again. . . . I keep thinking about that shark . . . .
> I didn't hear the stateroom door open, but she's beside me now while I'm writing. I can feel her.
> The moon (136).

While the status of these last few pages is not absolutely clear (a coda, a type of appendix to the confession now in Keyes' possession, left to be found in Huff's stateroom?) it provides a fitting end both thematically and formally to all that comes before.

This is a novel that positions itself somewhere between realism and gothic melodrama. The novel is set in Los Angeles, round about Hollywood. Huff lives in the Los Feliz hills area, Phyllis in Hollywoodland. But, if references to the movie business sprinkle the text, it is everyday California living that the novel primarily depicts: the Nirdlingers' "Spanish house, like all the rest of them in California" (1) and its living room, with nothing in it "that any department store wouldn't deliver on one truck, lay out in the morning, and have the credit OK ready the next afternoon" (2); Walter's work for General Fidelity of California, with fifteen years' experience in the insurance business, selling automobile cover, arranging public liability bonds (63), and the like; Nirdlinger's job in the oil industry. The novel, too, is full of common-or-garden descriptions of everyday life: Walter "gulp[ing] down . . . orange juice and coffee" before going upstairs to read the paper (65); Phyllis buying ice-cream at the drug store (80); Walter's Filipino house-boy giving him "steak, mashed potatoes, peas and carrots" for his dinner, with "fruit cup" to follow (45–46), before Walter then goes out to commit the murder.

But the story of that murder, and what then follows, brings another quite different dimension to the book as realism and gothic excess meet head-on. Phyllis, it turns out, is a serial murderer. She and Walter dispose callously of her husband, Walter breaking his neck with – we assume – one of the husband's crutches (Nirdlinger has previously broken his leg in a minor neighborhood accident). Phyllis shoots Walter, who is himself planning to murder her (both act separately in this to ensure the absence of any witness to their joint crime). But the book moves into gothic overdrive earlier than this, with its description of Phyllis carrying her husband's body to its dumping spot on the railroad tracks (she and Walter intend it to look as though Nirdlinger has fallen from the train supposedly taking him to his class reunion at Stanford). Walter – who has been impersonating Nirdlinger on the train, using crutches and with his lower leg bound as if in a cast, before then safely jumping off (the train is travelling slowly) – describes what he sees:

> I heard a panting. Then . . . footsteps. . . . It was like being in a nightmare, with something queer coming after me. . . . Then I saw it. It was her. The man must have weighed 200 pounds, but she had him on her back . . . staggering along with him, over the tracks. His head was hanging down beside her head. They looked like something in a horror picture. (59–60)

It is Phyllis who is primarily associated with the gothic in the novel, as her representation (and dramatic self-representation) at a number of key points in the book suggests. I have spoken of the femme fatale in the context of other crime fictions, but it is here that we see this figure at her most vividly intense. Phyllis is driven by what Freud called the death instinct (Thanatos), her erotic potential (she has "a shape to set a man nuts," 5) combined with, and outweighed by, her deadly intentions toward others and her barely suppressed desire for her own death. Jonathan Dollimore, in his study of *Death, Desire and Loss in Western Culture*, writes that "death inhabits sexuality: perversely, lethally, ecstatically" (1999: x), words that seem particularly appropriate to Phyllis' case (whether or not we agree with the psychological or metaphysical basis of such a claim). So, Phyllis tells Walter as they start to plan Nirdlinger's murder that "there's something in me that loves Death. I think of myself as Death, sometimes. In a scarlet shroud, floating through the night. I'm so beautiful, then" (Cain 2005: 20). Lola later tells Walter how she has come in on Phyllis in the latter's bedroom dressed in red silk (also described as "like a shroud"), with "white powder and red lipstick . . . smeared" on her face, and "with a dagger in her hand, making faces at herself in front of a mirror" (101). And, when Walter and Phyllis make what amounts to their final suicide pact, Phyllis then gets ready – in her words – to "meet my bridegroom. The only one I ever loved" (135). Walter describes her preparations:

> She's made her face chalk white, with black circles under her eyes and red on her lips and cheeks. She's got that red thing on. It's awful-looking. It's just one big square of red silk that wraps around her. . . . She looks like what came aboard the ship to shoot dice for souls in the *Rime of the Ancient Mariner*. (136)

This is powerful stuff, and one cannot help but think that Cain has again been influenced by the cinema here. Perhaps he was recalling its portrayals of "vamps" (an abbreviation of vampires, referring to women who ensnare and victimize the men attracted by their vibrant sexuality) in the 1920s and just before. So Theda Bara, for instance, whose films spanned the 1914–1926 period, was known by this term ("the vamp") as a result of her role as a sexual predator, one she performed with pallid face and heavy black makeup around her eyes. Cain may, though, have been thinking of a more recent film such as Tod Browning's *Mark of the Vampire* (1935), in which Caroll Borland's white face is dramatically contrasted with her full and sensual glossed lips and where her full-length diaphanous gown confirmed her sexual allure. The descriptions of Phyllis, and of her various murders – together with the fact that Walter finally realizes that he has been duped by her, that she "had used me for a cat's paw" (96) – establish her at the deadly center of the novel: an "Irrawaddy cobra" (124) with whom Walter gets entangled. Her powerful womanhood is the very center of the novel's disturbing quality, and the prime factor in the destruction of the family that it traces. I will expand on this shortly as it impacts on the larger meanings of the novel.

James M. Cain: Double Indemnity (1936)

But I return first to Walter and his motives. Rational explication, the very thing on which classical detective fiction depends, plays only a part in his narrative. For Walter is initially driven by strong *impulse* even despite his recognition of its considerable danger to the life and career he has established. So, when Phyllis raises the subject of accident insurance on her husband, to be taken out without the latter's knowledge, Walter says that, instead of "get[ting] out of there, and drop[ping] . . . everything . . . about her like a red-hot poker . . . [,] I didn't do it. . . . What I did do was put my arm around her, pull her face up against mine, and kiss her on the mouth, hard. I was trembling like a leaf" (13). Walter is clearly affected by a mixture of transgressive impulses here, one of which is sexual desire. But from this point, and strangely, there is little description of any erotic connection between the pair. So, quite the opposite, when they are planning the murder and staged accident, and Walter says, "I've got to know. Where I stand. You can't fool – with this" (19), the only physical gestures described are his putting an arm around her and patting her like a child as she lies in his arms, to still the tears she then sheds. This forms the prelude to the confirmation of their decision: "'Yes, we're going to do it.' 'Straight down the line'" (21). As they continue their planning, they are mutually aroused by the excitement this causes, and Phyllis asks Walter to kiss her (26), but his consequent (we assume positive) response goes undescribed. And that is more or less the end of it, as far as the sexual dynamics of their relationship go.

What else then motivates Walter? This is a text set in Depression America and it is tempting to look for some kind of socio-political context to, and explanation for, the crime. Richard Bradbury, indeed, argues that the "spectres of the crisis [of the thirties] stalk around the edges of [Cain's] fiction." The Depression, he continues, a time when "the quintessentially American posture of individual effort being rewarded with security has been shattered by the economic collapse," stands as "an external fact which shapes the broad contours of the internal action" of the author's 1930s' texts (Bradbury 1988: 89–90). This may be true to the extent that, in this novel, the big insurance pay-off that Walter and Phyllis look for will give them the type of security that cannot be guaranteed elsewhere. It does not, though, serve as a fully adequate explanation for Walter's actions, given the security provided by his job and the success of his business sideline, the "little finance company" he runs (Cain 2005: 33).

There does, however, appear to be a broader critique of the capitalist system and the way that it has come to work embedded within the text. For Walter acts, in good part, as a result of his alienation from the corporate world he serves (see Harvey 1980: 40). Professionally, he is a small cog in a very large machine. His personal agency (the ability to act in a constructive and life-defining manner) is, one might suggest, swallowed up by his job, in his role as a "reputable agent" (Cain 2005: 5) for the company that employs him. There is a fixed hierarchy here, from Norton, president of the company, to Keyes, head of the Claims Department, to salesman Walter. Caught within a rationalized corporate world of rigid rules and regulations, Walter complains of Keyes that "[y]ou can't even say that today is Tuesday without he has to look on the calendar, and then check if it's this year's calendar or last year's calendar, and then find out what company printed the calendar" (6). The whole insurance world is highly organized and bureaucratic, with its making of money based on exact knowledge and statistics, and with even death subject to tabulation – with charts (as Keyes reveals in discussing Nirdlinger's death with Norton and Huff) classifying suicide not just "by race, by color, by occupation, by sex, by locality, by seasons of the year [etc.]" but also by "method of accomplishment subdivided by poisons, by firearms, by gas, by drowning, by leaps [etc.]" (70). All the odds have been worked out here to ensure a business that works like clockwork, where corporate profit is guaranteed and where Walter acts as "a croupier in [the] game" (27), merely raking in the money on his company's behalf.

The gambling metaphor Walter uses is significant. He sees his company as operating a type of roulette wheel where there is a pay-out on genuine claims but with profits guaranteed because of the knowledge of the odds on which the wheel depends. There would seem to be a contradiction here between the worlds of corporate business and games of chance. But references in the novel to the oil business and gold mining suggest a certain connection between the two – that the creation of large industrial companies depends upon some kind of initial lucky strike (of either natural resource). But Huff's main point is that, once a large corporation is established, little gambling in fact takes place, at least on its part. The insurance companies know how their business, dependent on "the biggest gambling wheel in the world" (26), works – have figured out all the percentages in advance to take in far more money than they ever pay out.

This, then, is a game of long and short odds ("You bet that your house will burn down, they bet it won't," 26) stacked on the side of big business. And these insurance companies are particularly on their guard against those who try and "crook the wheel" (27), to get large pay-offs from them on the basis of fraudulent claims. So Walter turns from croupier (raking in money for his company) to crooked gambler, from patrol guard to transgressor, looking to fix the wheel on the basis of his professional store of knowledge, and placing his bet with the help of Phyllis, his "plant" (27). Walter discovers a type of freedom, an exhilarating sense of personal agency, in playing a double game, representing the company as he deceives it, and "hit[ting] it for the limit"

(42); in escaping the fixed routines and regulative boundaries that have conditioned his life as an employee. If little of this is actually verbalized, Bradbury speaks persuasively of the way Walter turns from a "world of calculation" to an "almost furious space of his released desires and fears" (1988: 98).

Another way of putting this, bringing us back to the two strands that compose the book (Phyllis as femme fatale, Walter as going off the company rails to take extreme risks for maximum personal profit), is to see the novel – as both Claire Johnston (1980) and Sylvia Harvey do – as thematizing an attack on patriarchal values. This works in two ways. First, however, we should note "the motif of doubling" in the book. So, "Lola . . . is the good girl to Phyllis' femme fatale, and Keyes . . . is the straight-shooting insurance man consistently set against his failed protégé Walter's rogue salesman" (Leitch 2004: 138–139). We should remember, too, Lacan's words: that "Law and repressed desire are one and the same thing" (Johnston 1980: 102).

Patriarchy is based on the way that the whole apparatus of the state – from government, law, and business all the way down to the individual family unit – places absolute authority in the figure of the father, and relies on that authority for the stability and sustenance of the entire social order. Here the femme fatale, Phyllis, and her sexual presence stand as "the 'fault' inherent in patriarchy as an order," the force that "cannot be contained" within its repressive structures (Johnston 1980: 92–93). Walter, too, challenges patriarchy at the corporate level – sets himself up against the authority figure of Keyes (and, by implication, all those in the hierarchy above him), shattering the rules on which the smooth efficiency of his company depends and casting aside the straightjackets of conventional morality and the law in the process. But he and Phyllis also overturn the domestic order: they destroy the family in the name of desire (sexual, financial, and what we might call existential), literally killing the father (Nirdlinger) in the process.

Lola, in such terms, stands at the other end of the spectrum from Phyllis. A "sweet" (Cain 2005: 96) and "devoted" (93) nineteen-year-old daughter, she – it is implied – is also completely content to become a submissive and loving wife (to Nino Sachetti, whom she finally marries). Walter falls in love with Lola, while she and Nino are temporarily estranged, and compares the "unhealthy excitement" he feels when he sees Phyllis to the "sweet peace that came over me as soon as I was with [Lola]" (102). But, if Walter's relationship with Phyllis is, in terms of patriarchy, impossible (based on the killing of the family head), his relationship with Lola is doubly so – based on two forms of transgression (the murder of her father and, given his relationship with her stepmother, a type of symbolic incest). If the family is "a microcosm, containing within itself all the patterns of dominance and submission that are characteristic of the larger society" (Harvey 1980: 24), Walter – in helping to destroy Nordlinger's – has permanently barred himself from the potential comforts and security of both worlds.

In Cain's conservative universe (for that is what it is), there is only one way out of all this. I earlier quoted Cain's statement that "my stories have some of the quality of the opening of a forbidden box" (qtd. in Bradbury 1988: 90). But what is opened up is firmly closed again at the novel's end. Phyllis, the figure whose death drive and erotic excess (released outside normative family bounds) has prompted all the events of the novel, ends up in union with Death, the only "bridegroom" who can satisfy her, in her suicide. Walter, too, commits suicide alongside her, though his own intimacy with her is long past. Keyes finds out the real facts of the case but covers them up in the interests of the insurance company for which he works. (Cain's cynical view of the way the social system functions is clear in the fact that no policeman or detective appears in the novel. For we are asked to assume that "the officers sworn to uphold the law have much less interest in its enforcement than the insurance companies who stand to lose financially from any fraud," Leitch 2004: 135.) Lola marries Nino, thus restoring the family and social order disrupted by her mother's and Walter's acts. Cain's powerful novel of transgression ends with the two words "The moon" (135), the moon that will provide the light to see the "black fin" of the shark "[c]utting the water in the moonlight" (135) as it follows the ship from which Walter and Phyllis are about to jump. The violent dismemberment about to occur (Walter is bleeding from a previous wound) will provide – we can assume – just punishment for the deep social upset for which they are both responsible.

Patricia Highsmith: *The Talented Mr. Ripley* (1955)

Of course they all came to France a great many to paint pictures and naturally they could not do that at home, or write they could not do that at home either, they could be dentists at home.

Gertrude Stein on the American expatriates of the 1920s
(qtd. in Bradbury 1982: 31)

There are no dentists in Patricia Highsmith's *The Talented Mr. Ripley*. Tom Ripley, the novel's main protagonist and first-person narrator, has, though, in his past American life, worked at an "accounting job in [a] department store" (Highsmith 2001: 38–39) and in a warehouse in New York. He was sacked from the latter because he was not "as tough as the gorillas who worked with him" and lacked their physical strength (39–40). When Mr. Greenleaf – the father of Dickie Greenleaf, whom Tom has murdered and whose identity he has stolen – visits Tom in Venice, he is described as having the "taut face-of-an-industrialist" beneath the "grey homburg" he wears, and "looking like a piece of Madison Avenue" (247). And, when Tom and Marge (Dickie Greenleaf's former sort-of-girlfriend) go to a party held by the American Rudy Maloof in that same city, Tom describes the "checked suit of loud English tweed" Maloof wears as "the kind of pattern, Tom supposed, the English made, reluctantly, especially for such Americans" (244).

Stein's above remark dismisses America as dull and soulless, and those who live and work there as lacking the aesthetic consciousness – the concern with art and literature – she associates with Europe. The same view of America dominates Highsmith's later novel. When Ripley thinks back to the

The Crime Fiction Handbook, First Edition. Peter Messent.
© 2013 John Wiley & Sons, Ltd. Published 2013 by John Wiley & Sons, Ltd.

existence he and the people he knew had had in New York, he is scornfully dismissive of the "dismal life they led, creeping around New York, . . . standing in some dingy bar on Third Avenue . . . , watching television" (249). And, earlier, when he thinks of Dickie Greenleaf and of Dickie's father's attempts to persuade him (through Tom's ambassadorship) to come home and run the family boat-building firm, he asks himself: "Why should Dickie want to come back to . . . starched collars and a nine-to-five job?" (52). Reconsidering his past life, and his occasional visits to a Madison Avenue bar or a good New York restaurant, Tom can only think of their dullness "compared to the worst little trattoria in Venice with its tables of green salad, trays of wonderful cheeses, and its friendly waiters bringing you the best wine in the world!" (249).

Tom says that "it [is] not so much Europe itself" that makes him feel that he might never go back to America as the leisure time he has spent there, just by himself, "lying around on sofas thumbing through guidebooks" (249) and (after Dickie's murder) enjoying the various luxuries of his new life. But in fact it is indeed Europe that stands in symbiotic relationship to this life change. And, when an old American acquaintance writes to ask how long he will be staying there, Tom's response is to think "[f]orever" (249). We cannot help identifying author and character here, for Highsmith left America for good in 1954 (in her early thirties) to make "a life's work of her ostracisation from the American mainstream and her own subsequent self re-invention" (Frank Rich, qtd. in Žižek 2003: 1). We remember, too, that Highsmith occasionally signed letters "Pat H., alias Ripley" (see Nicol 2010: 509).

This transatlantic thematic, and the shortcomings of America when measured against European life, connects with the Jamesian motif in the novel. For Highsmith references *The Ambassadors* (1903), with Ripley hoping to search out the book in the ship's library, as he leaves America for Cherbourg. Indeed, he, like Lambert Strether, the main protagonist of Henry James' novel, who is sent to bring Chad Newsome back from Paris to take up his place in the family business, is an ambassador of a similar type. Like Strether, he too learns to appreciate the cultural richness and civilized quality of European life, and the opportunity for personal fulfillment it offers. However, ironically, Tom never gets access to James' book, as it is not available in first class (where Mr. Greenleaf has paid for Tom to travel) but only in the cabin-class library. Nonetheless, Highsmith follows James in reversing traditional American images of immigration and the experience associated with it. So Tom, sailing from New York, "felt as he imagined immigrants felt when they . . . left friends and relations and their past mistakes, and sailed for America. A clean slate!" (Highsmith 2001: 35). It is Europe here – not America – that serves as the place for new beginnings and fresh starts; sets excitement beating in Tom's heart.

For Tom, Europe is indissolubly linked to the existential sense of fulfilled identity he creates there: "He existed. Not many people in the world knew how to, even if they had the money" (249). This newly minted selfhood is composed of a curious mixture of aesthetic and cultural belonging and self-improvement and the satisfaction of material desire. Dickie Greenleaf has come to Europe to be an artist, but he is not very good at it: Tom thinks his landscapes, for instance, "all wild and hasty and monotonously similar" (60). Dickie appears not to know how to make the best of his leisured life, seems "bored" (60), and has not bothered, apparently, to learn Italian properly (136). In short, he has not made the most of the opportunities offered him. So it is significant that, when Tom first sees photographs of him, he feels they reveal Dickie's lack of intelligence (19). Once Tom has murdered Dickie – first to assume his identity and later, as he adapts to circumstances, to once more assume his own name but now buoyed by Dickie's money – he makes much more of the European opportunities *he* has now been given (or rather, has seized). He develops a "sureness in his taste," evidenced in part by the "palazzo overlooking San Marco" he rents in Venice, with its "indelibly beautiful" old garden and its internal furnishings: the "carved fronts of [its] armoires and chests and chairs . . . polish[ed] . . . until they seemed alive with dim lustrous lights" (214–215).

Tom makes the very most of Europe. "To me," Highsmith commented, "he's a social climber ever trying to refine himself" (1977: 34). This refinement is to a large degree aesthetic. When he has a simple sandwich and hot milk in a Paris bar-tabac, he describes the milk as "almost tasteless, pure and chastening, as [he] imagined a wafer tasted in church" (Highsmith 2001: 129). There is, indeed, something almost sacramental in his experience, and consumption, of France and Italy: in France, his slow taking-in of the "atmosphere" (125), his stopping in Arles "to see the places that Van Gogh had painted there" (129), and his imagining of people in an out-of-season Monte Carlo, "light and brilliant as a Dufy water-colour" (129). He sounds, indeed, like one of Henry James' perhaps-too-sensitive souls (maybe the main protagonist of "The Altar of the Dead") when he imagines the inside of the cathedral in Palermo, "its musty, sweetish smell, composed of the uncounted candles and incense-burnings" of many centuries (180). Tom annihilates his personal past (127) as he constructs this new self, entirely attuned to what is for him a new and wonderful world. Dickie's money – for Tom forges Greenleaf's will to his own benefit – gives him "the leisure to see Greece . . . , to read his Malraux . . . as late as he pleased, because he did not have to go to a job in the morning" (250).

Tom's changed life, then, depends on Dickie's money. Gatsby-like (for Tom's representation echoes that of Fitzgerald's protagonist in a number of ways), it is a new life built on material luxury as much as it is on aesthetic enjoyment. Indeed (as I suggest above), money and aesthetic pleasure are necessarily linked here. Again like *The Great Gatsby* (1926), this is a novel about class. Tom – like Wolfsheim in Fitzgerald's novel, who "just saw the opportunity" (Fitzgerald 1958 [1925]: 76) to fix the World (Baseball) Series – just sees the opportunity to improve his social and economic status, even if it is at the cost of Dickie's life, and he seizes that chance. In New York, Tom shares a "grimy single room" that has a "smelly john down the hall that didn't lock" in a "dingy brownstone" with Bob Delancey, totally dependent on the latter's generosity for even this living space (Highsmith 2001: 11). His house in Venice is the very opposite of such squalor. Once Dickie is killed, Tom surrounds himself with luxury: new Gucci suitcases (138); Dickie's "grain-leather shoes" (140) and hand-made shirt with monogrammed pocket; the "white, taut sheets" on his overnight train to Paris, that "seemed the most wonderful luxury he had ever known" (111). Like Gatsby, Tom uses the commodities only the very rich can buy to construct his newly successful self. Like Gatsby, too, his view of selfhood is not as something solid, coherent, and genuine but – to quote Jackson Lears on the development of American consumer culture – "an empty vessel to be filled and refilled according to the expectations of others and the needs of the moment" (1983: 8).

There is a revealing moment early in *The Talented Mr. Ripley* when Tom is lying in his deckchair on his boat to Europe, "fortified morally by the luxurious surroundings" (Highsmith 2001: 38). "Morally" is a very odd word to use here and suggests how Tom's values have a very different base than that we would normally expect. Tom "love[d] possessions" – that is, highly select possessions of the very best "quality" – because "[p]ossessions reminded him that he existed, and made him enjoy his existence" (249). Again here, we have that same sense of Tom as an empty vessel, forming his subjectivity from the objects that surround him, and adorning it with the art and culture that he learns both to appreciate and to imbue. But the fact that he sees morality in terms of luxury suggests that the priorities that drive him have nothing to do with conventional ethics. Indeed, he uses violence and murder to further fortify himself "morally": to achieve his desire for the finer things of life and the self-transformation they bring with them, and to preserve the self that is accordingly created.

Rzepka calls Ripley "a pleasant, polite and morally vacuous young murderer and confidence man" (2005: 230). Highsmith talks about him as having "a singular lack of conscience" (1977: 33). This is a transgression narrative, focusing on the first-person representation of Ripley and the serial murders he commits (just two in this text but more follow later in the novel sequence). But it is also a book that completely upsets our expectations of the way crime fiction works and prepares the way for later protagonists such as Thomas Harris' Hannibal Lecter, who shares Ripley's emphasis on fine living and good taste, and who, like Ripley, lives to reap the benefits of his crimes rather than ending up imprisoned, hunted down by representatives of the law. Murder is represented here as a relatively matter-of-fact response to immediate needs. As Žižek again writes, "[Tom's] crimes are based on simple pragmatism: he does what is necessary to attain his goal" (2003: 3) – the step-up from relative poverty to affluence and the refined pleasures that affluence can bring. Horsley suggests that Tom acts out a darkly comic version of the traditional American Dream, his murders linked to "the optimistic American belief in fresh starts" (2005: 135) – and, again, we might remember here that Gatsby's self-creation depends on criminal activity.

Though Ripley lives in ongoing fear of discovery, the law fails here. The police are mystified by his (undiscovered) swappings of identity and the false trails he lays. Greenleaf's father hires an American private eye to sort things out but he, too, is metaphorically blind, unable to adapt to the Italian setting (he barely speaks the language) and lacking any of the penetrating insight with which those in his fictional role are normally credited. Ripley imagines the worst when exposure threatens him (for there are clear clues to what has really happened available), but McCarron, the P. I., goes back to America with the case unsolved. As Horsley says, in calling the novel "a blackly comic manipulation of the basic ingredients of the [detective] genre," and in also pointing to its unusual construction of gender roles:

> The masculine ethos of more traditional detective narratives is constantly undercut in [Ripley's] . . . feminized world. . . . The intellectual endeavour and rational investigative structure of detection have little success in comparison to flair, intuition, dressing well, and shopping discerningly, all of which are satisfyingly rewarded. . . . (2005: 132–133)

Crime here is divorced from punishment. So the novel ends with Ripley, unchallenged, in possession of Dickie's income and possessions, and on his way to the best hotel in Athens. From there he plans to "see the [Greek] islands" but "as a living, breathing, courageous individual – not as a cringing little nobody from Boston" (Highsmith 2001: 277).

Ripley is hollow at the center, a self composed of external props. This, though, is an advantage in the world through which he moves. If Gatsby springs "from his Platonic conception of himself" (Fitzgerald 1958: 202), so too does Ripley, with a little help from Dickie Greenleaf on the way. From the start of the novel, he shows his adeptness at imagining false (and better) identities: in this case a Princeton background (Highsmith 2001: 18). He inspects the self he projects to Greenleaf's parents (and which helps him to gain his ambassadorship) in the mirror (21). And, on the boat to Europe he begins to play the role "of a serious young man with a serious job ahead of him. He was courteous, poised, civilized and preoccupied" (34). Tom further adapts and defines the part he wants to play on the world's stage once he meets Dickie, to whose wealth and way of life in Italy he responds "with a heart-breaking surge of envy and of self-pity" (52). Listing his talents to Dickie (when they are talking about possible jobs), he includes his ability to "forge a signature" and to "impersonate practically anybody" (58). Realizing his close resemblance to Dickie (66–67), Tom starts to play at being him: part of their falling-out, indeed, comes when the former finds him trying on his clothes (78–79). And, as Dickie starts to "shov[e] him out in the cold" (100), in part because he has begun to think Tom may well be "queer" (80, 98–99), Tom has the sudden thought of murdering him; to "become Dickie Greenleaf himself," living in Paris or Rome and forging Dickie's signature to cash the monthly checks that would then come his way; to "step right into Dickie's shoes" (100). Almost no sooner than this is thought, it is done. The rest of the novel is then spent in a type of theatrical performance (see, for instance, 219), as Tom mimics and appropriates Dickie's habits, gestures, and ways of thinking, taking up and – when necessary – discarding the personae of Dickie and Tom in turn. One identity becomes just as much a role-play as the other in this process ("he wore Tom Ripley's shy, slightly frightened expression" 176), and Tom, once in a while, even confuses which particular role he is in (224). Ironies proliferate as Tom plays his dangerous game, one where he is often on the edge of discovery. So (when he is being Dickie), Marge tells him in a letter – and with more truth than she knows – that she has told the police "that you and Tom are inseparable and how they could have found you and still missed *Tom*, I could not imagine" (181).

Much of the tension in the novel lies in Tom's narrow escapes from discovery, the moves and improvisations he makes in the process, his vacillations "between confidence in his luck and fear of nemesis" (Horsley 2005: 133). Tom is a double murderer: he also kills one of Dickie's American friends who is getting too close to the truth. But the fact that this is a first-person narration nonetheless encourages the reader to take his perspective on events, feel a degree of relief when he evades capture. Horsley focuses on Tom's aesthetic appreciation, his inventiveness, his ability to create his own life-narrative (in an "open-ended process of self-creation"). She claims, indeed, that Tom "acts metaphorically as an embodiment of cultural freedom and as a celebration of the transgressive imagination" (2005: 136).

Ripley is a risk-taker, and in taking risks he finds the excitement that gives his life much of its meaning. At the book's start he is defrauding the

American tax system as a type of "[g]ood clean sport" (Highsmith 2001: 14), despite the fact that he cannot cash in the (always small) checks that result, and even though he lives in fear of discovery and arrest. And, when he thinks of the dangers in his juggling of the two identities, Dickie's and Tom's, and how the police might discover the truth, he thinks: "Risks were what made the whole thing fun" (179). Gambling with his own life, Tom discovers an intensity of feeling that is absent from conventional lives. He becomes, despite (perhaps because of) the murders he commits, attractive: a type of existential figure, finding fulfillment in the rejection of what he sees as bourgeois (American) mediocrity, his acts of violence a spontaneous asser-tion of what Norman Mailer would call in "The White Negro" (1957) "the rebellious imperatives of self" (1961: 116).

There is, as I have suggested, more than a hint of Thomas Harris' Hannibal Lecter here, another serial murderer and man of excellent taste, another who abhors the dullness of the everyday. Žižek suggests that, in *The Talented Mr. Ripley,*

> Highsmith foreshadows today's rewriting of the Ten Commandments as recommendations which we don't need to follow too blindly. Ripley stands for the final step in this process: thou shalt not kill, except when there is really no other way to pursue your happiness. (2003: 3)

He becomes, accordingly, a blackly parodic illustration of where "American adaptability, other-directedness, and upward mobility" can lead, once released from conventional moral restraints (Horsley 2005: 134). Ripley is the most "civilized" person in the novel. So, like Thomas Harris and his depiction of Lecter, Highsmith challenges us to rethink the nature of our belief in what "civilization" actually means, just how far (if at all) we have moved beyond the savagery of its supposed opposite (and see Baker 2009 here). Ripley's happiness and taste come at the expense of the legal and moral codes of our everyday world, but it is this world that is represented as worthless in the novel: with "its injustices and stupidities, its deadening conformity, and its lack of imagination" (Horsley 2005: 129). In such a context, Ripley becomes both villain and hero: a "psychopath who doesn't give a damn about killing anybody" (Highsmith 1977: 33) but also a gambler who plays for the highest stakes, an expatriate life of taste and beauty, of self-creation and self-fulfill-ment. And, in setting these goals, he rejects what Highsmith presents as an unattractive American world: one dominated by convention and largely inhabited by "the riffraff, the vulgarians, the slobs" (Highsmith 2001: 30); one where economic lines are fixed, with those who have the wealth lacking the drive and/or imagination to make the most of the possibilities it brings.

Highsmith is very different from Cain. Both write fictions of transgression, but Highsmith moves away from the deterministic frame that governs Cain's fiction to a world of risk and danger but also of escape, attractive possibility, and good living. Ripley, too, considers hurling himself from a ship at the end of the novel (282). (There may possibly be an intertextual reference to Cain's Walter and Phyllis here.) But he stays on board and remains free, with Australia, India, Japan, and South America on his list of places to explore, looking positively to the future: "[m]erely to look at the art of those countries would be a pleasant, rewarding life's work" (284). While Cain puts his emphasis on plot and action, Highsmith puts hers on psychology: the mind of Ripley and the way it looks to adjust to, and use to best advantage, life's circumstances.

Bran Nicol describes Highsmith's style as "distinctive, measured, emotionless," one that "maintains the same pace and detached perspective no matter what she is describing" (2010: 508). Occasionally, however, Tom's "twitching nerves" (Highsmith 2001: 282), feelings of imminent discovery and arrest, and sexual fastidiousness disturb this smooth surface. Violence, too, can suddenly and swiftly break in on this stylistic composure. So, Tom's irritation with Marge when she is staying with him in Venice takes a sudden, vicious turn when, anticipating the ride in a gondola he is to take with her, he thinks: "If she dangled those hands in the water, he hoped a shark bit them off" (233). So, too, faced with Freddie Miles' belligerence, he quickly shifts from a smiling and polite deflection of the latter's suspicions to the violent obliteration of the threat he poses: "Tom slammed the edge of the ashtray into the back of Freddie's neck. He hit the neck again and again" (143). In this move between measured calmness and occasional but deadly eruption of violence, Highsmith's distinctive stylistic signature can be found.

Chester Himes:
Cotton Comes to Harlem (1965)

Crime fiction writers from minority groups or from those who are in any way marginalized or oppressed by the dominant social system have a particular problem in their writing. For, as we have seen, the genre works by and large by illustrating how ruptures in the social fabric (caused by criminal action) are resolved and repaired through detective work; how the social status quo as it previously exists is accordingly reinstated. In the case of minority authors (or even authors who represent the majority of the population in, say, a colonial situation), such a reinstatement can only be problematic.

W. E. B. DuBois, the important turn-of-the-century African American intellectual, compared being black in the United States to being "shut out" from the surrounding white world "by a vast veil," torn in two by a dual identity as both "American" and "Negro": "two souls, two thoughts, two unreconciled strivings; two warring ideals in one dark body, whose dogged strength alone keeps it from being torn asunder" (1999: 10–11). A dominant and ongoing metaphor for black life in the United States, implied by DuBois' reference to that veil and elaborated by Ralph Ellison in his 1952 novel *Invisible Man*, is that of invisibility. So, when in Himes' *Cotton Comes to Harlem* the Harlem witnesses to the after-events of a robbery have nothing to say, are said by Coffin Ed Johnson (along with Grave Digger Jones, the main detective protagonist of the novel) to be "[a]ll stone blind," Jones then continues, "What do you expect from people who are invisible themselves?" (Himes 1974: 43). *Cotton Comes to Harlem* serves in part to document this invisibility: the failure of American society to recognize the human worth of its black population (to this point in its history) or to give them the same

The Crime Fiction Handbook, First Edition. Peter Messent.
© 2013 John Wiley & Sons, Ltd. Published 2013 by John Wiley & Sons, Ltd.

living opportunities as their white counterparts, separated off as they are in an immiserated Harlem environment by fundamental racial (and social) injustices that dominate every aspect of their lives. Himes' two black detectives are consequently themselves torn by conflicting demands, employed to uphold the (white) dominant society and its laws while at the same time looking to serve the needs of the black community with which they identify. The novel works in part as an exploration of how such conflicts might (temporarily) be resolved.

"Himes' most important contribution to the detective fiction genre," David Schmid writes, was "to 'make the faces black' and so place 'racial ideology' at centre stage of the genre" (Schmid 1995: 255; he quotes J. A. Williams and Robert Gooding-Williams respectively here). Race dominates *Cotton Comes to Harlem*, as one would expect in a text set, as all Himes' "Harlem domestic" series are, in that part of New York City generally recognized as the capital of black America. For the most part, it is the demeaning quality of Harlem life on which Himes focuses. The description of the area around Eighth Avenue and 112th Street where Jones and Johnson stop at a "dingy bar" reads, indeed, like a scene out of hell, with its prostitutes and drug addicts, children running loose on filthy streets, and workmen "stagger[ing] down the sidewalks filled with aimless resentment, muttering curses, hating to go to their hotbox hovels but having nowhere else to go." When Grave Digger, "his voice cotton-dry with rage," takes in the scene to say that he wishes that "for just one mother-raping second" he were God, Cotton Ed understands his meaning: "I know. . . . You'd concrete the face of the mother-raping earth and turn white folks into hogs" (Himes 1974: 47).

While it is clear that not all of Harlem is like this particular neighborhood, Himes nonetheless emphasizes that, for the non-criminal population, this is generally a place of some desperation, of slum overcrowding (6) and high rents (8), where half a million African Americans struggle for existence, many in the meanest of circumstances. Lieutenant Anderson, Jones' and Johnson's white superior, comments on the way Iris (the main female protagonist of the novel) – pressured by the two detectives – has turned against her former partner, Deke O'Hara (aka Deke O'Malley), saying: "I hate to see people tearing at one another like rapacious animals." Jones replies simply: "Hell, what do you expect? . . . As long as there are jungles there'll be rapacious animals" (138).

Harlem is, then, represented here as a jungle, where crime is endemic and where police intervention is less than full scale. Himes' portrayal of the poverty of black lives, and of commonplace criminality and violence, may explain the unease felt by other African American writers and critics in his literary presence (see Schmid 1999). But, for Himes, to ignore such realities would be to give a false representation of African American life in America.

Violence and crime act as a means of survival and one of the few avenues of possible material advancement in a brutish and Darwinian world. But the reason for the existence of such a world, and the distortion of the black psyche that it evidences, is racism: the way in which a whole sector of the American population has been systematically oppressed and denied full social justice. Himes himself spoke of the need to "know the truth" about black life in America, saying that "[i]f this plumbing for the truth reveals within the Negro personality . . . homicidal mania, . . . a pathetic sense of inferiority, . . . uncle tomism, hate and fear and self-hate, this then is the effect of oppression on the human personality" (qtd. in Schmid 1999: 291). When Anderson tells Grave Digger to hold back on the use of "brute force" as he and Johnson go about their duties, the latter – deeply angered – replies:

> We got the highest crime rate on earth [here in Harlem]. . . . And there ain't but three things to do about it: Make the criminals pay for it – you don't want to do that; pay the people enough to live decently – you ain't going to do that; so all that's left is let 'em eat one another up.
>
> (Himes 1974: 18)

This sense of racial and social defeat inhabits the whole book: it explains the constant tension between black and white within it; why, when a young black man is prevented from throwing a brick through the plate-glass window of the (white-run) Back-to-the-Southland office during a street protest, with the words "[n]one of that son, we're peaceful," he answers "What for?" (91). This is the same answer we might assume Himes himself would have given: see, for instance, his statement that "I have always believed . . . that the Black man in America should mount a serious revolution and this revolution should employ massive, extreme violence" (qtd. in Fuller 1972: 18).

Himes' stance here may be extreme but was not unusual for its time, and stemmed from the long-standing sense of racial injustice in America. This directly reflects on the position of Grave Digger and Cotton Ed, employed as police detectives to uphold the law, and thus protect a social system that has betrayed their fellow black men and women; caused their whole racial group to be "sick at soul" (Himes, qtd. in Schmid 1995: 257). The two, Lieutenant Anderson's "ace detectives" (Himes 1974: 16), can do nothing about the larger "crime" in this novel: the effects of racism on the black population. But they can do something in looking to solve the immediate criminal act that drives the action of the novel and that adversely affects their black community – the theft of 87 000 dollars that rightly belongs to those people of Harlem who have invested it in the (fraudulent) "new Back-to-Africa movement" (20) fronted by Deke O'Hara (in his assumed role as Reverend Deke O'Malley).

Even here, though, the two black detectives only get results by acting outside the limits of the law. Warned by their white superior about the excessive use of force, they know that in the crime-ridden Harlem environment only extra-legal tactics, backed up where necessary by violent action, have a chance of bringing any kind of justice. Grave Digger and Coffin Ed, as Michael Denning points out, are very different from Philip Marlowe and his like: "vulnerable but tough, wise-cracking but sentimental," dominating the texts in which they feature as "the consciousness that holds the characteristically first-person narrative together" (1988: 11). In Himes' third-person narrative, the two detectives, more often than not, lack this type of authority as they struggle to retain their balance and are faced with confusing, even chaotic, facts and events that constantly threaten to overwhelm them. So, for much of the novel they are on the back foot, looking for some kind of key to explain the carnival of crime that has erupted, and where the missing money might be. After they have questioned a potential witness to a truck wreck (the truck is carrying the stolen money that has consequently disappeared), we are told that the two detectives are "frustrated and deadbeat, and no nearer the solution than at the start" (Himes 1974: 74). The notion of individual agency is questioned here as Coffin Ed and Grave Digger simply react to the chain of events as much as they have any kind of positive control over them. And the authority and ability to control events that they *do* have come from their ability to meet violence with violence (see 74) and through a well-organized group of stool-pigeons without whom the majority of crimes would go unsolved (45).

We know little about Grave Digger and Coffin Ed from this novel except that they are married (Grave Digger with two daughters) and live in Astoria, Long Island. There is little space here (as in Chandler) for attention to these detectives' private sensibilities. Rather they are defined by their race and their job, and the pressures that this combination, and their presence in the Harlem "jungle," brings. The two men are quick to turn to violence (as Coffin Ed says, "[b]etter to be quick than dead," 17), and both are clearly constantly on edge, characterized by their ticks – Coffin Ed's twitching acid-scarred face and Grave Digger's swollen neck and prominent temple veins. They survive and succeed in their job only because of their toughness, their unconventional (and often legally unacceptable) responses to the problems confronting them, and the willingness of their white superiors to turn a blind eye to such tactics.

The two detectives are, moreover, no respecters of gender difference. So, when Iris – in response to a violent slap from Grave Digger, infuriated by her warning O'Malley of their presence – then slaps Coffin Ed, only a blow on the back of his neck by his partner makes Ed release the hands he then puts on her throat, just an instant before he would have "crushed her windpipe" (39). The two men meet resistance (itself often excessively violent) with violence in a dangerous and lawless Harlem world where "coloured hoodlums had no respect for coloured cops unless you beat it into them or blew them away" (41–42). And this last is exactly what the two detectives do when they eventually find Deke – held by rival criminals in his 121st Street church. Responding to sawed-off shotgun fire with their own tracer bullets, they not only wreak physical havoc (one of Grave Digger's shots breaking the leg of one criminal just "like a wooden stick," 200) but set both their opponents' bodies and the church itself on fire as they do so. It is Grave Digger and Cotton Ed alone who have the ability to keep some kind of order in this savage and conflicted environment. So, too, it is they who face down rival mobs of Black Muslims and Back-to-the-Southland supporters when open conflict between the two groups seems inevitable (158–162).

If the two detectives are employed to uphold the (white establishment's) law, then, they do it very much in their own way. And the justice they mete out has little to do with official legal procedure. Grave Digger and Cotton Ed's dominant motive throughout *Cotton Comes to Harlem* is to recover the missing 87 000 dollars in order to pay it back to the eighty-seven families who have lost their lifetime savings on what, anyway, was an impossible dream. They discover eventually that Uncle Bud, a local junk collector, has found the missing money in the bale of cotton in which it has initially been hidden and has indeed returned to Africa on the proceeds (to live a life of dissolute wealth). They get "justice" for their fellow black men and women, however, not by recovering this stolen money but by threatening Colonel Calhoun – leader of the Back-to-the-Southland movement – with exposure of his criminal activities (a murder committed in the Colonel's own pursuit of the loot) unless he himself restores the now-irrecoverable sum. The Colonel calls their actions "incredible," asking "Is it because they [the victims] are nigras and you're nigras too?" to get the response "That's right" (213). But the ability of the two detectives to arrange such unofficial justice, to protect the interests of their racial community, is a one-off exception to an ongoing situation of unfairness and oppression. And (as I have shown earlier) their position as upholders of the law becomes increasingly untenable as the "Harlem domestic" series continues. Here, however, there is at least some positive resolution to the case in which they are involved.

This is a novel rooted in African American political and cultural history. Deke's Back-to-Africa scam looks back to Marcus Garvey and the earlier years of the century and Garvey's consequent conviction (probably politically motivated) for mail fraud (see 35). But it also references the murder of Congolese independence leader Patrice Lumumba in February 1961 (159).

This event was deeply significant for the emergent African American nationalism of the period, and its view of Lumumba as a victim of white colonialism and its political interests. Among the manifestations of this black nationalism was the National Memorial Book Store, established by Lewis H. Michaux in Harlem and headquarters of a new 1960s resurgence of the same Back-to-Africa idea (see 33 and 159; for a photo of the storefront see "Lewis Michaux's House of Common Sense and Home of Proper Propaganda" 1964). Another sign of this nationalist impulse was the rise of the Black Muslims, fictionally introduced in Himes' novel on pages 159–162.

The Muslims here are placed in opposition to Colonel Calhoun's Back-to-the-Southland organization. The latter is a wholly fictional organization, but one based on long-established white Southern patriarchal attitudes to race: that the best interests of the child-like Negro were best served by slavery before Emancipation and tenant farming after it, with the white master housing and feeding and caring for his black workers in a competitive economic landscape where they would otherwise flounder. Thus, Calhoun (Himes plays here on the name of ante-bellum pro-slavery apologist John C. Calhoun) is the very image of the Southern patriarch with his "white mane of hair, . . . white moustache and white goatee" and the "shoestring tie" he wears (77). His Back-to-the-Southland campaign, meanwhile, employs all the images of Southern white benevolence and the material comforts of the region as it looks to reverse the twentieth-century African American northward movement, to tempt the black population back "home." So the glass frontage of Calhoun's Harlem headquarters is covered with brightly-colored "paintings of conk-haired black cotton-pickers . . . delicately lifting enormous snow-white cotton balls . . . and grinning happily with even whiter teeth" and the like, with other smaller images of Southern soul food (grits, hog maw stew, hoppin john, etc.) given the label "ALL GOOD THINGS TO EAT" (77). Images of the 1960s (the conked hair, other pictures of "happy darkies" doing the twist) merge here with traditional Southern racist apologetics to satirize any notion that the South, with its racial attitudes and traditions, could ever serve the African American as the homeland it projected.

Himes saturates his novel with a wealth of detail specific to African American culture. At the same time, he uses a generally standard American English narrative base to keep the novel accessible to an intended white readership. There is, nonetheless, considerable use of black slang and of a gritty vernacular here: enough to have caused, one imagines, some degree of shock to its initial readers. The use of the adjective "mother-raping" by Grave Digger and Coffin Ed – a thinly-veiled euphemism for "mother-fucking" – litters the text. And, when Himes describes the seduction of a white detective by Iris (he is meant to be guarding her in her apartment), he uses the language of a raw sexual power: "The odour of hot-bodied woman, wet cunt and perfume came up from her and drowned him" (100). Black street vernacular, too, constantly features in the text – "the boss man got salty" (143); Coffin Ed's disguise of "black weedhead sunglasses" under pulled-down red cap, consequently looking "like one of the real-gone cats with his signifying walk" (188) – but carefully deployed so as not to overwhelm the novel's dominant linguistic register.

As he refers to the specifics of African American culture in the text, Himes points to some of the more positive aspects of black Harlem life, even despite its various problems. He describes the soul food at Mammy Louise's "barbeque joint" – "ribs, . . . black-eyed peas, rice, okra, collard greens . . . , yellow corn bread" with its hot sauce accompaniments – and makes it clear how much the two detectives enjoy its tasty pleasures (139–142). It is at Mammy Louise's, too, that the two men "[s]uddenly" listen when they hear Lester ("Pres") Young, Harry ("Sweets") Edison, and Roy Eldridge's "Laughing to Keep from Crying" (1958) playing on the jukebox. They are clearly moved by this (unknown to them) jazz track, and the episode recalls their earlier comments on the live jazz music at Big Wilt's Small Paradise Inn at 135th Street and Seventh Avenue. (This was a long-time Harlem night-club, Small's, bought by basketball star Wilt Chamberlain in the 1960s, thus the new name.) At Big Wilt's, Coffin Ed and Grave Digger listen to the band, "the horns . . . talking and the saxes talking back," and have the following conversation:

"Somewhere in that jungle is the solution to the world," Coffin Ed said . . . .
"Yes, it's like the sidewalks trying to speak in a language never heard. But they can't spell it either."
"Naw," Coffin Ed said. "Unless there's an alphabet for emotion."
"The emotion that comes out of experience. If we could read that language, man, we would solve all the crimes in the world."
"Let's split," Coffin Ed said. "Jazz talks too much to me." (45)

There is a sense of jazz, here, as a type of alternative black vernacular register – an untranslatable tongue that, nonetheless, provides a glimpse of utopian possibility, of a better world than that currently existing for the African American people (and see Gair 2003). This is, though, just a rare indication of such promise in what is an otherwise bleak novel as far as improving racial possibilities goes.

But what is evident in what I have already said is how much this novel varies in tone and content: what a rollercoaster of a ride it is. Jam-packed with action, much of it violent, the book swings between actual historical event (black nationalism in the 1960s) and satiric invention (the Back-to-the

Southland movement). It swings, too, between gritty realism and comic exaggeration: the church sister having a hole silently cut from her skirt to reveal her buttocks "encased" in "rose-colored rayon pants" (Himes 1974: 24) in the course of the "holy dream" robbery scam (51); Iris leaving the white detective standing "buck-naked" with just a paper sack (with eye-holes) over his head as she makes her escape from her apartment (96–102); Uncle Bud setting himself up in Dakar, with "100 wives of moyen qualite [sic]" (222) and a herd of cattle, on the proceeds of the stolen money he has pocketed.

This move between realism and a type of comic absurdism is the distinguishing mark of Himes' fiction. And Himes defined himself in terms of both the above traditions. Speaking of his earlier protest novel, *If He Hollers Let Him Go* (1945), he said that "it is my small self-appointed task to write the truth as I see it. As long as this nation is what it is and its human products are what they are, then that is what I will write about, beautiful or not" (qtd. in Schmid 1999: 292). This statement also applies to *Cotton Comes to Harlem* in terms of its depiction of the lack of opportunity, racial and social degradation, and pervasive criminal violence that distorts black lives in Harlem. But, as Himes was the first to admit, Harlem was in fact a place where he himself had never lived. And, while his portrayal of the effects of racism can be taken as realistic, as can the impact of a pervasive violence on American culture as a whole ("there is no way one can evaluate the American scene and avoid violence," qtd. in Williams 1973: 329), such realism is contained within a largely surrealistic fictional method. "The Harlem of my books," Himes said, "was never meant to be real, I never called it real" (qtd. in Schmid 1995: 258). So, while he makes it clear in *Cotton Comes to Harlem* that a sense of "homelessness" and desperation marks the mass of the lives of the inhabitants (all those who invest in O'Malley's scam), and while he uses actual places and real historical events as the backdrop to the novel, both its plotting and its action swiftly move onto a different, and absurdist, plane.

So, a central strand of Coffin Ed and Grave Digger's investigation centers on the whereabouts of the bale of cotton in which the stolen money was originally hidden. The symbolic value of this bale is clear. For, as Grave Digger comments, "[t]his mother-raping cotton punished the colored man down south and now it's killing them up north" (Himes 1974: 152). The very appearance of such an object, however, in a New York setting acts as a type of surreal joke: as a white cop says, "[w]hat the hell's a bale of cotton doing here in the street?" (29). At one stage of a novel filled with a mixture of violent mayhem and comic event, Grave Digger says, "so much nonsense must make sense" (148). We could argue that the sense Himes in fact makes is twofold. First, the proliferation of the absurd in the urban life he represents may act as an indication of the greater absurdity of racism itself (for Himes' recognition of the way "[r]acism introduces absurdity into the human condition" see Schmid 1999: 286). Second, the humor involved in such representations acts as a type of correlative to the jazz (and blues) music that is at the core of African American cultural life: a celebration of comedy even in the face of oppression and pain; a way, in the words of the music track named in the novel, of "Laughing to Keep from Crying." There may be something contradictory, and even compromising, in the way Himes jams the two different traditions together in his work. But, in keeping his reader off balance in this way, Himes brings a highly distinctive method to the detective fiction genre and one that undoubtedly serves his African American aesthetic needs. His novels stand as a significant contribution to African American writing in the period, and to the developing history of the crime fiction form.

Maj Sjöwall and Per Wahlöö:
The Laughing Policeman (1968)

The Laughing Policeman (*Den Skrattande Polisen*) is the fourth novel in Maj
Sjöwall and Per Wahlöö's ground-breaking ten-novel *Report of a Crime*
(*Roman om ett Brott*) series featuring Martin Beck, published in Sweden
between 1965 and 1975. In this and in my later chapter on Stieg Larsson,
I work with the translated versions of the novels, here by Alan Blair.

Sjöwall and Wahlöö, both journalists, were writing from a "distinctly
Marxist perspective" (Winston and Mellerski 1992: 17) in the context of
what they saw as the then-failures of the Swedish welfare state. This needs
some explanation, though my comments are necessarily brief. Sweden, from
the outside, has generally been seen as a model of a fair and egalitarian
society with its social welfare system (an education and health system,
pension rights, old age care, and the like) established over the course of
the twentieth century and made possible, in part, by its neutrality during the
two world wars and the relative affluence that this brought. In 1928, Prime
Minister Per Albin Hansson spoke of Sweden as "the people's home"
(*folkhemmet*) – a term that came to be generally recognized as describing
the Swedish state, and this system of care and support for its citizenry, as a
type of metaphorical extended family. In 1936, American journalist Marquis
Childs published his highly influential book *The Middle Way*, arguing that
Sweden had, accordingly, found an effective and unique way of combining
capitalism and communism. By the 1960s, this system was generally recognized as a highly successful application of social democratic ideals. Those on
the political left, however, such as Sjöwall and Wahlöö, were prescient in
identifying the cracks and compromises in the Swedish welfare state. Though

The Crime Fiction Handbook, First Edition. Peter Messent.
© 2013 John Wiley & Sons, Ltd. Published 2013 by John Wiley & Sons, Ltd.

they tend rather to accept the premises of the two authors' own position, Winston and Mellerski's provide accurate comment:

> The investigations of Martin Beck and his colleagues on the National Homicide Squad enable their creators to indict the conspiracy between a supposedly socialist government and the capitalists in whose interests they govern. As crime spreads throughout Sweden, the police are confronted with an increasingly alienated population that denies the myth of a homogenous and harmonious society based on "cooperative individualism." Marginal groups within the population – the elderly, the adolescent, the poor – are systematically scrutinized as targets of exploitation by the combined forces of the state and private enterprise. (1992: 10–11)

Sjöwall and Wahlöö develop and harden their critique of Swedish society over the course of their series and (especially in the earlier novels) effectively disguise their own political agenda within a complex, well-written, and gripping crime fiction format. And the ideological position they take is not the reason for their novels' success. Rather, they introduce a particular type of police novel: one that has been highly influential (especially in a European context) and has acted as the forerunner for the larger successes of Scandinavian crime fiction in the period since. Thus, the novels of fellow Swede Henning Mankel, for instance, are scarcely conceivable without their example. And the recent prominence of Scandinavian crime fiction generally – Swedish writers Mankel, Camilla Läckberg, Stieg Larsson, Liza Marklund, Håkan Nesser, and Leif Persson; Icelandic writer Arnaldur Indriðason; and Norwegians Karin Fossum and Jo Nesbø are some of the best known – also has its roots, though to varying extents, in their work. (For more information on Scandinavian crime fiction, see Nestingen and Arvas 2011.)

I would not, however, want to suggest here that all the above authors are alike, or that the different cultural and historical backgrounds of the Scandinavian countries from which these writers (and others from Denmark and Finland) come do not make a difference to their work. But there does seem to be a certain distinctive quality to the detective fiction of this entire region. Arvas and Nestingen's assessment may be broad-scale, and even contentious, but it indicates something of this commonality:

> Scandinavian crime fiction . . . has been dominated by the police procedural. . . . The novels often articulate social criticism, critiquing national institutions and gender politics in particular. And they are frequently gloomy, pensive and pessimistic in tone. These factors are evident in other crime fiction traditions, but combined in the Scandinavian crime novel they form a unique constellation. (2011: 2)

I would add here that the dynamics of geography and climate also form an important part of this distinctiveness. (And see *Death in a Cold Climate: A Guide to Scandinavian Crime Fiction* by Barry Forshsaw (2012) for more on this matter.)

We can think of *The Laughing Policeman* in such terms. The title itself provides a type of ironic commentary on lead detective Martin Beck and his somewhat jaded attitude to life. As Sean and Nicci French say:

> Martin Beck [is] the prototype of the brilliant tormented detective: Thomas Harris' Will Graham, Ian Rankin's John Rebus, Henning Mankell's Kurt Wallander, and many others, owe their existence to him. Beck's malaise is all the more effective for being only partially articulated. There is almost a surfeit of causes: his weariness after years as a detective, his failures as a family man and, suffusing everything in all the books, a sense that something has gone profoundly wrong in social democratic Sweden, as if the crimes he faces are superficial symptoms of a much deeper historical crisis. (2007: vii)

Beck's "malaise" is evident in the general run-down state of his health. We remember, at this point, Moretti's description of Sherlock Holmes as a doctoring presence tending the good health of the Victorian social body. Here the putative doctor is in fact a sick man, with his cold (Sjöwall and Wahlöö 60–61), coughing attacks (18), poor appetite (84), insomnia (180), and stomach pains (210–211). This condition mirrors the generally unhealthy state of the social body he serves (of which more later). Beck cuts an unprepossessing figure, as his self-mocking description of himself ("the snuf-fling Martin Beck," 65) suggests. And, when he looks into the mirror, it is as if into an unfamiliar, saturnine, and even disturbing, reflection: "a tall sinister figure with a lean face, . . . heavy jaws and mournful grey-blue eyes" (66).

As with so many police detectives to follow, Beck's family relations too are poor (this, too, may act as a subliminal reflection of the larger social whole, when we recall that "people's home" tag). Though he gets on well with his daughter Ingrid, his relationship with his wife has completely run out of steam. "He had met her seventeen years ago, made her pregnant on the spot and married in haste. He had . . . repented at leisure" (105). Accordingly, when Beck uses the excuse of his late hours on the job to sleep on a sofa bed in the living room, he finds it "a relief not to have to share a bed with her" (18). Beck takes part in the family celebrations at Christmas (the festival around which the book is in part structured) but has no emotional connection to them – is a type of alien within his own home.

The title of the book relates in part to this family Christmas. Ingrid has noticed her father's general melancholy ("I haven't seen you laugh since last spring," 181) and looks to change this with her Christmas present to him: a record of "The Laughing Policeman," sung by British music-hall and radio comedian Charles Penrose. The song (which at the time of writing can be heard on YouTube), first recorded in 1922 but still relatively well-known today, has a series of verses each of which are followed by a chorus of extended laughter. Martin's family find its humor infectious and "how[l] with mirth" while it plays, but Martin himself is "left utterly cold" (212). If this functions as sign of his general weariness and malaise, it also has a larger function. The starting lyrics of the song run as follows:

> I know a fat old policeman / He's always on our street. / A fat and jolly red-faced man / He really is a treat.
> He's too kind for a policeman / He's never known to frown. / And everybody says / He is the happiest man in town!
> He laughs upon point duty / He laughs upon his beat. / He laughs at everybody / When he's walking in the street.
> He never can stop laughing / He says he's never tried. / But once he did arrest a man / And laughed until he cried!
> Oh ho ho ho ho ho ho. Ha ha ha ha ha ha. Ho ho ho ho ho ho ho. Ha ha ha ha ha ha.

The B-side of the record – also mentioned in the text – is "Jolly Coppers on Parade" ("[T]heir uniforms are blue / And the brass is shining too. / A finer lot of men were never made . . . ," 212). If "The Laughing Policeman" represents a certain inanity on the part of its title character, nonetheless the general image that come to mind here – and is reinforced in the second-named song – is of the traditional British bobby, highly visible, contented in the job he does and valued by the public: his own overweight but happy body at absolute one with the (assumed) "unitary and knowable body" (Moretti 1983: 145) of the community he serves. And this is exactly what is no longer the case in the policing of Martin Beck's 1960s Stockholm.

This is where we return to the status of Sjöwall and Wahlöö's novel as a police procedural (and one that "articulate[s] social criticism, critiqu[es] national institutions"). I have argued earlier in my chapter on the police novel in Part 2 that, where a police novel exposes the failures of the state and challenges dominant social values, it is usually through an identification with an abrasive individual figure (such as Ian Rankin's John Rebus – and see my later chapter on Rankin) who is, in one way or another, at odds with the larger institution of the police force in which he serves. Sjöwall and Wahlöö are exceptional in writing police novels that focus on the collective inter-actions of a team of detectives yet that nonetheless challenge the apparatus of the state on whose behalf that team is ultimately deployed. I examine here both how this novel works in terms of team detection and also the narrative techniques that allow its social critique to occur.

The police novel often operates in terms of the description of the "collective, grim and often untidy" business of the day-to-day procedural investigation of a crime, and *The Laughing Policeman* fits this model. The authors evidently took their lead here from the American Ed McBain's example. The main criminal act, occurring near the start of the book, is startling and exceptional: the mass murder of nine people including the driver (and one other victim who dies in hospital later), by sub-machine gun fire, on board a red double-decker British Leyland bus late on a 1967 November evening in the outskirts of Stockholm. This type of massacre is more readily associated with American than with Swedish patterns of violence (see Sjöwall and Wahlöö 2007: 109–111), and initially completely baffles Martin Beck and his team of investigators. The case is further complicated by the fact that one of Beck's youngest colleagues, Åke Stenström, off-duty at the time and not officially working on any case in hand, is one of those murdered – and is found with his service pistol at the ready. The clues left for the police to interpret are very few and one of the victims is initially unidentifiable, his face having literally been shot away (40).

Beck's team follow up what leads they can but for a good time their efforts seem to be going nowhere. A week after the "bloodbath" (119), "[t]he investigation had so far produced nothing" (122). More than a week later, Beck's closest colleague, Lennart Kollberg, can still say, in response to the Swedish Minster of Justice's published comment about the "intensive manhunt" taking place, that "[i]t . . . would be nice to know whom one was hunting and where the hunt ought to be carried on" (125). As late as page 209, Beck still thinks that "[t]he investigation had stuck fast. And technically . . . it looked like a pile of rubbish."

The authors spend considerable time building up the profiles of the different members of Beck's team, and describing the different avenues they pursue in helping to solve the crime. The white-haired Ek responds to what has happened by noting the oddness of having a British rather than German bus on the route in question, and is well-informed on the technical specifics of the vehicle. His intervention is met with ridicule but later in the case his knowledge proves useful. He explains the positions of the various switches and levers that work the bus doors (thus implying a certain knowledge about these procedures on the killer's part) and explains, too, the mechanism by which the driver knew the number of people on the upper deck of the bus (56–58). Indeed, it is exactly this kind of detailed vehicular knowledge (though not deployed by Ek) that finally cracks the case. For Kollberg realizes the crucial importance of the word "Morris" in Stenström's notebook: that (as by that point is beginning to emerge) it is the latter's private investigation of a previously unsolved case that has led to his death, and that this case could be solved through the car used in that earlier murder – a Morris Minor, virtually indistinguishable from a Renault 4 (the car previously identified as used by that killer) when seen from the front.

All the members of Beck's team have their own distinguishing features and each contributes to the case in different ways. The happily married Kollberg takes on the main handling of Stenström's girlfriend, Åsa Torrell, following his and Beck's discovery of sexually explicit photos of her in the dead detective's desk. Kollberg recognizes his own sexual attraction to Åsa and "vaccinat[es]" (133) himself prior to their meeting by having sex with his own (willing and understanding) young wife, Gun. His determination to break through Åsa's obvious distress and "isolation" (145), the honesty of his dealings with her, and his genuine care for her wellbeing (his and Gun's generosity in taking her into their own home start her process of psychological recovery), break through her frosty resistance to questioning to produce further vital evidence in the case (information about the photos, which – as it happens – are centrally related to it, and further knowledge of Stenström's movements and motives).

As the novel continues, so the hard work and different strengths of the various members of the police task force pay off. Nordin – brought in from Sundsvall (northern Sweden) to assist, and ill at ease in the Stockholm environment – follows up a tip that has a "ninety-nine per cent certainty" of being "useless" (124). Due to his persistence in this task, a small detail (the particular quality and loudness of a man's laughter) leads him to discover the identity of the victim left without a face, and this in turn helps to unlock the murders (both in the unsolved past case and the bus massacre). Meanwhile, Rönn, "not one of the shining lights of the age" but "a useful and capable policeman" (76–77), nonetheless follows up with equal keenness the partially articulated and initially incomprehensible answers to the questions he has asked the man who dies in hospital following the bus shooting. He discovers that the man's words do make sense (and help point to the killer) once he realizes that the American-born victim has reverted to his native English in these final moments.

There is more to say here about the other detectives' roles, but basically what we see here is Beck (who has his own insights too) leading a very tricky investigation that, through a mixture of luck, dogged investigative work, the skilful putting together of evidence, and brain-storming teamwork, eventually reveals the culprit: Björn Forsberg. Forsberg, once a crook and now a respected businessman, has murdered the nine people to disguise his direct involvement with just two of this group, the faceless man, Görannsson, and his tracker, detective Stenström. Görannsson, it turns out, is the only person who knows that Forsberg murdered Teresa Camarão, the victim in the much earlier (1951) unsolved murder case, and Stenström was openly following

Görannsson, looking to panic him into revealing the killer. The plot is complicated, but the movement back from one crime to another earlier one that stands behind it (as in Martín Solares' recent and highly accomplished *The Black Minutes*) is highly effective. The novel, then, works extremely well as a police procedural, showing the interactions (often tense and touchy) between the various team members, and the gradual if untidy move toward the resolution of the crimes, and the justice that follows.

This still, though, leaves the matter of the novel's social criticism to be considered, for this, as I have earlier suggested, is a novel about the state of Sweden in the late 1960s, as well as about the solving of two particular crimes. We might approach this matter first by way of the narrative tactics employed. The narrative is cleverly constructed, shifting between perspectives but subject to the overall authority of a third-person voice. This voice gives a factual overview of the situation at hand; thus, at the start of chapter twelve we are told that "[s]even hours later the time was ten o'clock in the evening. . . . Nothing special had occurred. . . . [T]he state of the investigation was unchanged. The dying man at Karolinska Hospital was still dying" (59). But this voice also encourages the reader in the direction of social critique. So, in a key passage in the novel (and one to which I will later return), we are again told about the current state of the investigation prior to an – apparently irrelevant – interjection about the upcoming Christmas holiday and the frenzy of consumption it brings with it. After commenting on the drying up of tips from the public about the bus murders, the narrative continues:

> The consumer society and its harassed citizens had other things to think about. Although it was over a month to Christmas, the advertising orgy had begun and the buying hysteria spread as swiftly . . . as the Black Death along the festooned shopping streets. The epidemic swept all before it . . . , poisoning and breaking down everything and everyone in its path. . . . [F]athers of families were plunged into debt. . . . The gigantic legalized confidence trick claimed victims everywhere. The hospitals had a boom in cardiac infractions, nervous breakdowns and burst stomach ulcers. (119)

If such explicit commentary is the exception rather than the rule – and here the effect is particularly jarring – nonetheless there are a good number of occasions when such social and political critique is apparent.

The book works through short and snappy chapters (a technique that has now become much of a norm in the genre) and a combination of the third-person narrative voice, a series of different character perspectives, and sequences of dialogue recorded therein. Chapter two of the novel is particularly unusual in presenting events through the eyes of Stenström, and ending at the exact point that his murder is to occur. Chapter sixteen alternates between Beck's and Kollberg's points of view to contrast their very different domestic lives. Beck's late-night phone call to Kollberg, interrupting the latter as he makes love to his wife, stands as a signal both of Beck's own failure to find such intimacy and of the inappropriateness of his intrusion into the domestic space of a colleague.

The move between different perspectives (all of which belong to the detectives on the case) also allows for social criticism. So Nordin compares the hospitality and good-neighborliness of his own (smaller) home town to the "jostling crowds and . . . unfriendly people" of Stockholm, their general hostility to others brought about (at least in part) by fear and insecurity, and the "rowdyism and . . . petty crimes" that go unpunished in the city (123, and see 134–136). Similarly, Stenström notes the "large shabby flats" and "bleak esplanade" (5) he passes, which, together with the signs of the coming winter, make Stockholm an unattractive place to be. The social and political criticism in the text takes a number of forms. So (as above), it is aimed at Stockholm and the poverties of urban living: the failures of urban planning (see 83) and the loneliness and lack of community spirit evident; the "violence, narcotics, thieves, [and] alcohol" (141) that blight everyday life; the immigrant population (here North African and Turkish) and their exploitation and poor treatment by their Swedish hosts (112–117); and the "broken-down and destitute" (122) who live their lives on the city's margins. Such complaints – or variants of them – are common to modern city life in general but take on additional weight in the context of a welfare state society and its assumptions of a government and a citizenry committed to community values and the common good.

But the novel also critiques the position of the police force in terms of its changing role and relation to the larger political order. The novel starts with conflict between the police and those demonstrating outside the American Embassy against the Vietnam war. Many of the police involved "hadn't a clue as to what they were doing or why they were doing it," while others used various excuses, or merely dodged, what they saw as an "unpleasant assignment" (2). The narrator satirizes the motives behind this police presence – with regular police duties neglected because, in the words of the police commissioner, "they were obliged to protect the American ambassador against letters and other things from people who disliked Lyndon Johnson and the war in Vietnam" (4). The scale of the equipment and weaponry (1) used by the police and their abuse of innocent young protestors (their dragging of a thirteen-year-old girl into a squad car "where they twisted her arms and pawed her breasts," 2) is also the subject of sharply ironic comment. The authors return to their title in describing the morning after another Vietnam protest and the "spectacular and utterly chaotic fight" with the police that follows, when they write that "there were very few laughing policemen on this dismal and chilly morning" (202).

We can assume here, I think, that what had been the recent creation of a nationalized Swedish police force (see 66) has gone hand in glove with an increased use of the police as the agents of politics and the state. But it is clear, too, that – more generally – public attitudes to the police have changed: that, in detective Melander's words, "[t]here's a latent hatred of the police in all classes of society" (119, and see 120). This connects with the Penrose song, and its traditional version of the friendly presence of policemen at the very center of community existence. Now, as Beck's daughter reports, she keeps quiet about her father's profession, rather than being able to "boast and be proud" of it as in her earlier childhood years (17–18). Again, we might see this change in attitudes toward the police, and in their public deployment, as one that has been common across the European and American scene since the 1960s. But it takes on a special significance in Swedish society, where it suggests the undermining of a social democratic state by more autocratic and anonymous forms of centralized power.

Sjöwall and Wahlöö save their most intense criticism, though, for the rise of capitalist values in their country and the damage thereby done to the socialist principles on which the welfare state was founded. I have already noted the overt criticism of a consumer society that occurs as the Christmas "buying hysteria" is described, together with the "poisoning" of individual and social health it signifies. More significantly, it is a commitment to the possession of individual wealth and status that helps to explain the main crimes in the novel, both Teresa Camarão's murder and the massacre on the bus. Forsberg has killed the "nymphomaniac" (187) Theresa because of her continued pursuit of him once he has slept with her, and the threat this posed to his plans for a better life through marriage to a wealthy woman. (The sexual politics of the novel are confused – the representations of Gun and Åsa suggest an acceptance of the healthy results of sexual liberation in Sweden; that of Teresa evidences, rather, a more puritanical attitude.) And, when Forsberg kills Göransson and Stenström, it is for private and individualist motives: to save himself from personal ruin and to protect his "children's future" (243); to defend – in his words – "myself and my family and my home and my firm" (246).

Earlier in the novel, Kollberg speaks of a man's killing of a wife who was dissatisfied with their material circumstance as a "[t]ypical welfare-state crime": "A lonely man with a status-poisoned wife who kept nagging at him because . . . they couldn't afford a motorboat and a summer cottage and a car as upmarket as the neighbors" (159). Again the failure of socialist aspirations of a more equal and less competitive society associated with the welfare state gives a specifically Swedish twist to what would elsewhere be seen in terms of the conspicuous consumption of late capitalism, and its other-directed society. So, too, with Forsberg: for, all the repetitions of "my" in the quotation above lead us straight to Gunvald Larsson (another important member of Beck's team), who sees Forsberg's actions in terms of the larger social whole, seeing inequalities of wealth, status, and power as the very key to Swedish crime:

> How I loathe that bastard. . . . I feel sorry for nearly everyone we meet in this job. . . . It's not their fault everything goes to hell and they don't understand why. It's types like [Forsberg] who wreck their lives. Smug swine who only think of their money and their houses and their families and their so-called status. Who think they can order others about because they happen to be better off. There are thousands of such people. . . . We only see their victims. This guy's an exception. (247)

This is the view of just one character but it fits the wider politics of the novel and the authors' Marxist agenda (Wahlöö himself stated that they looked to "use the crime novel as a scalpel cutting open the belly of an ideologically pauperized and morally debatable so-called welfare state of the bourgeois type," qtd. in Winston and Mellerski 1992: 16). Perhaps fortunately, the skill of the two authors in constructing crime novels that are well-plotted, genuinely unusual, and develop the police novel in important new directions tends to disguise their agit-prop agenda. And, though their politics become more evident as the series continues (the very last word in the final novel they wrote is "Marx"!), it is hard to see a point at which their criticism of an existing social system could possibly lead the way to any purer Marxist alternative (the ultimate aim of any truly revolutionary writer).

But it is with Martin Beck that I wish to end. *The Laughing Policeman*'s final twist comes when Månsson – drafted in to help with the investigation, searching for a document held by Stenström, and still unaware that the crime has in fact been solved – phones Beck to say that he has found Forsberg's name written in pencil under the blotter on Stenström's desk (this has been missed by Kollberg and Beck in their earlier search). In other words, the solution to the crime was available right from the start and the whole tortuous investigation and retracing of Stenström's investigative steps in the earlier murder case has been unnecessary. Månsson's question about his information – "Does that tell us anything?" – sets up the last lines of the book: "Martin Beck made no reply. He just sat there with the receiver in his hand. Then he began to laugh" (248). To place Beck finally in the role of the laughing policeman is an effective and witty conclusion to the novel. But it also reminds us of the highly exceptional quality of such laughter. Beck's position throughout the series is that of a thoughtful and self-aware police detective disillusioned by the nature of the social system that he has given his life to protect, and responding, together with his closest colleagues, to their "modern police work" with a mixture of "defeatism [Kollberg will later quit the force] and resignation" (Tapper 2011: 23). Beck "carries out a constant, and mostly losing, battle against loneliness" (Söderlind 2011: 162). He is "troubled but ultimately loyal to his profession" (Winston and Mellerski 1992: 48). Loyal to his colleagues, too, and at the center of the team he leads but all too aware of the flaws and failures of the social system and authorities he serves, Beck nonetheless carries on regardless, doing the best he can in his job and protecting his society as well as he can against disruption (whatever the faults of that society and its own complicity in such crimes). What else, the implication is, is an honest and committed policeman to do? As Rohan Maitzen sums up:

> Beck does not walk down the main streets of Stockholm either untarnished or unafraid. But he still goes to work every day . . . because he believes in [what he calls in *The Man on the Balcony*] . . . 'the protective mechanism of society.' . . . Though he is neither an ideal nor an idealist, his daily drudgery in the service of a system he knows to be deeply flawed is its own dogged kind of moral heroism. (2011: n.p.)

James Ellroy:
The Black Dahlia (1987)

James Ellroy is one of the most distinctive and influential crime writers of the contemporary period. *The Black Dahlia* is the first novel in his *LA Quartet* (*The Big Nowhere*, *LA Confidential*, and *White Jazz*, published in 1988, 1990, and 1992 respectively, complete the sequence). As a whole, the series provides an "explosively charged map of the historical and geographical dynamics" (Cohen 1997: 170) of Los Angeles in the period from 1943 to the late 1950s. In doing so, it lays out not just a bleakly disturbing "alternative history" of the city (Ian Rankin, qtd. in Wroe 2004: 22) but one that speaks resonantly to the social and cultural anxieties and concerns of our own day.

Ellroy's work is quite unlike that of any of the crime writers who preceded him. Ellroy, self-described "demon dog" of American crime fiction, is an astute self-publicist who revels in presenting himself and his writing in terms of outrageous extremes: "these books are written in blood, seminal fluid and napalm!" (qtd. in Jayanti 2001: 7); "I write books for the whole family. . . . That is, if you're the Manson family" (qtd. in Dussault 1999–2000: n.p.). (It is well worth seeing Ellroy in verbal action: there are a good number of examples on the web; see, for instance, Ellroy's official website at http://jamesellroy.net.) One should not, however, be taken in by this. His novels are indeed shocking, violent, and sexually explicit, but always for a highly serious purpose, as he shows "bad white men doing bad things in the name of authority" (Ellroy, qtd. in Wroe 2004: 22) and thereby conducts his exposure of what Horsley calls "the hidden guilt at the core of the American dream" (2005: 147).

Josh Cohen describes Ellroy's novels as "Gothic dramas of criminal excess" (1997: 168). Ian Rankin, happy to acknowledge his own personal

The Crime Fiction Handbook, First Edition. Peter Messent.
© 2013 John Wiley & Sons, Ltd. Published 2013 by John Wiley & Sons, Ltd.

debt to Ellroy, speaks of his "incredible staccato, edgy style that provides extraordinary pace and dialogue" (qtd. in Wroe 2004: 22). *The Black Dahlia* works in part through the intensity and excess to which Cohen alludes – with its compulsively obsessive patterns of behavior, violently broken and rotting bodies (77, 182, 212, 250), face-slashing (344), grave-robbing and necrophilia (287, 326, 328), gruesomely perverted sexual abuse (230), incestuous or quasi-incestuous relationships (319–321, 324, 333), and the like. Such high-octane material drives the narrative forward with the type of dramatic intensity rarely found elsewhere in the genre. As it does so, it also provides an allegorical counterthrust to any expectation of everyday normality, and the individual and social health with which it is associated. For this is a narrative of violent disintegration, of dark doubles, dysfunctional families, and the abuse of power. LA stands here in microcosmic relation to the national whole: "The LA Quartet books use Los Angeles and its limitless potential [a phrase that cuts two ways] as a metaphor for America" (Ellroy, qtd. in Wroe 2004: 23). Any comforting version of the way the American social, economic, and political system works is ruthlessly demolished in the process.

This, too (like *The Laughing Policeman*), is a police novel, and one that raises a series of extremely uneasy questions about American society and its various forms of power and authority. The compulsions and compromises of Ellroy's main protagonists and the fragmented nature of their sense of personal identity, however, together with the complexities, contradictions, and internal fissures of the social and institutional world that surrounds and positions them, make any straightforward reading of the novel in terms of its acceptance of, or resistance to, the social and political status quo seem curiously irrelevant and even outdated (and see Pepper 2000: 26–31). Instead, the "deep-seated indeterminacy . . . , lack of fixed moral guiding posts" (Pepper 2000: 26), and unsettling bleakness of vision that lie at the heart of this fiction have served to make it an appropriate match for the reading tastes (and worldview) of its contemporary and post-modern audience.

Before commenting further on this, however, I return to Ellroy's style and the way in which his critical vision of American social reality is conveyed. In one sense, his novel's popularity is surprising. Ellroy's plot is labyrinthine and the relations between the large cast of characters complicated. He filters events through the consciousness of Bucky Bleichert, the leading protagonist and first-person narrator of this "memoir" (Ellroy 1987: 3) and remembrance of Elizabeth Short, the Black Dahlia, the murdered girl at the text's center. And Bucky's and his colleagues' use of police acronyms and colloquialisms lend a certain resistance to the immediate understanding of the text. So, the first summary report on Betty Short – one that in fact contains a vital clue that the police ignore – reads in part: "Sergeant Shears and I [Russ Millard] will be going to San Diego to question [Elizabeth's] K.A.'s [known associates] there. Between the APB [all points bulletin] on "Red" [a reported male acquaintance of the dead girl] and the L.A. K.A. questionings we should get salient information" (104). And the narrative pace generally of the novel is fast, as the reader is bombarded with information in that "staccato, edgy" manner that Rankin suggests:

> Newton Street Division was southeast of downtown LA, 95 percent slums, 95 percent Negroes, all trouble. . . . Footbeat hacks carried metal-studded saps; squadroom dicks packed .45 automatics loaded with un-regulation dum-dums. . . . The kids on the street were scrawny and bloated, stray dogs sported mange and perpetual snarls, merchants kept shotguns under the counter. Newton Street Division was a war zone. (277)

One of the most distinctive qualities of the novel are its shifts between fact and fiction. The book starts with the zoot suit riots (conflict between Mexicans and white servicemen) of June 1943 (see, for example, "People & Events: The Zoot Suit Riots of 1943" n.d.) and refers in passing to local and national celebrities of the period: boxer Joe Louis (15), jazz-man Stan Kenton, film-star Ray Milland, LA Mayor Fletcher Bowron (38), and many others (including Howard Hughes). More crucially, the fictional Lee Blanchard, Bucky's part-ner, is mixed up with Jewish mobster Ben (Bugsy) Siegel. Similarly, Emmett Sprague (partly responsible for Short's murder) is in a business relationship with Mack Sennett, whose Keystone Kop films play a significant part in the unraveling of the mystery surrounding Betty Short's death. Sennett, too, is – with Sprague's help – responsible for the building of a housing project in the Hollywood hills, and has had the famous Hollywoodland sign erected "to ballyhoo it" (146). The final four letters of this sign are, in fact, being removed by the local chamber of commerce as the book's climax takes place: so making it into the icon and landmark it still is today. If Sprague is a fictional character (Sennett's actual business partner was Harry Chandler, publisher of the *Los Angeles Times*), the main historical details here are accurate.

The most important carryover from fact to fiction, however, is Elizabeth Short, the Black Dahlia, herself. Her 1947 murder remains one of the most famous of Los Angeles' unsolved crimes. Betty had come to the city from Medford, Massachusetts, aiming (like so many others) to enter the film business. Her nickname, probably a result of press sensationalism following her death, came from the black clothes she customarily wore to match her hair – and was probably inspired by the previous year's release of the Veronica Lake movie *The Blue Dahlia* (with screenplay by Raymond Chandler). Short's body (like that in the novel) was severed, her mouth slashed in an apparent grotesquely extended smile. If Ellroy centers his novel on this crime, the historical was (for him) also the present and personal. For, as he has frequently said, his own obsession with the unsolved murder of his own mother (Geneva Hilliker Ellroy) in 1958, when Ellroy was ten (he dedicates *The Black Dahlia* to her), stands behind Bleichert and Blanchard's mutual obsession with the case here. Ellroy would go on to write *My Dark Places* (1996) – part memoir, part investigative attempt to discover the identity of his mother's killer – and would connect his writing of the two texts as follows: "I had to go through a very long journey with Elizabeth Short and write *The Black Dahlia* before I could get to my mother. Elizabeth Short was always the fictional stand-in for my mother. And my mother and she transmogrified, it was quite a heady brew. They are as one, in my mind, much of the time" ("The Black Dahlia: Production Information" n.d.: 5). There is indeed a heady brew here, and one that helps to account for the fierce intensity, and artistic complexity, of a novel that accordingly moves, and to highly successful effect, between fact and fiction, public history and personal obsession, murder mystery and psychodrama.

The doubling of the above murders (Betty Short's and Geneva Ellroy's) gives us an entry point into an analysis of a text constructed around the notion of dark doubles, and working through the blurring of the oppositions that conventionally structure the genre. The compulsive doubling found in and around the text starts with the story of Bucky Bleichart's partnership with fellow policeman Lee Blanchard. Both men, we are told, were successful boxers before becoming cops, but – though very aware of each other's presence and reputation – do not really get to know each other until they are thrown together during the zoot suits riots. Initially a patrolman, Bucky gets to join Lee in the prestigious Central Warrants, following the fight between the two men organized by their superiors to drum up public support for a public bond proposal to upgrade police salaries: as Deputy District Attorney Ellis Loew says of the need to impress the electorate with the quality of the force, "[w]holesome white boxers are a big draw" (Ellroy 1987: 22). The fight is built up by the press (the popular media and its various manipulations of actual events constitute a key theme of the novel) on the basis of the men's different fighting styles: Lee, "Mr. Fire," "the poet of brute strength"; Bucky (so-called for his buck teeth), "Mr. Ice," "the counter poet of speed and guile" (20).

Though Bucky loses the fight, he gets his promotion. He and partner Lee then cement their public reputation in a shoot-out with four suspected "[h]opheads" (68) – three black, one white, all of whom are killed – in the course of their search for a particularly vicious criminal in their jurisdiction, "Junior" Nash. Their new partnership, though, Bucky tells us early on (and retrospectively), was "nothing but a bungling road to the Dahlia. And in the end, she was to own the two of us completely" (11). As this quote suggests, the apparently strong contrast between the two men (fire and ice) disappears as their friendship develops, and as both become obsessed with the murder case. They become instead, and despite continuing differences, a type of twins, even living together in "a sort of triad" (61) with Kay Lake, whom Lee has earlier rescued from an abusive relationship with a convicted bank robber (Bobby De Witt). This household serves – with both men in love with Kay but neither sleeping with her – as a type of perfect (62) alternative family.

The two men's obsession with Elizabeth Short starts with her murder. Lee's intense and single-minded hunt for the killer is driven by the earlier disappearance of his nine-year-old sister, Laurie, when Lee was fourteen (35), his unease with the way he has dealt with her death, and the guilt he feels over it (51, 82). Laurie's fate may mirror Elizabeth's in that Lee assumes "[s]ome degenerate strangled her or chopped her up" (82) – thus Bucky's description of Laurie as "Lee's ghost" (79). Lee's tough masculinity – already suspect given the nature of his non-sexual relationship with Kay and the sobs that Bucky hears coming from his and Kay's shared bedroom (65) – breaks down under the pressure of the intensity he puts into the Dahlia case; and as, taking amphetamines, he pushes himself beyond his limits (Bucky calls him "the Benzedrine man from outer space," 117). As he, once again, breaks down and weeps, his Mr. Fire persona collapses in his assumption of a different, and mentally tortured, identity. Ellroy's exploration of the unfix-edness and fluidity of identity (of Bucky's, Kay's, and Betty's, too) is, indeed, a concern that runs throughout the book – here suggested by Bucky's words as he looks at the weeping Lee, "just [standing] there like the straight man to his own blood kin" (118). Lee's violent outburst when he sees a porno-graphic film in which Betty Short has featured (and in which we assume he imagines his dead sister in Betty's place – see 165–166) is followed by Bucky's discovery that Nash, the man they were meant to be trailing, has meanwhile killed two people in a further armed robbery. Furious with Lee for letting his "ghosts" (171) deflect him from their proper task, Bucky loses his ice-cool sense of self-control and takes on the fiery aspect of his partner, letting the "crimson loose" to smash "my best friend until . . . he was senseless at my feet" (171). Lee then takes off for Mexico, apparently following up the pornographic film connection (for the film seems to have been shot there, and by a Mexican director). He is also looking, though, to stop De Witt, now just released from prison and down in Tijuana (in search of heroin), from taking revenge on both Kay and Lee himself, for it was Lee who was responsible for De Witt's arrest for the bank job. Lee then disappears from the picture until Bucky goes down to Mexico to look for him, only to find his corpse "[c]hopped up with an axe" (248) in an Ensenada burial dump. When his body is dug up, Bucky recognizes the body: sees "Lee smiling like the Dahlia" (250) as worms crawl from his mouth and empty eye sockets.

The fact that Lee's face and victimized condition are compared to the Dahlia (another doubling) symbolically endorses his loss of masculine authority and agency in the emotional and sexual trauma the Dahlia case has caused him. Bucky's finding of his body is also a massive shock in terms of the narrative trajectory of a book that, until this point, has mainly focused on the Lee–Bucky partnership and love triangle. And it is our sense of Bucky's identity that now shifts as he assumes his partner's prior obsession with the Dahlia. If my analysis focuses so much on the complexities of the plot, this is because it is plot that drives this novel, and it is through plot and what it reveals (not through character or authorial point of view) that the text's social critique becomes most apparent.

Bucky, then, takes over Lee's obsessive role. His motives are hard to identify. Initially it seems that he looks to save Betty from the way her death has been sensationalized in the media, with its affixing of that "Black Dahlia" tag. So the Los Angeles *Herald* represents her as "a black-clad, man-crazy delinquent known as the Black Dahlia . . . a slinky femme fatale in a tight black dress" – a line followed by Bucky's "'No,' I said" (100). And his decision, immediately after Lee's disappearance, to stay with the case results from overhearing Ellis Loew's and Jack Tierney's intentions: not (primarily) to continue to give the case high profile to bring justice to the dead girl but to use its publicity to further their own political and police careers. For, as Tierney says, "[t]he girl's a gravy train" (187) in this respect.

Things, though, get more complicated (!) when Bucky meets Madeleine Sprague, daughter of wealthy property developer Emmett Sprague, and a "lookalike" (152) for Betty – and who, after the latter's death, arranges her hair, makeup, and dress to mimic her. If Betty's ambition is to be in the Hollywood film business and if the press play her up as femme fatale, it seems that Bucky, too, has been affected by such images and their cultural power. So, the first time he sees Madeleine, Betty's double, his intense sexual desire for her is sparked (123). The narrative then builds up a series of complex patterns. With Lee gone, Bucky finds himself with Kay in a "family sans patriarch" (191). The "stasis" that results – Bucky's desire for Kay but inability to move on from their prior domestic situation – drives him to Madeleine and to sex with her ("So I brought Kay with me to Madeleine," 191). Madeleine, however, acts as stand-in for the Dahlia. After an orgasmic sexual climax with her, Bucky says that her "Pollyanna grin" and "smeared

red lipstick" remind him of "the Dahlia's death smile" (169). And, again while having sex, he speaks of "coming from hunger. Or from the Dahlia." Seeing her with the lights left accidentally on, he makes "Madeleine Betty," and when Madeleine then tells him she is happy to be Betty Short or, indeed, anyone else he wants her to be, he says, "[s]o Elizabeth Short and I were formally joined" (192). A proliferation of disturbing doubles occurs here, with Bucky, Lee, Kay, Madeleine, and Betty all involved. This continues as Bucky's relationship with Kay then develops sexually and emotionally, following his flight back to her, highly disturbed, after a particularly sadistic and vicious episode of police brutality. At this point, he echoes his earlier phrase, though in this different but related context, in saying: "So were Kay . . . and I formally joined" (213).

From then on the novel swings back and forth between the Bleichert–Kay and Bleichert–Madeleine relationships. Bucky first ends the relationship with Madeleine to build a life with Kay, "content in our monogamy" (236). He then marries Kay. But – still driven by his psycho-sexual needs – he is unable to keep the Black Dahlia (and thus Madeleine too) from his mind, even as he makes love to his new wife (263). As his obsession makes increasing demands on him (264), he starts following Madeleine again as she goes through the routine they once shared (liaisons in her Dahlia get-up with motel sex to follow), but now with other men. After an episode of needless violence on his part when back on police duty (his police career goes up and down in the book's course), Bucky goes back to Madeleine. (Violence and sexuality exist in an uncomfortable relationship with each other throughout the book, and, as it proceeds, Bucky takes on the mantle of explosive violence previously identified with the fiery Lee – see 205, 281, and especially 290.) Kay walks out on him as a result. But it is at this point, too, that he regains his obsession with the criminal case – put aside when the fuller relationship with Kay takes off – and resumes his own (unofficial) enquires in earnest (though he keeps Russ Millard up to date with his significant discoveries, and works with him as he follows them through).

Bucky now makes a series of breakthroughs that lead him back to the Spragues. In a gothic climax, he discovers that Madeleine and her supposed father Emmett are lovers. He finds out, too, that Elizabeth Short (who, it turns out, knows and has slept with Madeleine), psychologically disturbed, short of money, moving from one man to another, had previously contacted Madeleine for help. He learns that Madeline and her father (who, it turns out, owns the house, made over as a Keystone Cops set, where Betty's stag film was also shot) then passed her on to George Tilden, "offer[ing] Betty money to date a nice man [Emmett] knew" (324). Tilden, Emmett's oldest and closest friend, has a perverse obsession with dead bodies and body parts.

But he is also a "disfigured wreck" (322), the result of Emmett's earlier violence on learning of George's affair with Emmett's wife, Ramona, and of George's identity as Madeleine's real father (Sprague has later repented of his actions and gone on to act as George's financial support and part-time employer). George is already interested in Betty, having "got crazy" (324) over her when he saw the pornographic film in which she features – affected in this way, at least in part, because of her resemblance to his daughter Madeleine. Bucky then acts on what he has found out, going to the house where George is living (a nightmare locale, filled with "jars of preserved organs," 328) and killing him in the struggle that ensues. It is only later that Bucky realizes that he has been set up by Emmett to act in exactly this way, as he looks to protect his wife, Ramona. For it is Ramona who has, in fact, instigated the killing of Betty, filled with rage by the "cruelest of jokes" (345) that sees the girl, so like her daughter, together with George (whom she still loves). She has bribed George to join her in this murderous act by promising him "parts of the girl to keep forever" (345).

Where, then, does all this take us? The novel works through a series of dizzying mirroring effects. Bucky and Lee are twinned figures, whose strong differences (fire and ice) dissolve in the course of the narrative as each is obsessively drawn into the Betty Short case. Traditional notions of stable subjectivity collapse in the book as characters merge into one another (Bucky into Lee, Madeleine and Kay into the Black Dahlia) and as we constantly learn that no one is quite what they seem. So Emmett, the powerful Sprague "patriarch" (142), is later revealed as a blubbering coward (323). And Lee, in one of the major surprises of the book, turns out to be a "rogue cop" (254) who himself committed the bank robbery originally attributed to De Witt; who orchestrated the early shootout with the four slain "hopheads" to eliminate the man who was blackmailing him over that crime; and who – it seems – also "had [De Witt] snuffed" in Mexico "to protect his own ass" (247). Madeleine is not just a Black Dahlia lookalike but, as Bucky finally realizes, Lee Blanchard's killer. For – unknown to Bucky – Lee had discovered Madeleine's and George's roles in the crime at an earlier point in the narrative but had kept his silence in exchange for a hundred thousand dollars of Emmett Sprague's money. But that "theft," and Lee's beating up of Madeline's stepfather/lover, had then (we learn) prompted Madeleine to act, both to recover the money and to take her own bloody revenge on Lee. Bucky also learns of Kay's involvement in all this. Her role of comforter and domestic haven, and her hatred of the whole Black Dahlia connection, turns out to be a fraud. For it is she who has collected the money from Emmett on Lee's behalf, knowing that Lee had discovered the identity of the Dahlia's killer (334–336).

Bucky, then, is very much the patsy in all this, taken in by the world of indeterminacy and shifting identities that surrounds him, and denied knowledge of its workings until the text's very end. Nonetheless, it is he who brings some kind of closure to the case even if he is dismissed from the police for his various unprofessional actions during the investigation, and even if Ramona goes publicly undiscovered and unpunished, Emmett has merely a slap on his financial wrists, and Madeleine's time in Atascadero State Hospital (for she has been judged a violent schizophrenic) will be relatively short compared to the severity of her crime. And, at the book's conclusion Bucky is flying to Boston to meet up again with Kay, pregnant with his baby – offered (through, as he sees it, the medium of Betty Short) his second chance at a rewarding domestic life.

This is a fictional world of shifting identities and one where the matter of individual agency is under acute interrogation, with Bucky driven by forces he doesn't understand and subject to events whose real meanings commonly elude him. It is also one where the opposites that normally structure crime fiction dissolve. So, traditional boundaries start to collapse right at the start of the novel when Bucky is involved in the zoot suit riots: when uniformed members of the US army and navy descend on LA's downtown area, using "two-by-fours and baseball bats" to brawl with "zoot suit wearing Mexicans." Faced with those charged with the defense of the nation acting in an illegally violent manner, Bucky is "terrified because the good guys were really the bad guys" (5). A similar confusion of realms inhabits the whole book. Cop Lee is also a crook and Kay has "shack[ed] on both sides of the law" (36). The definition of "bad guys" muddies moral and political categories: Bleichert says in a reported newspaper remark that he became a cop because he "wanted to fight more dangerous opponents [than those met in the boxing ring], namely criminals and Communists" (21). The word "wholesome" is linked to the word "white" implicitly throughout the novel and explicitly in reference to boxers Bucky and Lee (22). But whiteness throughout the novel (for it is the white legal, political, media, and business worlds that are represented in the text) is generally its very opposite. So a casual racism pervades the whole police establishment. The lines between the criminal community and both the business world and the police are constantly compromised (see, for example, 26, 47, 151, 262, 268, 288). The police generally employ a brutal and sadistic violence in the treatment of those who may or may not be criminals (130, 178–179, 207–213). Policing, more generally, is caught up in the pursuit of individual political position (65, 81, 187–188, 303) and in messy internal conflicts. The perverted sexual tastes of individual cops mirror the degradations of the porn industry they supposedly patrol (220 and especially 230). American servicemen, the representatives of their nation, are likewise portrayed engaged in basely obscene sexual practices

(245) in Mexico – and despite that country's assumed position as the racially inferior other to its northern neighbor. Hollywood comedy and the porn industry, too, are portrayed here as two sides of the same coin (313). Good and evil, then, in Ellroy's world become almost impossible to separate out. The indeterminacies of the world that surround Bucky compromise him (even if he remains a kind of hero): his own actions and (mixed) motives always caught up in this morally murky swirl.

The novel's larger critique of the American social and ideological whole – and one that relates to varying degrees to the contemporary period as well as the past – can be found in the cluster of themes centering round the Dahlia herself (and her slashed body), the family, Hollywood, property, and power. Betty is a victim of America's apparent promise. Desiring entry into the realm of romance and stardom, both of which Hollywood epitomizes, she ends up tortured and then dismembered – like the child victims in Victor Hugo's *The Man who Laughed* (a book found at the crime scene) who are similarly treated by the *comprachicos*. The latter, in Ellroy's version of them, are a fifteenth- or sixteenth-century group of Spaniards, who "kidnapped and tortured children, then mutilated them and sold them to the aristocracy so that they could be used as court jesters" (339). Betty's leering smile (her "mouth cut ear to ear") thus mimics Hugo's main character, Gwynplain, as also portrayed in a painting formerly owned by Ramona Sprague (339). Betty then is the victim of the very rich and "silenced by the dominant [social] order," "the atrocities inflicted on [her body] . . . inscriptions of the rage generated by the cruelties and humiliations inflicted within a family characterized by 'gothic hyper-dysfunctionality'" (Horsley 2005:150, quoting Cohen).

But her death implicates more than just a family. If Emmett is the patriarch of the Sprague family, it is the larger white patriarchal social order that is implicitly indicted here. Emmett – married to Ramona Cathcart Sprague, directly descended from "*the* California land grant Cathcarts" (Ellroy 1987: 191–192) – also deals in property: has "built half of Hollywood and Long Beach, and what he didn't build he bought" (136). His empire, though, is built on "greed" (344) and various forms of malpractice and corruption. So, Madeleine describes to Bucky how her father made his money: through

> [g]angster kickbacks and worse. Daddy bought rotten lumber and abandoned movie facades from Mack Sennett [a business partner] and built houses out of them. He's got firetraps and dives all over LA, registered to phony corporations. He's friends with Mickey Cohen [himself "thick with Bowron and half the Board of Supervisors" and other parts of the city administration]. His people collect the rents. (151)

In this power set-up, Sprague and Sennett act as tyrannous masters to their various employee "slaves" (146). And it is no coincidence that Elizabeth is both delivered to her killer by Sprague and murdered in one of his ill-built properties.

Neither is it a coincidence that this property is in the Hollywood Hills, and that "Hooray for Hollywood" (played by the Hollywood High School band to celebrate the alteration to the Hollywood sign) is heard as Bucky makes his way to the murder scene (315). For Hollywood, the very symbol of the American culture industry, is portrayed here as in a perversely unhealthy relationship with the young female victims it attracts (Betty among them). If Sprague's relationship with his daughters has incestuous connotations, Hollywood's relationship with the girls and young women drawn to the industry is, it is suggested, similarly corrupt. This is hinted at early on, with Linda Martin, one of Liz's fellow Hollywood wannabes: for, when Marjorie Graham, with whom Linda has lodged, realizes "God, she's only fifteen," Bucky laconically repliers, "Middle-aged for Hollywood," 115). Such corruption is also implied in the fact that Hollywood has two sides to it: the porn films featuring both these girls as they look to enter the movie business proper are shot on an old Sennett Hollywood set, and one that Sprague himself has worked on (in its Keystone Cops manifestation). Betty's hideous extended smile, moreover, is a grotesque parody of what America expects of its screen goddesses; the violence loosed on her body a sign of the "masculine anxiety and rage," the "violent misogyny" (Cohen 1997: 174, 179) that together form the dark underside of a glamorized Hollywood sexuality – the drive behind the pornographic urge that here goes hand in glove with it. As Lee Horsely says, "the Dahlia's dismembered corpse [ultimately] resists all tidy and reassuring interpretations" (2005: 150). Ellroy uses its grotesque dismemberment to focus what should be read as a searing indictment of the worst (though not the only!) side of American white patriarchy and power.

Thomas Harris:
The Silence of the Lambs (1988)

Thomas Harris is one of the most popular crime writers of the 1980s and 1990s, working in a form that combines crime fiction and gothic horror. The focus on serial killers and the realistic portrayal of the investigative process locate his texts close to the intersection of fiction and fact – especially in the first two of the four-novel Hannibal Lecter series, *Red Dragon* (1981) and *The Silence of the Lambs*. But their portrayal of excessive and transgressive behavior also takes them, in contrast, into the realm of the monstrous and shocking. Harris' most famous creation, "Hannibal the Cannibal" Lecter, has taken on a cultural life extending beyond the limits of any of his books (or the films made from them). So too, to a lesser degree, has his female lead and (in *The Silence of the Lambs*) F.B.I. trainee, Clarice Starling.

Harris' early career was as a crime reporter, and this prefigures the attention to realistic detail in his novels. His later practice, as a writer, of attending police training sessions and conferences speaks of the same concern, while his presence at the 1994 Florence trial of "Il Mostro" (the monster), the Italian serial killer Pietro Pacciani, provided a source for sections of *Hannibal* (1999), the third novel in the Lecter sequence. He also visited the Behavioral Science Unit at the F.B.I. Academy at Quantico at a time when the unit was first exploring the motivations of convicted murderers through interview and psychiatric profiling. This, we should remember, was also the time when serial killing was first being recognized, and named, as a significant form of contemporary crime. The knowledge Harris gained in the course of this first-hand research was strongly to influence his work. For *The Silence of the Lambs*, and *Red Dragon* too, though part police procedurals, also probe the

The Crime Fiction Handbook, First Edition. Peter Messent.
© 2013 John Wiley & Sons, Ltd. Published 2013 by John Wiley & Sons, Ltd.

psychological causes behind the actions of their serial killers: Francis Dolar-hyde in the earlier book; Jame Gumb in the second. There has been considera-ble debate concerning possible real-life models for Harris' protagonists. Dolarhyde and Gumb have characteristics apparently drawn from three serial murderers interviewed by the F.B.I.'s Behavioral Science Unit: Ed Gein, Ted Bundy, and Ed Kemper. Similarly, Lecter, to some degree, resembles William Coyner, a cannibal killer from the 1930s, well-known in Harris' Mississippi home region. Lecter has more in common, though, with figures from literature and myth, with Bram Stoker's Dracula coming particularly to mind.

For, in a shift that has become increasingly common in contemporary crime fiction, Harris moves between genres in his texts. He also departs in other ways from standard crime fiction models. *The Silence of the Lambs* can certainly be placed in this last category, structured round Clarice Starling's successful quest to discover the identity and whereabouts of serial killer Jame Gumb ("Buffalo Bill") before he is able to murder Catherine Baker Martin, the latest woman he has abducted. But (like Harris' previous novel) it is a peculiar type of crime fiction – a type of "anti-mystery" where the detective "still seeks to unmask a murderer, [but where] the killer is known far in advance by the reader" (Simpson 1995: 7). Though the main crimes are successfully solved in this text (and in *Red Dragon* too), the sense of focus, linear development, and strongly forged relationship between perpetrator and victim, all normally associated with the genre, are all placed under considerable strain. Thus, serial murder (Harris' theme) evacuates much of that sense of affect – that intensity of feeling, emotion, and desire – to be found in the relationship between victim and criminal in traditional forms of detective narrative, and of any sense of shared community to which they both belong. In consequence, its representa-tion reflects wider anxieties about contemporary social fragmentation and breakdown. As Barry Taylor comments:

> The absence of any discernible motivated link between killer and victim . . . leads to the criminological classification of serial murder as "motiveless," and so to the shattering of the links which forge the causal and narrative coherence of the "classic" murder. The serial murder is a crime about which no recognisable story can be told. . . . [Serial murder stands as] the sign of a threatening randomness, of a disappearance of meaningful inter-subjective structures, of demotivated action, of the collapse of authoritative models of explanation and interpretation. (1994: 216–217)

In Harris' books, the type of causal and narrative links that Taylor discusses are still, in the case of Jame Gumb – to a limited degree – recuperable. Thus, Gumb – looking to "harvest" (Harris 1991: 323) the skin of his various victims to "mak[e] himself a girl suit out of real girls" (157) – first kills a woman to whom he has got a traceable connection: Frederica Bimmel. For, he met her through his job with the "Mr Hide leather-goods company" (344), and has in fact had a close relationship with her (346). All his other victims, though, are geographically scattered, and have no personal connection to him. It is Lecter, helping Clarice with the case in exchange for information about her personal life, who gives her the clue that the crimes are "*desperately* random" (280): information (as she reflects upon the reason for that "desperately") that allows her to track Gumb down. Until that point, there are no traceable links between the crimes and their perpetrator.

Serial murder, and the discovery of clear reasons and strong personal motivation for its occurrence, becomes even more tricky in the case of Hannibal Lecter. Here, too, the normal trajectory of detective fiction is disrupted in a number of important ways. For, if the genre usually works through its uncovering of dark secrets and restoration of a disrupted social normality, this is not quite what happens in *The Silence of the Lambs*. Lecter's crimes (at least as they are represented in this novel) are motiveless in conventional terms, and the behavioral science that can give insight into Gumb's actions offers little explanation in his case. Indeed, as Lecter (himself a professional psychologist) tells Clarice, the psychology informing the findings of this science is "puerile . . . on a level with phrenology" (18). Lecter kills, maims, and mentally torments his victims seemingly "only for the fun" (124), for the "exquisite" (191) pleasure of tasting other people's pain. He kills Benjamin Raspail, flautist with the Baltimore Philharmonic and one of his clients, because "[f]rankly, I got sick and tired of his whining. Best thing for him, really. Therapy wasn't going anywhere" (57). Incarcerated when the novel begins, Lecter has – even in this confinement – managed to savage a nurse who is helping to treat him for supposed chest pains:

> When the nurse bent over him, he did this to her [Clarice is shown a photograph]. . . . The doctors managed to save one of her eyes. Lecter was hooked up to monitors the entire time. He broke her jaw to get at her tongue. His pulse never got over eighty-five, even when he swallowed it. (11)

We have, then, two serial killers in the text. One, Gumb, can be explained psychologically; the other, Lecter, cannot. Jack Crawford, Starling's F.B.I. boss, when asked "what [Lecter] is," replies: "I know he's a monster. Beyond that, nobody can know for sure" (6). And, when Clarice speaks to Lecter, "[a]bout why you're here [in the Baltimore State Hospital for the Criminally Insane]. About what happened to you," Lecter replies: "Nothing happened to me, Officer Starling. You can't reduce me to a set of influences. You've given up good and evil for behaviorism, . . . nothing is ever anybody's fault.

Look at me, Officer Starling. Can you stand to say I'm evil?" (20). Lecter, then, wounds and kills for no particular (good) reason, or on apparent whim. And it is his monstrousness that suggests how Harris' texts move (like Ellroy's, too) beyond the borders of the detective genre into gothic/horror territory. Thus, Taylor suggests that

> Lecter . . . is not a reviewed, placed and known subject, but a (fatal) object, some thing that happens (keeps happening) in an unrecuperable serial presentness. Generically, the relation of the Lecter narrative to the "classical" rationalist form of the detective story involves a shift toward the codes of Gothic and Horror. (1994: 220)

(Taylor here is speaking of the first two books in the Lecter series. In *Hannibal*, things start to change.)

Lecter's monstrousness, and the powerful charge associated with it, also affect the narrative trajectory of Harris' book. For, if Clarice's solution (with Lecter's help) of the James Gumb murders restores (in an expected way) the social normality disturbed by his criminal actions, as far as Lecter goes, quite the opposite happens. In jail when the novel starts, Lecter ends the novel having made his escape, the source of his monstrosity still unknowable, his powerful aura and freed state overshadowing Gumb's containment. I return to Lecter and his gothic monstrousness in due course.

But there are other ways that, in *The Silence of the Lambs*, Harris adjusts and disrupts narrative conventions normally associated with the crime fiction genre. The very fact that this is part detective novel (focusing on Gumb's murders and the investigative work of Clarice and the F.B.I.) and part transgressor narrative (focusing on the figure of Hannibal Lecter) is highly unusual. Its double structure leads to the different endings described above – with Gumb dead and Lecter drinking a glass of "excellent Batard-Montrachet" (Harris 1991: 350) wine before starting out under a new identity for Rio. As Harris moves between Gumb and Lecter, he explores too one of crime fiction's key subjects: whether psychopathic acts can be explained in terms of prior social and psychological conditioning or whether, rather, evil exists as a motivating principle in itself. That first interest, in the psychological profiling of the criminal mind, has formal implications here, with serial killer Gumb introduced comparatively early on (129) and with the probing of his thoughts to discover what has prompted his violent acts. The fact that we have three different (though interconnected) centers of interest – Clarice's investigation, Gumb's serial murders and their psychological explanation, and Lecter, a type of narrative wildcard, aiding the investigation (in his own self-interest) but also looking to escape confinement – marks this, together with *Red Dragon* (its predecessor in the series and one that follows a similar pattern), as highly innovative texts. Together, they have had a considerable effect on other writing in the genre since they first appeared.

Harris' novel works thematically – as so many gothic novels do – through both its doublings and its oppositional patterns. Thus, Clarice and Gumb are twinned in the text's depiction of parent–child relations. The novel is, in part, about Clarice's professional maturation, as (despite her trainee status) she becomes a successful F.B.I. investigator and gains Jack Crawford's plaudits: "You hit a home run, kid" (336). Crawford acts as one of her two (living) father figures in the novel: choosing her to interview Lecter at the novel's start, encouraging her pursuit of the clues she discovers, and "showing confidence in [her] where nobody can miss it" (65). Lecter, meanwhile, serves as Crawford's dark double, adding his "help" (59) to Crawford's as Clarice moves toward a solution of the Gumb case, and acting as a therapist in his plumbing of her family history, and the recognitions to which this leads.

As Clarice's past and its relation to her present being and state of mind are clarified, and as she successfully comes to terms with that past, she comes to stand (in terms of parent–child relationships) as the positive pole to Jame Gumb's negative. The failure of the mother–child relationship is a recurrent motif in Harris' work and, in Gumb's case, it has damaged him irreparably, acting as the psychological trigger for the murders he commits. His relationship with his would-be-actress mother was broken off when Gumb was two years old, when he was placed in a foster home (343). But Jame has never separated off emotionally from her, never moved on from what Lacan would call the realm of the imaginary to that of the symbolic. He watches video film of his mother in the 1948 Miss Sacramento contest (when he, in fact, was a month-old fetus in her womb) and, responding to her appearance, falls back into child-like mode: "Mom. There was Mom" (269).

Lecter explains Gumb's obsession with moths and their emergence from the chrysalis in terms of the "imago," a term that signifies the emergence of the adult insect into its full beauty but that also, in psychoanalytical discourse, describes "an image of the parent buried in the unconscious from infancy and bound with infantile affect" (157). Gumb's own vision of personal beauty is accordingly bound up with, and inseparable from, his mother's image. He kills the girls to create a suit of female skin (through his tailoring skills) that he envisions will allow him to replicate his mother's identity: as he says to his pet poodle, Precious, "Mommy's gonna be *so* beautiful" (270).

Gumb is trapped in an infantile state, desiring to be merged with his absent mother. But Clarice too has had a traumatic childhood, which (unlike Gumb) she works through in the novel's course. She only does this, though, by remembering and moving forward from that past, and through Lecter's (not disinterested) probings. In Clarice's case, her night-marshal father was killed by burglars/addicts and, two years later, she (at around the age of eight years old) was sent by her mother to live with relatives in Montana. As Lecter looks to discover what lies behind her present feelings of class resentment (21, 277), concealed "rage" (163), and deferred emotional distress (her persistent memory of the screaming of the lambs on her new guardians' ranch before they go to slaughter, 220), Clarice starts to understand that past more fully. In particular, she realizes that the repeated incident at her mother's job – where a crow stole from the motel cleaning cart as her mother scrubbed the bathrooms within (180–181) – provides a metaphor for her mother's failure to cope with the conflicting demands on her, and her consequent decision to send her daughter away for care (see 285).

In the course of the narrative, Clarice works her way through her feelings about the past – and her time in the orphanage where she eventually ended up – to accept what has happened to her, to find "courage" (312) in her memory of *both* her parents, and to move forward confidently into her own mature personal and professional future as one who is now "approved, included, chosen, and not sent away" (277). Harris' effective counterpoint of these two childhood stories forms one important structural strand of the novel.

Another way Harris structures the book is in terms of its oppositional patterns, which (just as in Ellroy's novel) are characterized by their instability. So, for example, the structural opposition between law and criminality – usually the very foundation of the detective novel – is thrown into some question here by the breaking down of the boundaries between Hannibal, the virus infecting the good health of the wider society, and the supposed vaccine, the F.B.I. and its upholding of the law. If Lecter's brilliance as a psychologist, astonishing knowledge, and profiling skills explain the F.B.I.'s use of him as an unofficial consultant, there is more to the blurring of opposites than this. For, throughout his work, Harris suggests that virus and vaccine, law and criminality, good and evil cannot be as neatly separated from one another as we generally like to believe. In *Red Dragon*, a peculiar kinship links F.B.I. special investigator Will Graham to the serial killers he tracks, his vision and imagination disturbingly mirroring that of such monsters: as Lecter tells him, "the reason you caught me is that we're *just alike*" (Harris 1983: 67).

Indeed, the relation between virus and vaccine progressively slips as the Hannibal Lecter series continues. In *The Silence of the Lambs*, Lecter literally becomes the image of the law, wearing a policeman's face (Harris 1991: 232–235), savagely torn from his victim, as a disguise as he escapes from Memphis. Similarly, his relationship with Clarice (and especially the way it develops in *Hannibal*) undoes the firm lines between detective and murderer; indeed, between good and evil. So, in *Hannibal*, it is the monstrous Lecter who punishes Mason Verger, evil representative of the mainstream capitalist and corporate American order, for his "crimes." Harris destabilizes the relationship between hunter and hunted, criminality and law, throughout his texts. His message – echoing the end of *Red Dragon* (see 354) – is that virus and vaccine are not neatly separate, and that the space between what we like to believe in and its opposite, between the civilized and the savage, what we acknowledge and what we suppress, may not be as firm or as wide as we might hope. Deep within each member of our apparently well-ordered society there may yet exist the potential for evil, mayhem, and murderous aggression.

Gothic motifs, then, are strongly foregrounded in *The Silence of the Lambs*, via its doublings, its representation of excess, and its undermining of the conventional oppositional patterns of the crime fiction genre. Such motifs take spatial form with Clarice's descent into the dungeon/labyrinth ("black warren," 345) of Gumb's basement, and move toward the "oubliette" (329) at its center, in the narrative's climactic scene. Harris' horror/gothic antecedents are clear, too, in the novel's self-conscious intertextuality. So, the *National Tattler* features Clarice in its "Bride of Dracula" series (346), unwittingly twinning her with the other victims into whom Lecter sinks his (here metaphorical) teeth. Similarly, Gumb is linked to Frankenstein in the patchwork monster – new womanly self – he would make from the body parts (more specifically the skin) of others (see Young 1991: 30 n. 17).

William Veeder suggests that the power of the gothic lies in its ability to explore and interrogate the cultural norms we take for granted and (at a psychological level) to express repressed desires (see 23). And Harris' most striking use of the gothic in *The Silence of the Lambs*, and indeed in this whole novel series, is with Hannibal Lecter himself and the cannibalism that defines him: thus, Starling knows of his reputation as "Hannibal the Cannibal" (4) even before she is pulled into his case. Hannibal is by far Harris' most significant fictional creation, and – to continue my emphasis on the oppositional patterns of the novel and their blurring – a protagonist who is defined, as Barry Taylor writes,

> through an oxymoronic implosion of definitions: brilliant scientist and bestial madman, a psychiatric case-study who, as a psychiatrist himself, ridicules the models which his captors apply to him, the serial-killer who is a consultant to the police. More fundamentally, Lecter confounds the monstrous and the civilized, the violence of nature and the refinements of culture, the raw and the cooked: he is a cannibal who we first see, in *Red Dragon*, reading Alexandre Dumas' *Grande Dictionnaire de Cuisine*. . . . [H]e is an ethical abomination with whom one is manoeuvered into identification. (1994: 219–220)

Lecter is, crucially, a man of considerable "taste" – a key word in Harris' fiction, and one that contains in itself the definitional implosion described above. Lecter appreciates the finer things in life. His taste is exquisitely developed, both in the material and cultural senses. He is a gourmet (Harris 1991: 26), has an extremely acute sense of smell (16), has drawings he has made of Florence (recaptured through his extraordinary memory) on the walls of his prison cell, and has a refined knowledge of art (17) and music (193) (and see *Hannibal* for more such examples). But, if we generally admire such forms of taste (as a sign of culture and high civilization), its other manifestation – Lecter's taste for human flesh – is an abomination. These two types of taste meet when Lecter, "known for the excellence of his table" (26), serves up the inner organs of Benjamin Raspail as edible delicacies at a dinner party he hosts for the president and conductor of the orchestra for which Raspail plays.

The crossing of boundaries here between the admirable and the abominable shocks and disconcerts the reader. The civilized and the savage, a core opposition in the symbolic system that structures our lives, is completely disrupted in this move. Cannibalism, in both its real and symbolic forms, is an important motif in the history of Western culture. We tend to associate cannibalism with others – with barbarous and uncivilized African or South American "savages." Modern anthropology and archaeology, however, argue that cannibalism was not limited in this way, and that *all* our ancestors were probably cannibalistic. Any division, then, between "us" and "them" – civilized Western European or North American and barbarous savage other – consequently starts to collapse in this recognition. The notion of cannibalism has also been used, though, symbolically: to describe a modern Western capitalism that feeds – in Karl Marx's terms – off the living bodies and blood of its workers (for more on this subject, see Messent 2008).

I would argue that Harris uses Hannibal, and the cannibalism motif, to challenge our contemporary assumptions about both individuality and the larger social order. His introduction of this gothic excess again acts here as a way of exposing what we would normally deny. Confidence in our own "civilized" status may be misplaced, masking hidden urges and appetites that still drive us. Cannibalism then becomes a *metaphor* for the worst aspects of (mainstream) Western culture: the excessive appetites through which we justify our desire to drain the lives of others to meet our own individual (or corporate – and see the representation of Mason Verger in *Hannibal* here) needs. As he is represented, then, in *The Silence of the Lambs*, Lecter becomes, in Maggie Kilgour's words, "a literally cannibal ego . . . the most exaggerated version of the modern Hobbesian individual, governed only by will and appetite, detached from the world and other humans, whom he sees only as objects for his own consumption" (1998: 248).

Lecter's cannibalism provides the key both to an understanding of Harris' novel and the way he uses gothic forms to serious cultural ends. His act – one of the most transgressive we can imagine – becomes a metaphor for the aggressive individualism that lies behind the capitalist system, and provides a way of questioning and turning upside down our normal understandings of our world. And it would be easy to extend the range of such cannibalistic metaphors. For, the fact that Lecter is a psychiatrist is also relevant here, his profession twinned with his cannibal identity. Hannibal penetrates minds as well as bodies: "specializes in getting . . . into one's thoughts [as well as "under one's skin"] and . . . mak[ing] little of the classic body/mind split as he eats bodies and sucks minds dry" (Halberstam 1991: 39). Clarice, here, is Lecter's particular victim, feeling him "like an alien consciousness loose in her head" (Harris 1991: 25). Again here, what we take for refinement (the analyst exploring the mind of the client in the latter's best interests) is revealed as something potentially quite different.

The hint in Lecter's name, too, and references to the excesses of tabloid journalism and its obsessive interest in serial killers, indicate that Harris is warning his readers of their own cannibalistic tendencies: questioning their gratification as they feed voraciously off stories of monstrous and violently perverse acts – and asking what this says about their own good taste. It is tempting too, as Kilgour does, to apply this same metaphor to critics: the critic as cannibal "eager to sink his teeth into fresh kill" (1998: 242).

Gothic motifs of cannibalism and monstrosity, then, are used here metaphorically to undermine the sets of cultural boundaries and differences (and especially that between civilization and savagery) by which we normally structure our lives, and to challenge fixed preconceptions we would normally take for granted, make us aware of possibilities and configurations we would otherwise deny. William Veeder's discussion of the gothic form perfectly fits the use Harris makes of it:

> committ[ed] to the simultaneous exploration of inner and outer, the psychological and the social. . . . Gothic is, of all fiction's genres, the one most intensely concerned with simultaneously liberating repressed emotions and exploring foreclosed social issues, since gothic presents most aggressively the range of outré emotions conventionally considered beyond the pale – incest, patricide, familial dysfunction, archaic rage, homoerotic desire. (1998: 22–23)

In Harris' case (over the course of the Hannibal Lecter series), we can modify this list to take in fratricide, pedophilia, the mutilation and refashioning of the human body, sexual dysfunction, murder, cannibalism, grotesque physicality, and the animal consumption of human flesh. Clarice solves the Jame Gumb case in *The Silence of the Lambs* and has (with Lecter's help) apparently resolved her childhood traumas – silenced the lambs (Harris 1991: 352) that previously woke her from her rest. But Harris' novel, nonetheless, offers a dark and disturbing vision of our contemporary world. And the fact that Lecter is on the loose at the text's end, and that his relationship with Clarice remains unresolved (writing of the night skies, he says to Clarice that "[s]ome of our stars are the same," 351), suggests that the crime fiction genre's conventional endings – and its reassurances of a safely restored normative social "reality," do not quite happen here. The nature of Hannibal and Clarice's relationship will change in *Hannibal* with Lecter's move (shocking in terms of our generic expectations) from dark father to living companion and lover (see Messent 2008: 26–29), and with no representative of the law remaining in sight. Lecter, the supposed embodiment of evil, is on the loose, now with "bride" Clarice in tow. Infection here appears triumphant, with any notion of vaccine cancelled. As he moves between the crime fiction and the gothic form, Harris achieves genuine shock in the vision of the world with which he leaves us, threatening our everyday conceptions of normality to the most powerful effect.

Patricia Cornwell: Unnatural Exposure (1997)

Patricia Cornwell is a prolific crime writer, best known for her creation of fictional protagonist Kay Scarpetta and the series of novels in which she features. Scarpetta is – until *Blowfly* (2003) – Chief Medical Officer in Richmond, Virginia. But she also investigates the murders she comes across in this role. Her detective work is accomplished in a close, and often intimate, working relationship with a few other key law-enforcement personnel.

Cornwell's enormous popular success stems from her use of a central and carefully developed female protagonist, and her representation of the ambiguities and conflicts of that protagonist's role. The close focus on Scarpetta's professional activity, the autopsies she conducts, her interest in the processes of bodily violation and decomposition, and her obsessive attitude toward the corpses she tends – hearing their "silent screams," imagining "the faces of victims in crowds she passed" (Cornwell 1994: 32) – clearly reflect contemporary anxieties about the vulnerability of the human body. They reflect, too, larger concerns about identity and agency in the post-modern world (and see "Crime and the Body" in Part 2). Cornwell also takes the police procedural form to a new level in her protagonist's considerable reliance on techniques of "scientific detection" (of which D.N.A. tracing is the most obvious contemporary example) and on a widespread investigative support network at both a local and a national level. In some (though not all) of her novels, we get a peculiar mixture of such scientific detection and gothic excess, where her "detailed descriptions of autopsy techniques, forensic science and computer technology" run in tandem with representations of "monstrous serial killers [such as Temple Gault and Jean-Baptiste

The Crime Fiction Handbook, First Edition. Peter Messent.
© 2013 John Wiley & Sons, Ltd. Published 2013 by John Wiley & Sons, Ltd.

Chandonne] whose Grand Guignol violence is offset and eventually contained" (Bygrave 2002) by Scarpetta's professional skills.

Throughout my book a main interest has been in how crime fiction addresses the social and cultural problems of its time. Cornwell stands – in many ways – at the conservative end of the crime fiction spectrum. Part of her success, though, comes from her re-writing of crime fiction from a female perspective, and she does challenge accepted gender norms within the genre (and in society at large) in this respect. So, in *Unnatural Exposure*, the eighth novel in the Kay Scarpetta series, Scarpetta's role is oppositional as far as "the discourse of patriarchal power" (Keitel 1994: 181) goes. As Scarpetta comes up against men – and women – who do not expect a woman to be in a position of authority, so Cornwell plays on the gap between such expectations and the challenge her main protagonist makes to them:

> "They said the medical examiner would get here, and for me to watch for him," he said to me.
> "Well, that would be me," I blandly replied.
> "Oh yes, ma'am. I didn't mean anything . . . " His voice trailed off.
> (Cornwell 1997: 20)

Scarpetta's intelligence, expertise, tough assertiveness, and success in her (conventionally "unfeminine") professional area are all consequently emphasized in the novel, and we should not underestimate the importance of such a representation.

Cornwell works to address the problems confronting a woman writing in what is generally recognized as a masculine genre in other ways too. Bodily violations and exposure, given Scarpetta's professional role as a pathologist, naturally play a major part in her fiction. And the appearance of a dismembered body in *Unnatural Exposure* on a landfill site on the outskirts of Richmond would initially seem to promise the connection between urban anxieties and female victimization on which the crime novel commonly relies – as in, say, *The Black Dahlia*. A similar pattern to that in Ellroy's novel appears to emerge here, with the bodily remains of a female murder victim symbiotically linked to the remnants of urban consumption; found among other "decomposing garbage" (22) on this landfill. Such connections, however, prove here to be something of a lure. The narrative swerves from its starting premise, an account of serial murder, as Scarpetta deduces that this death is, rather, a one-off "copycat" version of these prior killings, and as the case turns out to involve close professional and personal connections between the criminal and the investigator quite different from the urban pathologies with which the genre is so often associated. Phyllis Crowder, a microbiologist and medical colleague of Scarpetta, turns out to be the novel's murderer. Her motives include both her resentment of Scarpetta's professional success and the fact that she has been passed over for promotion in her own Richmond job. Though two of the four Crowder victims are female, neither is – as one might normally expect – young or attractive. And considerable play throughout the text is made on the gap between the assumed male identity of the murderer and her actual female status. If such moves are hardly ground-breaking, they do suggest that Cornwell does, to a certain extent, undermine "the unshakable hierarchical pairs of mind/body and male/female" (Nickerson 1997: 751) that traditionally structure the genre (at least in its hard-boiled manifestations).

Cornwell also gives a sympathetic representation of lesbianism in the novel, and what it means to work as a lesbian in a predominantly male profession, in her representation of Lucy, Scarpetta's niece and a computer expert working for the F.B.I. The displacement of Cornwell's own (reported) lesbian identity away from the main protagonist to her niece may suggest, though, that this is not the main item on her writerly agenda (and her readerly market may well play its part in making this the case). But the emphasis on Scarpetta's own heterosexual identity suggests, even in the realm of gender politics, the more conservative aspects of the book. Scarpetta's anxieties about the relationship between the private and professional demands in her life, centering round Benton Wesley, the F.B.I. executive whose on-off relationship with her forms a continuing strand to the series, are apparently resolved in this novel. That this resolution takes the form of Scarpetta's full romantic commitment (the novel ends with the words "'I love you, Benton,' I said," 338) is highly significant in this respect. This closure will in fact prove somewhat misleading (the ongoing relationship with Benton in the series proves complicated, to say the least). But it does reveal the importance of romantic conventions in Cornwell's novelistic armory. Scarpetta's search to match emotional self-fulfillment to a career-based version of female subjectivity turns out to end, over and over, in failure: a failure indicated on a formal level by the way the romance genre continually and uncomfortably intrudes (as it does in this novel) on the crime fiction form.

I would argue, more widely, that any interrogation Cornwell makes of the established social order is more than outweighed by her defense of it. *Unnatural Exposure* works as a police procedural in that Scarpetta is a consulting forensic pathologist for the F.B.I. Her investigative role is heavily reliant on both the local and national police powers at her disposal. As is the norm in the police procedural (and despite the more challenging examples I have given in this book), Scarpetta's actions ultimately and necessarily serve to preserve the status quo – and there is little question of her (or her creator's) own full commitment to that social and political order.

Thus *Unnatural Exposure* privileges, by and large, both whiteness and wealth. Despite Scarpetta's Italian American background, and the references in the novel to Tangier, a small island in Chesapeake Bay, and the archaic dialect of its inhabitants, there is little real concern here with poverty, or with ethnic, racial, or class difference (to recall Nickerson, the "thornier problems" of contemporary American life). Scarpetta lives in a wealthy Richmond suburb and this is symptomatic of a novel where – though one of Scarpetta's clerks is called Cleta (and so may be African American), a Coast Guard chief is called Martinez (but with the first name Ron), and an army colonel is called Fujitsubo – such indications of multi-cultural and (possibly) socio-economic difference count finally for very little. Indeed, there is an odd, and perhaps revealing, passage in the novel when Scarpetta checks out the various chat rooms available on the internet (the criminal, Crowder, teasingly communicates with her via that medium, as well as by e-mail) to comment that

> [t]here was truly something for everyone, places for flirts, singles, gays, lesbians, Native Americans, African Americans, and for evil. People who preferred bondage, sadomasochism, group sex, bestiality, incest, were welcome to find each other and exchange pornographic art. The FBI could do nothing about it. (210)

There is just a hint here, in the slippages of Scarpetta's language, and despite the sympathetic representation of lesbianism in the novel, that the further away from a heterosexual white American norm one ventures, the closer one gets to "evil"; and that, in terms of moral and sexual preference, bondage is on the same scale as bestiality. Equally, the move from particular social types to a metaphysical category (evil) and from various forms of unconventional sexual practice to a trans-cultural taboo (incest) may suggest something of the conservative novelistic imagination at work here.

This is similarly implicit in the description of criminal activity the text portrays. Anxieties about the violent underbelly of urban American life might be raised in the initial discovery of the severed female corpse. But rather different anxieties are consequently triggered about the ability of a single crazed individual to hold a nation (and even the world) to ransom through a form of germ warfare. (It is the fact that the virus Crowder creates is non-replicating, and not Scarpetta's detective work, that prevents widespread disaster.) The eruption of crime in this novel is signaled by the "eruptions" (55) and "fulminating pustules" (330) that mark the bodies of its victims. In a somewhat extravagant plotline it emerges that Crowder has loosed a mutant version of the smallpox virus on her chosen targets.

Cornwell consigns this crime to the category of pure evil, dependent on the purely personal motivation and disturbed psychological condition of the single criminal figure. And to do this removes it effectively from the world of social cause and effect. At the start of the book, an administrator at the Dublin (Ireland) coroner's office tells Scarpetta that "American violence is so exotic to us." She replies, "That's rather much like calling a plague *exotic*" (7). This, together with the book's prefacing quote from the book of Revelation (about "seven angels [with] . . . seven vials full of the seven last plagues") and the release of the smallpox variant as its main plotline, come together to suggest that *all* criminal violence is plague-like, always waiting to be loosed, part of a Manichean battle between good and evil that is inevitably waged in human societies, and takes an extreme form in America with its prevalence of serial murders ("the Gacys, the Bundys, the Dahmers," 333) and its conspicuous acts of random and widespread violence ("the Unabomber," 143). This way of representing crime is endorsed by Cornwell's constant use exceptionalist discourse – of evil and the monstrous – in the text. Thus, the victims of the initial serial murderer are described as "nothing but symbols of his private, evil credo" (11), while Crowder (still at this point an unknown killer) is simply "the monster" (199). When her identity is finally known, Crowder's eyes are described – in a peculiar trope – as narrowing "like evil" (327), and she is punished not by law but by a more immediate form of (divine?) justice, dying in the same way as her victims.

All this suggests that, though Cornwell is concerned with the various types and extreme forms of violent crime in America, her work does not fully engage (to return to Catherine Nickerson's phrase) "the most anxiety-producing issues and narratives" (1997: 744–745) of American culture. For to consign crime to the world of pure evil and individual moral monstrosity is to isolate it from all economic, social, or political causes, and to explain it as a psychopathic and freakish exception to all that we know to be "normal." Cornwell's is a black-and-white world where evil is pure "other," finally defeated partly just by luck (or perhaps by God's will, for we should remember that Scarpetta is a Catholic, Cornwell 1997: 219), partly by the (mostly) rational, analytic, and commanding figure of the female detective working on behalf of the established social order. As Mike Bygrave sums up:

> Cornwell's world-view closely follows US Christian fundamentalism with its Manichean split between good and evil. She endorses the death penalty, dismisses social explanations for crime and seems to believe that serial killers – an extremely rare phenomenon – are the norm. While clearly the product of her traumatic childhood rather than a developed political philosophy,

Cornwell's views fitted the mood of Reagan's America when she had her first success. (2002: n.p.)

If this implies a somewhat closed socio-political mind, and one that is confident of white Republican righteousness, Cornwell does, however, tap into contemporary cultural anxieties in what is the main focus in the Scarpetta series: the vulnerability of the human body. For there is undoubtedly something deeply disturbing about a series of fictions with a main female protagonist who is "consumed . . . by the dead" (Cornwell 1990: 166), who speaks of understanding their "language" and "muster[ing . . . their] silent armies" (Cornwell 1994: 269, 272), and whose main professional (and, at times, emotional) life centers on the dissection and exploration of their butchered bodies.

The series of explicit references in this novel to the body as infected by H.I. V. and A.I.D.S. might seem to provide an immediate textual engagement with the highly pertinent social problems of its period. Cornwell's depiction of Wingo, the gay man who works with Scarpetta and runs the Richmond morgue, and his status as H.I.V. positive, though, only give us more evidence of a subliminal conservatism. At first glance, Cornwell's attitude would appear to be a highly sympathetic one. When Wingo first comes to Scarpetta to tell her he is H.I.V. positive, she prefaces his confession by saying that

> your life is no secret to me. I don't make judgements. I don't label. In my mind, there are only two categories of people in this world. Those who are good. And those who aren't. But I worry about you because your orientation places you at risk.
>
> (Cornwell 1997: 64)

Scarpetta's liberal credentials are then amply reinforced by her empathy and support when Wingo tells her of his condition and of his fear of A.I.D.S.: "You will not go through this alone. You have me. . . . I will take care of you" (65). However, the fact that Wingo is the one member of Scarpetta's staff who is infected by the virus loosed by Crowder suggests a different reading. For, in a novel where a reference to a divinely inspired plague is introduced in the prefacing quote and where the notion of the criminal spreading of a (potentially) worldwide epidemic of a highly infectious disease stands as a central plotline, that it is H.I.V.-positive Wingo who catches the smallpox variant (and dies from it) is surely far from coincidental. In the chain of connections developed here, the social and moral subtext seems clear. The A.I.D.S. motif is a needless irrelevance in the novel unless it, too, is to be linked to the sense of criminal revulsion and moral condemnation associated with the other "epidemic" (223) threatened. Cornwell's apparent liberalism proves on closer inspection to be somewhat misleading (whatever her authorial intentions): the codes and values of the so-called moral majority are those that are ultimately endorsed.

But I return now to the prevalence of bodily mutilation, dissection, decay, and death in Cornwell as the symbolically disturbing core of her fictions. I have written on this wider subject in the chapter "Crime and the Body" and so will only recap as necessary in the context of this novel. It is Scarpetta's role as a pathologist that defines her – and that makes Cornwell's novels so distinctive. So, particularly detailed attention is paid to the body of the first victim in this novel, and to its dissection for medical and investigative ends. Scarpetta's "painstaking examination" – and realization that "[t]he faces of the pubic symphysis [of the victim], or the surfaces where one pubis joins the other, were no longer rugged and ridged, as in youth" (48) – enables her (unexpectedly) to identify the "hideous stub" (24) found on the landfill site as the body of an old, rather than young, woman. But it is the more gruesome side of such examinations that are, it would seem, a major source of Cornwell's readerly appeal. This works on a relatively low-key level in this novel: Scarpetta making "a half-inch incision" with her scalpel "on the torso's right side" at the site where the corpse is discovered to find "the core liver temperature" and time of death (24); her "sawing off the ends of arms and legs" in the morgue with a Stryker saw (56) to then "deflesh and degrease them" (58, and see 98) so she can examine exactly how the limbs had been severed from the torso. Elsewhere, such details are more grisly (see "Crime and the Body" for examples). This fascination with the physical vulnerability and violent dismemberment of the human body marks both crime fiction and gothic horror: genres (as I have argued) with increasingly permeable boundaries. The interest takes a particular and scientifically detached form in Cornwell's case, as the descriptions of mutilations resulting from the act of murder give way to a primary focus on Scarpetta's own cuttings and dissections of the human body as she conducts her forensic examinations. To recap: there are a number of ways to interpret why readers are drawn to such descriptions. It is, for instance, possible to explain this fascination in terms of larger anxieties about the status of the subject in our contemporary world – our fears of a collapse of the sense of individual authority and control in an ever-more-complex and determining social world, and the accompanying feeling of individual helplessness this brings. Alternatively, it may be that in reading of the dissection and destruction of the bodies of others we allow ourselves, rather, to reconstruct a sense of the wholeness and impregnability of our own bodies, to reaffirm a reassuring (if perhaps misleading) sense of our own autonomy, independence, and secure selfhood.

In my earlier chapter, I noted the gothic doublings that occur in Cornwell's fiction: how Scarpetta's role as detective-pathologist comes uneasily close to that of her criminal counterpart. Both, in their different ways, "brutal[ly] reduc[e] . . . the body into constituent parts" (Horsley and Horsley 2011: 16). This relationship is emphasized in *Unnatural Exposure* as, communicating with Scarpetta electronically (and sending photos of her first victim via e-mail under the name "deadoc"), the murderer, Crowder, establishes her identity as Scarpetta's dark double. Indeed, the autopsy saw marks made on the first victim are a close match to those made by the saw Scarpetta herself uses: "I could not tell which saw marks had been made by the killer and which had been made by me" (Cornwell 1997: 98). "Deadoc," moreover, describes her or himself in the A.O.L. (America Online) Members' Directory using Scarpetta's own personal and professional details: "'It's like deadoc's saying he's you,' Lucy said" (109). The motif of invasion and contamination – one raised early in the text (54) – is evident here, with Crowder ("[a] killer who's like us," 82) turning the professional talents she shares with Scarpetta against, rather using them for the protection of, the law. This twinning – one e-mail message to Scarpetta runs "death doctor death you are me" (208) – raises challenging questions about the precise nature of Scarpetta's professional interests in death, savaged bodies, and bodily decay. It also indicates that Scarpetta's own sense of her own identity may be insecure, deeply fissured. Thus, Lee and Katherine Horsley speak of the Scarpetta/deadoc relationship in terms of its "worrying parallels": of Scarpetta's "constant sense that her work [like that of the murderer] makes her a transgressor, a violator of nature"; that (again like the killer) her closeness to dead bodies may contaminate her links with the larger human community; that her version of "the ambitious, powerful woman" may also have its dark underside (2011: 20–21). Cornwell's texts are riven by such disturbances, such ambivalence about Scarpetta's identity and her relationship to the larger social order. And it is here that the true power of her writing lies.

My final comments on this novel have to do with its representation of urban space and the types of detective work associated with Scarpetta. It is noticeable that both Cornwell's use of a female protagonist and the type of crime fiction she writes work in their different ways to significantly alter the traditional relationship between city space and detection here and elsewhere in her work. First, the battle to police crime in this novel is, in geographical terms, wide-ranging and international. Thus, the forms that crime and crime-solving take here seem to render – in a move increasingly apparent in recent crime fiction – traditional notions of threatening criminal presence in a particular urban domain an outmoded paradigm. Thus, *Unnatural Exposure* starts in Dublin (with serial murders that parallel cases in Scarpetta's

Virginia home territory). Once Scarpetta has returned to Richmond, the novel moves geographically from there to Tangier Island (a small island in Chesapeake Bay), Atlanta, Memphis, Janes Island State Park in Maryland, and Utah. Travel by air becomes more significant than local car journeys as the book proceeds. For, if crime – in a reminder of wider processes of globalization – is no longer contained within the boundaries of a single city or even country, neither is the process by which it is solved.

Cornwell makes it clear here, too, that methods of detection have changed dramatically as a result both of technological change and the necessary reliance on a wider expertise in the solving of crime than that possessed by any one individual investigator or local policing agency. In other forms of detective fiction – and see my earlier chapter on "Vision, Supervision, and the City" – the relationship between the detective and a particular urban space is crucial. Here, though Scarpetta works in Richmond, we read little description of its street-level environment. For the most part, when the narrative is set there, we move between Scarpetta's home ("in the city's wealthiest neighborhood," Cornwell 1997: 238) to the Consolidated Lab Building in which she works. We get almost nothing here of that trawling of city spaces and the reading of the signs to be discovered there that we find, for instance, in Chandler's Marlowe and Walter Mosley's Easy Rawlins novels. Scarpetta is located for much (though not all) of the novel in a series of interior work-spaces – in a hospital isolation ward or behind her own locked front door (155) – and most of her "detective" work occurs in such locations. Almost all we do see of Richmond's urban spaces is through the windscreen of her black Mercedes.

This in turn alerts us to the importance of advances in science and forensics in the solving of contemporary crime. A particular sentence from the novel provides a useful critical prompt here. Exposed herself to the variant smallpox virus, part of Scarpetta's response, when questioned by Benton about her own possible fate, is that "[i]t's easier to worry about stalkers, serial killers, people you can blow away with a gun. But the invisible ones are who I've always feared" (241). If crime fiction has traditionally placed much emphasis on the power of the eye and the I (the perceptive lone detective), the sophistication of modern crime-solving techniques and an increasing emphasis on signs and clues that are *not visible* to the naked eye has led to a major shift of emphasis, and one that is strongly apparent in Cornwell's case. (This connects, of course, with the shift from private eye crime fiction to the police procedural, and its related forms, in the recent period.)

Thus, it is crucial here that Scarpetta has both local and national police and F.B.I. powers, and the high-tech support they can offer, at her disposal in her investigative work. Lucy, involved in the managing of C.A.I.N.

(the F.B.I.'s Criminal Artificial Intelligence Network) and a whiz in the I.T. field, monitors the e-mail messages being passed from Crowder to Scarpetta to discover the geographical location of the message source. Scarpetta does read clues as she visits the scenes of crimes (the facial spray, 175; the corncob pipe, 317), and these help to solve the case. But, for the most part, the available clues are invisible ones – legible by means of microscope or D.N.A. testing rather than the naked eye of the detective – and can only be read with the assistance of a wide variety of police, state, federal, and medical agencies (most referred to by their acronymic labels) scattered over a wide geographical area. Thus, to mention just one of numerous examples, Scarpetta flies to the C.D.C. (the Centers for Disease Control and Prevention) in Atlanta to get exact information on the variant of the smallpox virus she thinks she has discovered in the murder victims. The metaphor of panoptic surveillance and street-level knowledge of a particular urban space loses much of its informing force here. A more complex and multi-dimensional spatial and visual model is necessary to explain contemporary detective fiction and the way it works.

Similarly, the stress on computer technology, and the representation of direct communication with the criminal through such means, sets immediate geographical space against what we might call, to recall Elizabeth Grosz's words, "the screen interface" (1995: 100). Computer technology plays a crucial role in this text. Scarpetta uses the chat room to keep the criminal, who has made contact with her through this medium, online long enough for Lucy to locate her – and this does lead to a crucial breakthrough in the case. Prior to this, though, the criminal stays "coiled in cyberspace" (210), communicating with Scarpetta and frustrating her with the games she plays. Lucy – in a highly distinctive move – actually gets Scarpetta to enter cyberspace, when she takes the e-mail photo Crowder has sent of the room in which her victim lies, and uses the virtual environment lab at Quantico (the F.B.I. Academy) to "immers[e] [her aunt] in [t]he crime scene" (148). Scarpetta, accordingly, finds herself "standing on the floor in the room, as if the photograph had come to life, three-dimensional and large" (150). Though Scarpetta finds this both disorienting and disturbing, it does help in her final recognition of the crime scene. We see, then, in this novel a certain by-passing of the urban spaces conventionally associated with crime fiction in favor of an emphasis on the managing of scientific detection through specialized policing agencies, located over a widespread geographi-cal area, and a focus on hyperreality ("the reduction . . . of the face-to-face encounter to the terminal screen," Grosz: 110). Such changes point to a significant shift of emphasis in the way that contemporary crime fiction generally gains its effects.

Ian Rankin:
The Naming of the Dead (2006)

In my chapter in Part 2 on the police novel, I referred to Lee Horsley's argument that there are two main types of police novel. In one, the emphasis is on the work of a team of police detectives working together to solve a case. In the other, the focus is on just one detective, often a somewhat prickly non-conformist with his (or her) own particular set of values, and (usually) working to one side of, and resistant to, official procedures and interests. In the latter case, Horsley argues, we are also more likely to find a challenge to "the official machinery of law and order" and some realization of its "injustices and failures." "[T]here are many writers," Horsley continues, who use the various forms of detective fiction (*including* the police novel) to "explore the contradictions of contemporary existence" to create "a 'discontinuous' tradition that in a variety of ways has challenged normative thinking (existing social and racial hierarchies, the assumed power structure, establishment values)" (2005: 102).

My readings of Chester Himes, Sjöwall and Wahlöö, and James Ellroy have worked to complicate this picture. Nonetheless, Horsley's focus on the abrasive single detective working on the margins of the larger team of which he is supposedly a part, and challenging assumed power structures and establishment values, remains important – and in many respects Ian Rankin's Detective Inspector John Rebus fits such a bill pretty much exactly. Earlier I argued that the term "police novel" was more inclusive, and provided a better description, of this type of detective fiction than "police procedural." Ian Rankin, perhaps the most popular writer in Britain working in this field (though his main protagonist, John Rebus, is Scottish and based in

The Crime Fiction Handbook, First Edition. Peter Messent.
© 2013 John Wiley & Sons, Ltd. Published 2013 by John Wiley & Sons, Ltd.

Edinburgh, facts crucial to his identity) would seem to agree, emphasizing his own distance from the "procedural" model:

> [T]he thing about the procedural is that at its purest it should be about a team – real-life police-work is very much a team effort. You don't get the "driven loner cop" solving the case single-handedly (nor do you get Chief Inspectors doing basic policing with a sergeant as their "Watson"). Since I am not Joe Wambaugh (I've never been a cop), I make Rebus operate almost as a private eye within the police force – he runs his own investigation parallel to the team effort. This means I don't need to know too much about actual police procedures, since Rebus is seldom going to follow them!
>
> (Rankin 2007: n.p.)

In the sixteenth (of the seventeen) novels in the Rebus series, *The Naming of the Dead*, there is – almost inevitably – some degree of concern with team work and procedure. So Rebus looks for details on the unsolved Cyril Colliar murder case. Colliar, earlier convicted of a vicious rape and now working for Edinburgh crime boss Morris Gerald Cafferty, has been killed by a blow from behind, with a syringe filled with pure heroin injected into his body for good measure. Rebus spreads the bulky paperwork the case has produced across a series of desks in the C.I.D. (Criminal Investigation Department) suite he is using so that, as he walks around the room, he can accordingly "shift between the different stages of the enquiry: crime scene to initial interviews; victim profile to further interviews; prison record . . . ; autopsy and toxicology reports" (Rankin 2006: 32). So, too, Ray Duff's work in the Howdenhall Road Lothian and Borders Forensic Science Unit enables Rebus and Detective Sergeant Siobhan Clarke (his sidekick) to realize that it is not just one murder they are dealing with in the Colliar case but three (66–68). (Rebus reflects wittily here on the way police procedures and media representations of them intertwine, thinking about the "detrimental effect . . . [the] *CSI* franchise had had . . . on all the Howdenhall boffins. Despite their lack of resources, glamour and pounding soundtrack, they all seemed to think they were actors," 66.)

Slightly diverging from Horsley's model, Rebus is not a lone detective, working here in tandem with his junior officer, Siobhan. Her career, though, has been heavily influenced by him and, by and large, she shares his values and ways of doing things. Indeed, in the last few novels in the Rebus series, as Rebus nears retirement – here he has only a year to go (22) – the split focus on the two characters is all about their similarities and differences: whether Siobhan will become another version of Rebus; whether she, too, will be infected by a relationship with Cafferty.

But, if Rebus and Clarke depend to a certain extent on the work of their police colleagues, it is Rebus' non-conformism and resistance to official pressures and interests that primarily characterize him. This novel is, in part, about the anarchist groups that look to cause political havoc at the 2005 G8 Gleneagles Summit – the political event Rankin places right at the structural center of his text. And the author sees his main protagonist as a type of anarchist himself. This is clear in a comment in which Rankin also foregrounds his (related) authorial interest in addressing key social and political issues in his series, and especially as they figure within their Scottish cultural context:

> Since I set out to write books about contemporary Scotland, I try to ensure that each novel focuses on a different aspect of life in Scotland – the economy/oil industry (*Black and Blue*); racism (*Fleshmarket Close*); bigotry (*Mortal Causes*); local politics (*Let It Bleed*); geopolitics (*The Naming of the Dead*); educational divide (*Question of Blood*); etc. . . . . Rebus, of course, is aware that as a policeman he operates on behalf of the establishment, but he is also something of an anarchist himself, more likely to give a small-time crook an even break than some figure of the establishment. Ironically, he does not operate well in an institutional environment, yet has spent his whole life in such (school, then army, then the police).
>
> (Rankin 2007: n.p.)

Indeed, Rebus is also described as an anarchist within *The Naming of the Dead* itself. When he is frustrated by the wall of silence he meets when Labour MP Ben Webster falls to his death from the ramparts of Edinburgh Castle during an official dinner there, and is looking for some kind of business and/or political connection to that death, his journalist friend Mairie Henderson says: "Know what I think? I think all of this is because there's a bit of the anarchist in you. You're on *their* side, and it annoys you that you've somehow ended up working for 'The Man.'" While this may in fact exaggerate Rebus' position as we see it being played out, his response, "I do my best work on the margins" (Rankin 2006: 166), is highly significant. For Rebus is not a team player. "[O]bsessed and side-lined; thrawn [contrary or perverse] and mistrusted" (260), he knows his place in the police hierarchy, "somewhere down amongst the plankton," is the result of "years of insubordination and reckless conduct" (32). And both these last-named qualities mark his behavior in this novel: deliberately flouting the Special Branch as he pushes to find some kind of political conspiracy behind the Webster death; confronting the Minister of Trade over the same issue, while seriously under the influence of alcohol, as the minister dines with his wife at a local restaurant; suspended (along with Siohban) by his chief constable for their persistent refusal to shut down their various investigations – along with the various annoyances they cause in the process – during the summit week.

Rebus (and Siobhan to lesser extent) fit exactly the model of lone cop(s) to which Horsley refers. "Perched" on a very narrow "ledge" (327), and provocative toward his supposed superiors, both inside and outside the force, Rebus is a loose and often unpredictable cannon in the regulated official world of which he is (also) a part.

How then, in *The Naming of the Dead*, does Rankin (through Rebus) interrogate "the assumed power structure" and "establishment values," ask penetrating questions about the larger condition of society? The title of the book carries considerable significance here, for it suggests chains of connection between the personal and political: between individual criminal behavior, dysfunctional family units, and the larger social and political system.

The novel starts with the personal: the funeral of Rebus' own brother, Michael. After the ceremony, Rebus, driving to the crematorium, contacts Siobhan in response to a series of missed calls from her (see Plain 2002: 23–24 and 49–50 on their earlier professional relationship). But the quality of the call is affected (presumably by reception problems) as the scene ends: "'You're breaking up,' Siobhan said. Not if I can help it, Rebus thought to himself" (9). Rankin immediately, then, introduces his detective-protagonist's own intimate relationships and emotional balance as a subject in the book.

The focus on Rebus' family (for his failed marriage is also mentioned at this point) and the various difficulties described concerning his relationship with his dead brother are echoed in the relationship between undercover Special Branch agent Stacey Webster and her brother Ben. Rebus and Stacey are twinned, too, in the sense of commemoration and loss then associated with their respective siblings. When Rebus meets Stacey to talk about her brother's death, his own emotional guard almost slips (on Rankin and the representation of masculinity, see Plain 2002: 52–62). Later in the book, he does "ope[n] up" (61) to Stacey (who – because of her job – has not even been able to attend her brother's funeral) and tells her of his own loss when they go for a drink in a pub. This acts as a release for her suppressed emotions. Asking Rebus, clearly troubled, if what is bothering him is the fact that he never told his brother he was sorry about their difficult relationship (this refers directly to Rebus' having shopped Michael for his drug-dealing but has wider connotations), she herself then breaks down: "She got up . . . [and] fled to the toilets – one hundred per cent Stacey Webster now" – her undercover identity as Santal wiped away. Rebus, left to himself, widens his thoughts to take in some of the other cases in which he is involved, including the serial murder case (with its three victims) that provides the main criminal investigation of the text. Sitting, with his beer glass in front of him, he thinks "about families":

Ellen Wylie and her sister, the Jensens and their daughter Vicky [D.S. Wiley's sister is the victim of an abusive partner, Vicky Jensen is a rape victim], Stacey Webster and her brother Ben . . .
"Mickey," he said in a whisper. Naming the dead so they'd know they weren't forgotten.
Ben Webster.
Cyril Colliar.
Edward Isley.
Trevor Guest [the three men murdered by the supposed serial killer].
"Michael Rebus," he said out loud, making a little toast with his glass. (263)

I return later to the matter of criminality and Stacey's larger role in the book, but it is the stress on memory and commemoration for the dead, the damaged, and the lost on which I focus here. Such an emphasis recalls an earlier textual moment, but one that operates within the novel's political context. In using a real-life event – the G8 summit and the various protests, concerts, and events linked to it – as the locating political crux of his novel, Rankin suggestively shifts ground from a microcosmic study of individual crime and its social effect (and especially the ruptures within families described above) to the larger political and social unit. The coming of the summit to Gleneagles – with an agenda covering such issues as African poverty, climate change, the situation in the Middle East, global terrorism, and the proliferation of weapons – provides an opportunity for all those opposed to current policies in such areas, and to the condition of global politics in general, to demonstrate and protest in both peaceful and militant ways. A sense of crisis and social division (as the actions of those in power meet with large-scale popular resistance) is heightened by external terrorist threat: the 7 July London bombings, which occur while the summit is in session.

Rankin puts this subject matter right at the heart of his text. On its fringes, we have references to the Live8 concerts against global poverty (staged at ten international venues on July 2, 2005 and watched by a huge worldwide audience) and to the Final Push concert on July 6 (which Siobhan Clarke briefly attends). It is Siobhan herself – who as a teenager hitchhiked to Greenham Common, "singing 'We Shall Overcome' as she locked hands with the other women ringing the air base" – who suggests the impact of such events, and of the singers who organize them, on the political process: "Bono and Geldof had managed to breach the G8 security, putting their case to the various leaders. They'd made damned sure those men knew what was at stake, and that millions expected great things of them" (258). Rankin also describes the "[p]anic on the streets of Edinburgh" (128), the center of the city becoming "a war zone" (137) as the demonstrators – some peaceable, some violent anarchists – gather, and confrontations with the police take place. He describes the "[m]ayhem in Auchterarder" (235) as protestors try to breach the police cordon to reach the nearby Gleneagles estate when the G8 leaders fly in. The violence of some of the protestors (and disaffected Edinburgh locals who use their presence as their own excuse for savage riot) and their clever manipulation of the media is not downplayed. But neither are the Orwellian implications of a supervisory police presence, based on "visible strength . . . [v]isors and truncheons and handcuffs" (25), and the preventing of civil liberties being freely expressed. So the police use "Section 60 powers to stop and search without suspicion" (163) and wield batons with all their uniforms' identifying marks removed (178). Similarly, a patrolling soldier at Gleneagles has "no insignia on his uniform, nothing to identify his nationality, or which branch of the armed services he belong[s] to" (240).

Just as Siobhan is associated with civil resistance to establishment authority in her earlier youth, so Rebus too is distanced from the oppressive police actions in the confrontations all around him. He is (officially) kept well away from the novel's landmark political event: as Rankin says, "[i]t . . . amused me that amidst rumours of police reinforcements, limitless overtime for cops, etc, Rebus would be the one detective left out of proceedings – there was no way his bosses would want such a troublemaker anywhere near the G8" (Rankin n.d.: n.p.). Despite his disregard for authority and suspension from duty, Rebus nonetheless manages to remain very much at the center of things, even (unlike the demonstrators) breaching the protective cordon around Gleneagles itself in the course of his own investigations – his and Siobhan's sighting of George Bush falling off his bicycle (247) forms a kind of ironic coda to the book's concern with the working of large-scale political power.

It is clear that, as a result both of the use of Rebus' (and Siobhan's) marginalized points of view and Rankin's descriptive work, the reader is expected to question, and feel uneasy about, many of the ways in which official authority systems work. At a global level, the reference to the Iraq War, and the way that reference is integrated into a larger textual discourse about commemoration and loss, makes it clear that the attitude toward that war is critical rather than celebratory. Siobhan's parents – who had been "students in the 1960s, and had never quite shaken themselves free of the period" (Rankin 2006: 26) – are themselves in Edinburgh as anti-war protestors. Siobhan meets them as they listen to speeches, and – interrupting the conversation they are having together – her father puts a finger to his lips:

"They're starting," he whispered.
"Starting what?" Siobhan asked.
"The Naming of the Dead."

And so they were: reading out the names of a thousand victims of the warfare in Iraq, people from all sides of the conflict. A thousand names, the speakers taking it in turn, their audience silent.

Siobhan gives a "secret, rueful smile" as "the names continued," and connects this act of remembrance to her own police work:

Because this was what she did, her whole working life. She named the dead. She recorded their last details and tried to find out who they'd been, why they'd died. She gave a voice to the forgotten and the missing. A world filled with victims, waiting for her and other detectives like her. (112–113)

The word "victim" here carries the reader from those harmed in acts of criminal violence to those dead and missing in the Iraq war, as the boundaries between the legal and the extra-legal, the official and the criminal act are deliberately narrowed and blurred.

The blurring of such boundaries between what Rebus calls (in a different context) "the underworld" and "the overworld" (213) is, indeed, an ongoing motif in the novel. At the text's conclusion we find out that one of the deaths Rebus and Siobhan are investigating (Ben Webster's) may have been the suicide initially surmised or may have been accidental (399, 407). The other two sets of murders with which they are involved are, though, both private acts of vengeance. One (Tench's) is the result of his emotional betrayal of Denise Wylie, already previously psychologically damaged by her former abusive partner. The other set of serial killings turns out to be a type of red herring, the three killings taking attention from the one that really counts – that of Trevor Guest (the killer who had "torn the Webster family apart," 397) – killed by Stacey Webster to avenge the prior murder of her mother (and the death of her father that had closely followed from it).

Thus, as is so common in all types of crime fiction, murder – an act that usually belongs in the private rather than the public domain – finally draws the reader away from any concern with the larger public and political system. But the flaws in, and anxieties about, that larger system cannot be as easily discounted in this novel as they are in so many others. For the textual space given to "the overworld" of public and legal affairs, and to questions about the way it functions, is considerable. As Rebus first looks to investigate Ben Webster's death, his suspicions focus on Richard Pennen, a businessman with strong British and American government connections. The more he investigates Pennen (many of whose activities are completely legal), the more he uncovers a *moral* morass. Pennen's activities in the field of what is supposedly "foreign aid" (320) are in fact predominantly associated with the arms industry, and particularly with the "[m]oney sloshing around"

(299) as that industry gets involved in the supposed "reconstruction" of Iraq (298–299). The export potential of his various operations is directly tied to the G8 meetings, which facilitate the contracts he is looking to sign (136). His interests are protected both by the British secret service (Steelforth) and by the private (and illegal) security unit he controls. And, though Rebus uses a journalist contact (Mairie Henderson) to expose the extent and nature of his operations, and thus to undermine them, the assumption is that this would not have otherwise happened at any "official" level, where such machinations are (at least to some degree and in some government quarters) accepted practice.

Such questions about the real difference between the way official systems and their criminal counterparts work are insistently raised throughout the text. "Big Ger" Cafferty, the Edinburgh underworld boss who plays a major part in the whole Rebus series – and is associated with a "virus" (352) that damages all with which he comes in contact – is paired with Tench, a local Councilor battling him for control and "muscling in on [Cafferty's] turf" (210). But, despite Tench's work on behalf of the local community, this is no matter of a simple opposition between virus and vaccine. For Tench uses the criminal element in that community to his own ends, and his desire for power and control is seen as a similar version of Cafferty's own drives – and indeed those of all "[t]yrants and politicians" (213). Indeed, though Cafferty's voice cannot be entirely trusted, when he says to Rebus "Sometimes I think that's how half the globe operates. It's not the underworld you should be watching – it's the *over*world. Men like Tench and his ilk" (210), his message is one that is, by and large, endorsed by the text as a whole, leading to Siobhan's conclusion that "the rich and powerful . . . get away with anything they like" (341–342).

The oppositional notion of virus and vaccine as applied to the world of criminality and the law as a whole is also undermined when directly applied to Siobhan and Rebus' police work. For both are damaged by the nature of their relationships with Cafferty. Cafferty is Rebus' "nemesis" (210) – "a kind of devil always standing behind [him]" (Rankin, qtd. in Plain 2002: 13) – and he is compromised in his dealings with Tench as a result. In Siobhan's case, too, an alliance with Cafferty, as she looks to avenge the beating of her mother during one of the G8 demonstrations, comes close to contributing toward Tench's murder (see 341–342), and certainly compromises her status and official position. Ellen Wylie, another policewoman, initially protects her sister from discovery after she has murdered Tench, despite the uniform she wears. And Steelforth, a top Special Branch officer, helps his field operative Stacey Webster (the text's serial murderer) to escape the consequences of her acts. The fact, in turn, that Stacey has killed known sex offenders has meant that none of the other police (bar Rebus and Siobhan) on the case have pursued her crimes as carefully as they might. Rankin presents his readers with a murky world in which everything – Pennen, the G8, serial killing, and so on – is "connected" (408) but in which Rebus can never quite see "the mechanism" that holds them together (156). Rebus and Siobhan cannot do much "to change the bigger picture" (277) but – even despite their personal failings – continue to be (in Siobhan's words) "good copper[s]" (368), working against all the odds (277–278) to act morally and to see justice done, even while remaining aware of their own personal weaknesses and the problematic nature of the larger system within which that morality and justice operate. It is the complex and ambiguous nature of the contemporary world that Rankin represents that makes this novel so powerful and so troubling.

Stieg Larsson:
The Girl with the Dragon Tattoo (2005)

I again move out of chronological sequence here, a move justified by the gap between the first publication of Larsson's novel and its later translation into English, and the massive success that followed. Published as *Men Who Hate Women* (*Män Som Hatar Kvinnor*) in its native Sweden, and translated into English as *The Girl with the Dragon Tattoo* in 2008, Larsson's book has been the most successful crime novel of recent years. In 2010, according to the book-tracking service Nielsen Bookscan, *The Millenium Trilogy* (of which this is the first part) topped the year's bestseller lists, the Quercus edition of *The Girl with the Dragon Tattoo* selling 1 156 530 copies, *The Girl who Kicked the Hornet's Nest* (the final novel in the trilogy) 995 845 copies, and *The Girl who Played with Fire* 957 063 copies. *The Girl with the Dragon Tattoo* was also, as of early October 2011, "the all-time top seller" on Amazon's Kindle e-reader, while e-book sales for the trilogy as a whole stood at over a million (with Larsson as only the second author to break that barrier) (*Daily Mail* 2010).

It is difficult to say exactly what accounts for this success, though publishers' hype and good marketing no doubt play their part. It is the figure of Lisbeth Salander, though, that gives the novels their main distinctive difference from others in the genre. So Tim Parks says: "[o]ne character holds our attention throughout the trilogy . . . : Lisbeth Salander." Once she becomes Blomkvist's researcher, just over half-way through *The Girl with the Dragon Tattoo*, "[a]ll the real energy of [the book] will . . . come from her" (2011: 8). (Salander's

The Crime Fiction Handbook, First Edition. Peter Messent.
© 2013 John Wiley & Sons, Ltd. Published 2013 by John Wiley & Sons, Ltd.

crucial importance here, and in the books to follow, is also suggested by the title of a soon-to-be-published collection of critical essays on Larsson edited by Donna King and Carrie Lee Smith: *Men Who Hate Women and the Women Who Kick Their Asses: Stieg Larsson's Millennium Trilogy in Feminist Perspective*.) Larsson – who died suddenly at the age of fifty before his first novel's publication – structures his novel through a series of initially disconnected perspectives. So we move in its first stages from that of the eighty-two-year-old and as-yet-unnamed Henrik Vanger to retired Detective Superintendent Morell to political and financial journalist Carl Mikhael Blomkvist and then to the head of the Milton Security firm, Dragan Armansky. Salander, who works freelance in "personal investigations" (Larsson 2008: 31) for Armansky's company, is introduced, tangentially, in the context of a meeting called to discuss a report she has written on Blomkvist for Vanger, represented here by his lawyer, Dirch Frode. At this point in the novel, the reader has little inkling that the relationships between three of these five characters – Blomkvist and Vanger, and Blomkvist and Salander – will be crucial to its development. The main focus of Armansky's section is, rather, on the history of his own relationship with Salander, and on the report she then delivers.

Even at this early stage, we learn that everything about Salander and her behavior is both unconventional and unpredictable. She fits the conservative Milton business atmosphere "about as well as a buffalo at a boat show" (33) with her complete failure to conform to accepted forms of office behavior and her startling and unorthodox appearance: thin to the point of anorexic, her dyed black hair "as short as a fuse," "pierced nose and eyebrows," and with "a wasp tattoo about two centimetres long on her neck . . . [and] a dragon tattoo on her left shoulder blade" (33–34). She wears (on this occasion) Doc Martens and a black t-shirt picturing E. T., but with fangs, and the inscription "I am also an alien" (42). She is, however, a whiz at her job – the firm's best researcher, with an ability to gather information like "sheer magic" (32).

We learn more about Salander but little of her family background and history (mysteries to be held over until the next novel). Twenty-four years old but looking much younger, she has been – for the previous twelve years – "under social and psychiatric guardianship" on account of a family judged "dysfunctional," her own perceived "mental deficiencies," a propensity to violence (when provoked), and an apparently emotionally disturbed nature (141–142). Her reclusiveness (Blomkvist calls her "the most asocial being he had ever met," 464) and "sullen silence" in the face of authority – a "resistance to all attempts to measure, weigh, chart, analyse, or educate her" (141) – has helped to form such judgments. Salander is prickly in the extreme, subject to (apparently inexplicable) rages, and quick to withdraw from relationships at the merest hint of any emotional demand or dependency being made on, or expected of, her.

Andrew Nestingen, rightly, sees Salander as both courageous and self-assertive and as "an abject, melodramatic victim" (2011: 181), and it is this peculiar combination of traits that makes her such an unusual fictional figure. Her past is dominated by something that happened to her on the cusp of her teenage years, referred to in this first novel only as "All The Evil" (Larsson 2008: 206) (an event that takes center stage in the next novel in the sequence). Her extreme physical frailty (she is abnormally thin and only four feet eleven inches tall, 296), together with her lack of connection with the majority of those around her (she leaves school an "unloved girl with odd behavior," 206) and unconventional lifestyle and appearance, are perhaps what her sympathetic employer, Armansky, has in mind when we are told that he "had never been able to shake off the feeling that Lisbeth Salander was a perfect victim" (367). She is indeed victimized in a crucial section of this novel in which her newly appointed legal guardian, Advokat Bjurman, sexually assaults her (on what guardianship means in the Swedish context see 201–203). These assaults are depicted in shocking detail, as is appropriate in a novel that takes misogyny as its central subject. First, Salander is physically forced to have oral sex with him (199), and later she is handcuffed to his bed and penetrated with "a huge anal plug" (231) in an act of painfully sadistic "coercion and degradation" and "systematic brutality" (226). We are told, as Salander then does her research on her attacker and his sadistic type, that "[t]he sadist specialised in people who were in a position of dependence" (227). Indeed, Bjurman threatens her with the exercise of his legal power during the first assault, warning that she will be "put . . . away in an institution for the rest of [her] life" (199) should she attempt to make any trouble for him.

The fact that Bjurman has legal authority over Salander, and that she chooses not to report his assaults to the police because of her prior experiences of them as "a hostile force" (203) in her life, forms part of Larsson's critique of patriarchy, and its lopsided relationship between institutional power and morality, justice and individual rights. (We are a long way here from the optimistic vision of the Swedish welfare state that prevailed in the years immediately following World War II.) Always considered, from her school days on, as "unjustifiably violent" (204) due to her willingness to fight back when threatened, bullied, or physically attacked, Salander has learned an important lesson from her earlier (and sympathetic) guardian and mentor, Holger Palmgren: not to act impulsively as had been her previous practice, but to weigh the consequences of such actions before going ahead with them (198). Here she carefully plans revenge on Bjurman, and puts her early thoughts of murder to one side in favor of a more sophisticated strategy that effectively negates his legal power over her. Her revenge, though, (for Salander "always got revenge," 205) also entails a physical payback for the violence and pain he has inflicted on her: for she tasers Bjurman, uses the painful implement he has deployed (the anal plug) on his own body, and crudely tattoos the words "I am a sadistic pig, a pervert, and a rapist" (235) across his torso. She then makes demands, backed up by evidence of his crimes against her, that effectively end his control over her life. (This strand of the narrative is then completed as far as this text goes, but takes further turns as the series continues.)

Later in the novel, Salander saves Blomkvist's life after he has been imprisoned, and is on the point of death, in the hidden basement and "private torture chamber" (394) where Martin Vanger, one of the novel's two serial murderers, keeps his victims. The former abject victim again becomes a powerful agent of punishment and revenge here, as Salander beats Martin into submission with a golf club, "[t]eeth . . . bared like a beast of prey [and] . . . eyes . . . glittering, black as coal" as she moves against him "with the lightning speed of a tarantula" (409). The metaphors are mixed here as Salander becomes at one and the same time both an avenging beast and a venomous spider-woman, not only rescuing her partner but retaliating on behalf of the host of powerless female victims whose lives Martin Vanger has so casually and callously destroyed. Tim Parks sees much of Salander's attraction in her retaliatory function: "a retribution . . . to monstrous criminals . . . all the more satisfying when, in fine Old Testament fashion, it resembles the crime: an eye for an eye, a tooth for a tooth, an anal rape for an anal rape" (2011: 10).

What is interesting here, and throughout the novel, is the almost complete absence of the police in the various narratives of crime and punishment. After Martin has died at his own hands in the car wreck that follows the scene just described, Salander takes complete charge of the action (as Blomkvist, traumatized, finds himself "powerless to act," Larsson 2008: 421). She insists that she, at any rate, will not involve the police in the aftermath of Vanger's crimes – and Blomkvist reluctantly accedes. Her behavior matches the "vigilante individualism" (180) that Nestingen associates with her. Blomkvist, referring to her casual appropriation of (supposedly private) information on his computer, describes her as "an information junkie with a delinquent child's take on morals and ethics" (344). In a world where the power and authority of the state to act on behalf of its citizenry has been compromised in various ways (more on this later), justice appears to becomes the province of the lone vigilante acting largely out of self-interest and for piecemeal principles – but lacking the authority of any thoroughgoing social and moral code. So Salander's actions stem from a dedication to her investigative role (she "loved hunting skeletons," 243), her concern for Blomkvist, and a set of simple and highly personalized principles (of which one is "that a bastard is always a bastard and if I can hurt a bastard by digging up shit about him, then he deserves it," 308). Most importantly, though this is never explicitly said, she is also driven by a concern to avenge wide-ranging gender and sexual abuse. So we are told that "by the time she was eighteen, [she] did not know a single girl who . . . had not been forced to perform some sort of sexual act against her will" (204). And, accordingly, in the investigations she carries out, she uses knowledge gained about pedophilia (32) or abusive male behavior (36) to cause "catastrophe" (32) for those involved. When, too, she finally helps to bring Wennerström (of whom more later) to his death, it is – in considerable part – as revenge for the girl he forced, by an act of physical violence, into an abortion: for he is, as she says, and giving the original title to the book, just "[o]ne more man who hates women" (493, and see 524).

Michael Blomkvist is the yin to Salander's yang. Or rather, in terms of the models of classic detective fiction, his relationship with her echoes that between Holmes and Watson, but with neither party quite fitting the one role. Blomkvist is an astute investigative journalist whose thoroughness and sharp eye for investigative detail help him to make a series of breakthroughs on the Harriet Vanger case (the novel's main narrative), in which he gets involved. At a relatively late stage in the book he forms the partnership with Salander. Her photographic memory (379), "brilliant" research skills (454), and highly sophisticated computer intelligence (she is "the best [hacker] in Sweden," 355) complement his own strengths. Blomkvist is initially defined in Salander's eyes (in her investigation of him early in the novel) as one whose honesty is his "trust capital" and who directs that honesty to larger public ends: "the guardian of robust morality as opposed to the business world" (47). Unusually, the novel is not just about serial murder but starts and ends in the investigation of financial corruption – a field in which Blomkvist's critical methods and objective reporting are held in sharp contrast to the lack of rigor of most others in his profession (90–92). He works for the left-wing (though see 45–46) magazine *Millenium* where "he specializes in investigative reporting about corruption and shady transactions in the corporate world" (46). Indeed, the novel ends with Blomkvist's exposure in *Millenium* (with vital assistance from Salander) of one of his particular enemies, the powerful financier Hans-Erik Wennerström. Wennerström "and his young stockbrokers, partners, and Armani-clad lawyers" are revealed here to be fraudsters on the grandest of scales (517), involved in "all manner of shady [international] enterprises" (522).

Blomkvist, then, is motivated by larger political and economic interests than Salander, and interests vital to the continuing health of the Swedish state. On a personal level, however, and in his work on the Harriet Vanger case, he compromises his own moral and professional standards. He goes along with Salander's decision not to get the police involved once the serial murderers are discovered, on the basis that both killers – Martin Vanger and his father, Gottfried – are, anyway, now dead, and that Salander has insisted on a way (in fact, somewhat unlikely) in which compensation can be made by the Vanger Corporation for their crimes (461). Blomkvist is appalled by being part of what he sees as a "macabre cover-up" (461), with the murdered girls "forsaken" and the whole story buried (464–465). He does so, however, since he is by now emotionally committed to Henrik Vanger, the former (and now again temporary) head of the Vanger family firm, who employed him to discover Harriet's fate in the first place. More crucially, his commitment extends to Harriet herself – discovered alive and living in Australia – whose life would once more be destroyed if the full story were released. Faced with tricky choices between, as Henrik Vanger puts it, his "role as a journalist and . . . as a human being," Blomkvist chooses the latter. And, if Henrik judges this the behavior of a "mora[l]" (531) person, Blomkvist's own self-assessment is harsher. In a detective novel, though, where the machinery of the law is conspicuous by its absence or (later in the trilogy) by its failures, "justice" becomes a complex and ambiguous business, involving choices, costs, and compromises on the part of its imperfect (but, in Blomkvist's case, generally right-thinking and thoughtful) human agents.

I return to the differences, and connections, between Blomkvist and Salander later, and how they fit the novel's larger themes of private and public behavior and responsibility. The type of vigilante justice associated so strongly with Salander, though, forms part of her uniqueness, which gives Larsson's novel its special charge – a vigilante justice, though, that significantly stops short of representing Salander herself as a murderer (see Parks 2011: 10). Undoubtedly, too, the fact that Larsson skillfully adapts the previous conventions of the detective novel form to his own contemporary needs also contributes to the book's success. In my chapter on Patricia Cornwell, I spoke of the way that contemporary detective fiction, and the types of spaces that we associate with it, have been altered by recent technological change and by computer technology in particular. Salander, aka "Wasp" to her online community (354), is an expert in such fields. When Blomkvist is shot at on Hedeby Island (where she and he are staying), it is Salander who knows how to protect their house – with a pressure-sensitive doormat, motion detectors, and light-sensitive video cameras (Larsson 2008: 375–376). It is, though, her computer skills and especially her ability to hack into other people's computers (a crime punishable by two years imprisonment, 354) that are given the most attention here. She knows so much about Blomkvist in the first place because she has hacked into his personal computer. And a related action, the tapping of a private telephone by one of her hacker friends, Trinity, enables both her and Blomkvist finally to find out Harriet Vanger's whereabouts. Most importantly, though, it is her hacking into Wennerström's computer, and "Hostile Takeover" (472) of it, that sets up the whole of the novel's conclusion. For, not only does Salander penetrate the innermost recesses of Wennerström's financial world to expose the corruptions at its heart (money-laundering, the illegal weapons trade, etc.) but she also, with hacker colleague Plague's help, creates "a complete mirror image of the contents of his hard drive" (472) on another server, where she herself can take ultimate authority and control over the financier's whole operational base.

Salander's "bread and butter," we are told, is "spying on people" (297–298). Her ability to penetrate the computers of those she investigates – their supposedly private information and communication banks – makes her an updated version of the Sherlock Holmes type. Parks calls her "omnipotent . . . when [she] goes online" (2011: 12). We might recall here Moretti's discussion of Holmes' detection and that desire for social *transparency* it implies: Holmes' dream to fly out of windows and hover above the city, to "gently remove the roofs, and peep in at the queer things which are going on" (Moretti 1983: 136). Salander's computing skills, and those of her fellow experts, give her the type of liberty to peep in on people's lives that Holmes could never even imagine. The difference is that she uses the knowledge this brings her more for private than for public ends.

I return to this shortly. But I am looking to build up a picture of the various elements that might account for the popularity of Larsson's novel. We see above how Larsson effectively taps into, and updates, a number of key elements of the detective fiction tradition. And, throughout *The Girl with the Dragon Tattoo*, we notice his self-conscious use of his Anglo-American forebears. If Blomkvist has worked as a crime reporter, he also reads lots of crime fiction: Sue Grafton, Val McDermid, and Sara Paretsky – significantly all women crime writers – are name-checked in the course of the book (along with Larsson's main Swedish influence, Astrid Lingren). Blomkvist, too, comes across Mickey Spillane books in Gottfried Vanger's cabin. Henrik Vanger, meanwhile, is a reader of Dorothy Sayers.

Such intertextual references go together with the novel's adept play with different historical forms of detective fiction. So the Vanger case starts off as "a sort of locked room mystery" (Larsson 2008: 85), with a limited number of people trapped on an island (Hedeby) as suspects in Harriet's 1966 presumed murder. And Blomkvist's, and then Salander's, work on the case follows the paradigms of classical detective fiction as they examine old photographs, decode disguised Biblical references, pore over the Vanger corporate archives, and so on, to get the various "jigsaw piece[s]" (279) that compose the mystery to "fal[l] into place" (402). But, as Blomkvist starts to realize that the thirty-year-old case he is investigating is still in fact very much alive, the novel takes on hard-boiled characteristics as his life is put under threat by the serial killer (as Harriet's supposed killer turns out to be) and as he is drawn into active confrontation with one of the murderers. The main transition in the book, though, is from a type of classical detective novel, where the analytic detective carefully and patiently follows a series of clues, to the later use of the gothic mode. For, as Blomkvist discovers a narrative of family crime and serial murder, so the atmosphere of the book takes on gothic resonance, with its story of child abuse, incest, patricide, the sadistic killing of animals, and a buried history of savage and bizarre serial murders that grotesquely parody Biblical punishments. As this happens, and as we move to the climax of the Hedeby Island narrative in Martin Vanger's basement torture chamber, we are transported to a world closer to Thomas Harris than to Agatha Christie. And, though at times the novel creaks more than a little (see, for instance, Parks 2011: 8), Larsson generally manages the difficult transitions from the one missing girl to serial murder, from islanded family crime to nation-wide horror story, with some considerable narrative skill.

As all my comments above may suggest, *The Girl with the Dragon Tattoo* is something of a baggy monster of a crime novel – in particular as it segues from financial crime (Wennerström) to serial murder (Gottfried and Martin Vanger) and back again. This does mean, however, that Larsson is able to engage his reader at a whole range of levels. For there is a series of mysteries established in the course of the novel, the majority of which are resolved but some of which remain unsolved until later in the series. Some of these have to do with crime, others with the relationships between the book's various characters. A selection of these might be given in the form of a list. How does Blomkvist end up in a position where he is prosecuted and jailed for the slander of Wennerström? What are Wennerström's business crimes? How will Blomkvist get his revenge? What is Salander's past and does it help to explain her highly distinctive personality and social unease? What is the event that she names "All The Evil" that stands so significantly in her past? Why is her forty-six-year-old mother (who dies in the course of the novel) institutionalized in a nursing home? And what is wrong with her and why? What will happen to the romantic relationship between Salander and Blomkvist (seemingly at an end at the conclusion to this novel, when

Salander sees Blomkvist with long-time lover Erika Berger)? Who killed Harriet Vanger? Or, indeed, is she dead? Who has committed the ongoing series of serial murders that first Harriet and then Blomkvist discover and how is one to account for the chronology of the killings, which cannot, apparently, be explained by the existence of a single murderer? I could continue, but have done enough to suggest something of the large number of narrative hooks that Larsson builds into his multiple mystery story.

The main narrative of detection in the novel (the Harriet Vanger case) takes, as I have shown, a gothic turn as it continues. And the gothic (see the chapter on Thomas Harris) is a genre particularly suited to the exploration and interrogation of assumed cultural norms. Here the monstrous murders carried out by Gottfried Vanger and his son, the father's sexual abuse of the son, and both father and son's sexual abuse of their daughter/sister Harriet come to stand for the very worst abuses of patriarchy as it functions both within the family and in the larger social world. For the novel is a systematic critique of male power (when seen at its excessive worst). We are prepared for this by the statistics quoted at the start of each of its individual sections, which – taken together – suggest the (extraordinarily) high figures for Swedish male-on-female violence or sexual assault; and one assumes the general outlines of these figures are in no way nation-specific. The representation of Bjurman's assault on Salander and of Gottfried and Martin Vanger's abuse of Harriet (like Salander in Bjurman's case, Harriet eventually fights back, killing her own father in the process) then gives these abstract statistics graphic fictional illustration. The fact that Bjurman is a lawyer and Martin Vanger and his father are corporate executives works to link the worlds of private and public affairs. So Salander's distrust of the police stems, in part, from the fact that she knows they are one part of a larger male establishment and would take the word of a supposed (male) pillar of society over hers if she were to complain of Bjurman's criminal actions. Larsson, too, reopens suppressed aspects of Swedish history, linking Gottfried's father, Richard (brutally violent in his domestic life), to the Swedish Nazi movement of the 1930s (Larsson 2008: 79–80). (The fact that the victims of Gottfried's killings have Jewish names suggests that Gottfried has taken on his father's values.) Both political and corporate activity are here connected to patriarchal power and its sustained violence toward those labeled not just as gender inferiors but as social and racial inferiors too. Gottfried abuses his position in the Vanger firm, a firm that prides itself on the family principles it espouses (404), finding murder victims in its lower echelons, and while he is away at its various branches on business trips. Martin's "godlike feeling of having absolute control" (402) over his own female prey as he carries out his acts of serial murder speaks too of his deep misogyny. The book then is organized (right down to Wennerström and the pregnant waitress he abuses) around "men who hate women," around male power in all areas of society and the eventual payback by its female victims.

If Larsson's sexual politics clearly strike a chord in a contemporary world, they are nonetheless somewhat reductive and at times over-schematic (Tim Parks tends toward the dismissive in his review of the book but is right in seeing its sexual politics in terms of an opposition between the "grotesquely obscene and the charmingly promiscuous," 2011: 10). So Blomkvist is represented as an almost perfect illustration of liberal Swedish gender values, and a man who manages to avoid conventional and patriarchal forms of behavior. He has a long-term relationship with *Millenium* colleague Erika, but theirs is not "the old-fashioned kind of love that leads to a shared home, a shared mortgage, Christmas trees, and children" (Larsson 2008: 55). Erika is married. Her husband, though, accepts her relationship with Blomkvist, just as she accepts the relationships Blomkvist has with other women (staying out of his sexual life when he so signals). Salander falls in love with Blomkvist (528) after an adult lifetime, to that point, of sexual relations (with both men and women) that have taken place only "on her conditions and at her initiative" (211) and that have not been built on any strong emotional commitment.

Blomkvist, though, gets under her (considerable) emotional and sexual defenses. His gentle manner of taking authority on their first meeting disarms her (295) and his calm good humor, failure to react with anything but a literal or metaphorical shrug of the shoulders when she ignores his questions or abruptly walks from his presence, complete lack of any sense of threat or hostility about him (307), and willingness to play a submissive bedroom role (356) lead her quickly to accept him into her emotional and sexual life. And, though he is "baffled" (357) by Salander, Blomkvist holds out the hand of trust, equality, and friendship (380, 383) toward her and she accepts it since "He did not mess with her. He did not try to tell her how to live her life" (453). As someone who illustrates the very opposite of patriarchy's traditional forceful acting out of power, Blomkvist offers Salander good humor, a gentle friendliness, a working relationship based on the appreciation of each other's complementary strengths, and an acceptance of her unusual qualities without any attempt to judge them. Though the relationship founders (unknown, as it happens, to Blomkvist) when Erika re-enters the sexual picture, the relationship with Blomkvist has, nonetheless, brought Salander the kind of contentment (484) that it seems she has not previously experienced. All this may be, as I indicate, somewhat formulaic, but it does help to reverse the representation of the ruthlessly violent exercise of male power represented elsewhere in the novel.

But it is not just Blomkvist who is presented in sympathetic terms in the novel. In giving us twin lead protagonist (Blomkvist and Salander), Larsson offers (even despite the connections between them) two generally opposed views of the relationship between individual subject and the larger community in the modern Swedish state. Similarly, he balances out the negative view of patriarchy as it operates in a business world (Gottfried and Martin Vanger, Wennerström) in his representation of Henrik Vanger. For, and despite his age, Henrik provides a more traditional and sympathetic representation of a family and business patriarch than those others. "A cornerstone of Swedish industry. . . . The backbone of industry in the welfare state," Vanger has a reputation as "an honourable, old-fashioned patriarch" (64). Driven by an ethical conscience, he has put the interests of both the larger community and his particular family of workers alongside the business' own corporate needs. He tells Blomkvist that he has always been a man of his word and a keeper of promises, and continues: "I've never had problems negotiating with trade unions. . . . I was responsible for the livelihoods of thousands of people, and I cared about my employees" (78).

The word "old-fashioned" is significant here, for the assumption is that not just the family business ethics but Swedish business ethics as a whole have changed, as "short-termism and greed" (78) have come into the ascendant. Blomkvist, though, in his role as an investigative journalist, is associated with a desire to keep the best of Swedish business morals and good practices alive (as part of his own overall concern for the health of the larger Swedish community). His published attack on the crooked Wennerström, who masks his sharp practices behind an international web of different accounts and bank holdings, is marked by a genuine "fury" (522), supported by articulate media appearances. In one such appearance, when questioned on the possible catastrophic consequences for the Swedish economy of his revelations, he makes a distinction that strikes a particularly strong chord in our later troubled economic times. He identifies the real Swedish economy with production, "the sum of all the goods and services that are produced in this country every day," and sees this as unchanged by his exposé. The damage to that economy that might occur he puts down rather to speculation, the stock exchange (where "[t]here is no . . . production . . . only fantasies in which people from one hour to the next decide that this or that company is worth so many billions"), and an international share-market driven by "traitors" (520) to their country, concerned only with private profit.

This is a sympathetic (if somewhat unrealistic) position to take, and one that is given some endorsement in Harriet Vanger's new-found involvement with the family company at the novel's end. It speaks, too, of Blomkvist's concern for the state of his nation and its economy, and his desire for a better future on its behalf. Such high principle, however, is compromised – at least to a degree – by the fact that his damning report on Wennerström's business is based on a criminal act: Salander's illegal entry into Wennerström's computer system. Blomkvist and Berger publish their assault on Wennerström's empire on the basis that their sources are confidential and that any hacking cannot be proved, but their journalistic ethics are nonetheless compromised. The fact that they nowhere fully recognize this may signal the fact that in a complex global business world, and one in which electronic media play such a considerable part, the *only* way in which fraudulent and crooked businesses can be brought to book may be through such means.

If we see a concern for the larger community and the state present in Blomkvist's actions, the same is not true in Salander's case. Her distrust of the police and of all forms of state authority speaks of a very different Sweden from that we know from Sjöwall and Wahlöö's novels of the 1965–1975 period. If the Swedish welfare state and its bureaucracy is subject to serious critique in those earlier novels, it serves nonetheless as the measure of political and communal promise by which the social decline of that period can be measured. Here the welfare state is barely even mentioned – the principles on which it was based and its influence on forms of community life no longer, it seems, of much effect. The apparatus of the state is associated, rather (as will become clearer in the following books in the series), with the protection of special interest groups (usually comprising those already in a position of power), a disregard for the rights of those on the margins, an economic system marked by "systematic financial crime" (Nestingen 2011: 180), the existence of a secret security force whose operations run counter to every democratic and moral principle, and a largely ineffectual police force. Though one might argue about the biased nature of such a picture (for, to the outside view, Sweden remains comparatively a progressive and liberal country), undoubtedly – as across Europe – the socialist spirit that drove the welfare state has been replaced by a neo-liberalism marked by a far more individualistic, entrepreneurial, and materialistic culture. Wennerström, in this novel, represents such qualities taken to their extreme, least attractive, and thoroughly illegal limits. Until Blomkvist's intervention, however, he manages to disguise his operations under the mask of respectable and government-sponsored business practice.

Blomkvist's political and business morals find some measure of illustration in the actual practices of Henrik Vanger in *The Girl with the Dragon Tattoo*. Salander, though, and to much more disturbing effect, is twinned in such respects to Wennerström. Just as her "hostile takeover" of his business operations via his computer involves the creation of a "mirror image" of his hard-drive content onto a server over which she has control, so in her own actions Salander mirrors his entrepreneurial and ethically bankrupt individualism – unconcerned with any larger community interest, and flouting any constraints that the law might put in her way. For, in what is the final twist in the narrative, Salander uses her control over the multiple networks that compose Wennerström's business world to wipe out his financial holdings of two hundred and sixty million dollars (Larsson 2008: 525) and transfer it to her own accounts. (The description of her visit, in disguise, to the banks of Switzerland to manage this process, 504–511, is something of a tour de force in its own right.) What is more, Salander then helps to lay the ground for (though takes no active part in) Wennerström's murder, presumably by some of his less-savory "business" associates (524).

The fact that there would appear to have been no great moral shock on Larsson's readers' part to all this speaks to the positive charge he has managed, in the course of the novel, to attach to the figure of Salander – as a victim who has reversed roles with more socially and financially powerful opponents; who has taken on (rather like the protagonist of Thomas Harris' *Red Dragon*) the power of the image – that dragon tattoo – with which she is identified. The fact that Blomkvist is the one person who realizes that Salander has stolen Wennerström's fortune, and does nothing about it but to laugh hysterically (526), implicates him by association with her act. We have seen previously a similar contamination in the more private world of the Vanger family, where Blomkvist goes along with Salander's (and the Vangers') cover-up of Gottfried's, Martin's, and Harriet's crimes. Here it occurs at a much larger public level.

To re-use a previous phrase, Blomkvist and Salander provide the yin and yang of contemporary Swedish business and political life – the one looking back to a more responsible business system and shared sense of social and national wellbeing; the other unhindered by any sense of conventional morality or sense of social belonging and following the main chance when it arises. Both, though, are tied together: Salander in that she opens up the avenue for Blomkvist to expose Wennerström; Blomkvist in his earlier acceptance of Salander's decision regarding the final closure of the Harriet Vanger case and in his later knowledge of Salander's large-scale theft (for that is what it finally is). That Larsson ends his novel with such ambiguities suggests the difficulty he finds in bridging the two responses to the world that he describes, and implies that such an either/or choice may be, in contemporary times, impossible. As he tackles such problems, though, the author has created a character (Lisbeth Salander) who has dramatically caught the public imagination, and has built a detective novel (finally a transgressor narrative) of real power and complexity as he does so.

End Note

I end this book with a few short remarks. I am very aware that the selection of texts I have chosen to explore in Part 3 is to some extent arbitrary, and that many readers would have chosen differently. These particular texts do, however, usefully help to illustrate some of the ideas presented in Part 2. I was, however, torn in the choices that I made, and other authors who were particularly strong contenders at this point included Friedrich Dürrenmatt (*The Pledge*), P. D. James (*An Unsuitable Job for a Woman*), Elmore Leonard (*La Brava*), Henning Mankell (*The Troubled Man*), Georges Simenon (*Maigret in Vichy*), Peter Temple (*The Broken Shore*), Jim Thompson (*The Killer Inside Me*), and Don Winslow (*The Power of the Dog*). I recognize even here, though, the narrowness of my range, and immediately, too, want to add other writers to the mix. But I have to rest with the decisions already in place. There are two final points worth making. The first is to bring to the foreground something that has been implicit throughout: that though this book is dedicated to the crime fiction genre, the very notion of genre is a slippery thing, and perhaps especially in this particular case. Thus, it is the *hybrid* nature of crime fiction that emerges throughout this book, a factor that may indeed have contributed toward that fiction's market success. My numerous comments on the overlap between crime fiction and the gothic, on the absurdist comedy of Himes, and on the strategic use of romance in Conan Doyle and Cornwell all point in this direction. Second, it is worth mentioning the increasing globalization of crime fiction, with (in the United Kingdom and the United States at least) more and more novels appearing in translation and finding a ready audience. Signs of this can be found not just in the explosion of Scandinavian, and other European, crime novels in translation and the market for the very different novels

The Crime Fiction Handbook, First Edition. Peter Messent.
© 2013 John Wiley & Sons, Ltd. Published 2013 by John Wiley & Sons, Ltd.

of, say, Peter Temple (the important Australian crime novelist) and Qiu Xiaolong (whose work forms a bridge between his original Chinese and current U.S. homeland). This increasing recognition of the interest in crime fiction in its international dimensions can also be seen in the establishing of such publishing ventures as the small but significant Melville House "International Crime" series. All this indicates that the crime fiction field is in a particularly strong state of health and looks more than likely to retain its status as one of the most popular yet challenging forms of popular fiction around.

References

Arvas, Paula and Andrew Nestingen. 2011. "Introduction: Contemporary Scandinavian Crime Fiction." In Andrew Nestingen and Paula Arvas (eds.), *Scandinavian Crime Fiction*, 1–17. Cardiff: University of Wales Press.

Auden, W. H. 1948. "The Guilty Vicarage." http://harpers.org/archive/1948/05/
0033206 (accessed November 28, 2011).

Augusta Chronicle. 2005. "Sam Spade, 'Maltese Falcon' celebrate 75 years together."
http://chronicle.augusta.com/stories/2005/02/14/art_442754.shtml (accessed
November 28, 2011).

Auster, Paul. 1988 [1987]. *City of Glass*. In *The New York Trilogy*. London: Faber
and Faber.

Baker, Kerry. 2009. "Great Pretenders: The Performance and Commoditisation [sic]
of Masculine Identity in Patricia Highsmith's *The Talented Mr Ripley* and Bret
Easton Ellis' *American Psycho*." www.crimeculture.com/Contents/Articles-
Winter09/baker.html (accessed November 17, 2011).

Bradbury, Malcolm. 1982. *The Expatriate Tradition in American Literature*.
BAAS Pamphlets in American Studies 9. British Association of American
Studies.

Bradbury, Richard. 1988. "Sexuality, Guilt and Detection: Tension Between History
and Suspense." In Brian Docherty (ed.), *American Crime Fiction: Studies in the
Genre*, 88–99. New York: St. Martin's Press.

Branson, Allan L. 2010. "The Anonymity of African American Serial Killers." www.
crimeculture.com/Contents/Articles-Winter10/branson.html (accessed November 17, 2011).

Burke, James Lee. 2007. *The Tin Roof Blowdown*. Orion: London.

Bygrave, Mike. 2002. "Patricia Cornwell: The Paranoid Detective." *The Independent*, "Profiles," October 20.

Cain, James M. 1947 [1934]. *The Postman Always Rings Twice*. London: Jonathan
Cape.

Cain, James M. 2005 [1936]. *Double Indemnity*. London: Orion.

The Crime Fiction Handbook, First Edition. Peter Messent.
© 2013 John Wiley & Sons, Ltd. Published 2013 by John Wiley & Sons, Ltd.

Camacho, Austin S. 2008. "Why Do We Love Crime Fiction?" http://criminalmindsatwork.blogspot.com/2008/10/why-do-we-love-crime-fiction.html (accessed November 17, 2011).

Chandler, Raymond. 1949 [1940]. *Farewell, My Lovely*. London: Penguin.

Chandler, Raymond. 1962. *The Second Chandler Omnibus*. London: Hamish Hamilton.

Chandler, Raymond. 1979 [1939]. *The Big Sleep*. London: Pan Books.

Christian, Ed. 2010. "Ethnic Postcolonial Crime and Detection (Anglophone)." In Charles Rzepka and Lee Horsley (eds.), *A Companion to Crime Fiction*, 283–295. Chichester: Wiley-Blackwell.

Christie, Agatha. 2002 [1926]. *The Murder of Roger Ackroyd*. London: HarperCollins.

Christie, Agatha. 2007 [1921]. *The Mysterious Affair at Styles*. London: HarperCollins.

Cohen, Josh. 1997. "James Ellroy, Los Angeles and the Spectacular Crisis of Masculinity." In Peter Messent (ed.), *Criminal Proceedings: The Contemporary American Crime Novel*, 168–186. London: Pluto.

Connelly, Michael. 2010 [2009]. *The Scarecrow*. London: Orion.

Connelly, Michael. n.d. "FAQs." www.michaelconnelly.com/Biography/Interviews/FAQs/faqs.html (accessed November 17, 2011).

Conrad, Joseph. 1989 [1902]. *Heart of Darkness*. London: Penguin.

Cornwell, Patricia. 1990. *Post-Mortem*. New York: Avon.

Cornwell, Patricia. 1994. *The Body Farm*. London: Little, Brown.

Cornwell, Patricia. 1996. *Cause of Death*. London: Little, Brown.

Cornwell, Patricia. 1997. *Unnatural Exposure*. London: Little, Brown.

Cornwell, Patricia. 2003. *Blow Fly*. London: Little, Brown.

Creed, Barbara. 1995. "Horror and the Carnivalesque: The Body-monstrous." In Leslie Devereux and Roger Hillman (eds.), *Fields of Vision: Essays in Film Studies, Visual Anthropology, and Photography*, 127–159. Berkeley: University of California Press.

Daily Mail. 2010. "'Girl with the Dragon Tattoo' Author Breaks 1million Barrier for E-Book Sales." July 22. http://www.dailymail.co.uk/sciencetech/article-1296721/Girl-Dragon-Tattoo-author-breaks-1million-barrier-e-book-sales.html (accessed November 30, 2011).

DeCerteau, Michel. 1984 [1980]. *The Practice of Everyday Life*. Berkeley: University of California Press.

Denning, Michael. 1988. "Topographies of Violence: Chester Himes' Harlem Domestic Novels." *Critical Texts* 5:1, 10–18.

Dexter, Colin. 2007 [1991]. *The Jewel that Was Ours*. Basingstoke: Pan Books.

Dollimore, Jonathan. 1999 [1998]. *Death, Desire, and Loss in Western Culture*. London: Penguin.

Doyle, Arthur Conan. 1981a [1892]. *A Study in Scarlet*. London: Penguin.

Doyle, Arthur Conan. 1981b [1892]. *The Adventures of Sherlock Holmes*. London: Penguin.

Doyle, Arthur Conan. 2001 [1890]. *The Sign of Four*. London: Penguin Books.

Doyle, Arthur Conan. 2003 [1902]. *The Hound of the Baskervilles*. London: Penguin Books.

DuBois, W. E. B. 1999 [1903]. *The Souls of Black Folk*. New York: W. W. Norton.

Dussault, Ray. 1999–2000. "Books for the Manson Family: James Ellroy." www.ellroy.com/mansonfamily.htm (accessed November 17, 2011).

Ellroy, James. 1987. *The Black Dahlia*. New York: Mysterious Press.

Ellroy, James. 1988. *The Big Nowhere*. New York: Mysterious Press.

Ellroy, James. 1994. "The American Cop." *Without Walls*. British Channel 4 television program (November 29).

Fitzgerald, F. Scott. 1958 [1925]. The Great Gatsby. In *The Bodley Head Scott Fitzgerald, Vol. 1*. London: Bodley Head.

Forshaw, Barry. 2012. *Death in a Cold Climate: A Guide to Scandinavian Crime Fiction*. New York: Palgrave MacMillan.

Foucault, Michel. 1991 [1975]. *Discipline and Punish: The Birth of the Prison*. London: Penguin.

French, Sean and Nicci French. 2007. "Introduction." In Maj Sjöwall and Per Wahlöö, *The Laughing Policeman*. London: Harper Perennial.

Frisby, David. 1994. "Walter Benjamin and Detection." *German Politics and Society* 32, 89–106.

Fuller, Hoyt W. 1972. "An Interview. Chester Himes: Traveler on the Long, Rough, Lonely Old Road." *Black World* 21: 5, 4–22, 87–98.

Gair, Christopher. 1997. "Policing the Margins: Barbara Wilson's *Gaudí Afternoon* and *Troubles in Transylvania*. In Peter Messent (ed.), *Criminal Proceedings: The Contemporary American Crime Novel*, 111–126. London: Pluto.

Gair, Christopher. 2003. "Theory Comes To Harlem: The New York Novels of Chester Himes." *Twentieth Century Literary Criticism* 139, 314–319.

George, Elizabeth. 2005. *With No One as Witness*. London: Hodder & Stoughton.

Glover, David. 2003. "The Thriller." In Martin Priestland (ed.), *The Cambridge Companion to Crime Fiction*, 135–153. Cambridge: Cambridge University Press.

Grafton, Sue. 1982. *A is for Alibi*. New York: St. Martin's Griffin.

Grafton, Sue. 1990 [1987]. *D is for Deadbeat*. London: Pan Books.

Grafton, Sue. 2010 [2009]. *U is for Undertow*. London: Pan Books.

Grafton, Sue. n.d. "Kinsey Millhone Biography." http://www.suegrafton.com/ kinsey-millhone.php (accessed November 23, 2011).

Grosz, Elizabeth. 1995. *Space, Time, and Perversion: Essays on the Politics of Bodies*. New York: Routledge.

Gruesser, John Cullen. 1999. "An Un-Easy Relationship: Walter Mosley's Signifyin (g) Detective and the Black Community." In Adrienne Johnson Grosselin (ed.), *Multicultural Detective Fiction: Murder from the "Other" Side*, 235–255. New York: Garland.

Halberstam, Judith. 1991. "Skinflick: Posthuman Gender in Jonathan Demme's *The Silence of the Lambs*." *Camera Obscura: A Journal of Feminism and Film Theory* 27, 37–52.

Hammett, Dashiell. 1953 [1929]. *Red Harvest*. In *The Dashiell Hammett Omnibus*. London: Cassell.

Hammett, Dashiell. 1953 [1930]. *The Maltese Falcon*. In *The Dashiell Hammett Omnibus*. London: Cassell.

Harper, Douglas. n.d. "Gunsel." Online Etymological Dictionary. http://www. etymonline.com/index.php?term=gunsel (accessed November 28, 2011).

Harris, Thomas. 1983 [1981]. *Red Dragon*. London: Corgi.

Harris, Thomas. 1991 [1988]. *The Silence of the Lambs*. London: Mandarin.

Harvey, John. 1997 [1996]. *Easy Meat*. London: Mandarin.

Harvey, Sylvia. 1980. "Woman's Place: The Absent Family of Film Noir." In E. Ann Kaplan (ed.), *Women in Film Noir*, 22–34. London: British Film Institute.

Haut, Woody. 1999. *Neon Noir: Contemporary American Crime Fiction*. London: Serpent's Tail.

Haynsworth, Leslie. 2001. "Sensational Adventures: Sherlock Holmes and the Generic Past." *English Literature in Transition (1880–1920)* 44, 459–485.

Highsmith, Patricia. 1977. "Patricia Highsmith" (Conversation with Ian Hamilton). *The New Review* 4: 41, 31–36.

Highsmith, Patricia. 2001 [1955]. *The Talented Mr. Ripley*. New York: Alfred A. Knopf (Everyman's Library).

Himes, Chester. 1974 [1965]. *Cotton Comes to Harlem*. Harmondsworth: Penguin.

Himes, Chester. 1986 [1969]. *Blind Man with a Pistol*. London: Allison & Busby.

Himes, Chester. 1988 [1959]. *The Real Cool Killers*. London: Allison & Busby.

Hoag, Tami. 2010 [2009]. *Deeper than the Dead*. London: Orion.

Horsley, Lee. 2005. *Twentieth-Century Crime Fiction*. Oxford: Oxford University Press.

Horsley, Lee. 2010. "From Sherlock Holmes to the Present." In Charles Rzepka and Lee Horsley (eds.), *A Companion to Crime Fiction*, 28–42. Chichester: Wiley-Blackwell.

Horsley, Lee and Katharine Horsley. 2011 [2006]. "Body Language: Reading the Corpse in Forensic Crime Fiction." http://eprints.lancs.ac.uk/808/1/Body_Language.pdf (accessed November 16, 2011).

Howell, Philip. 1998. "Crime and the City Solution: Crime Fiction, Urban Knowledge, and Radical Geography." *Antipode* 30: 4, 357–378.

Irwin, John T. 1994. *The Mystery to a Solution: Poe, Borges, and the Analytic Detective Story*. Baltimore: John Hopkins University Press.

Jackson, Rosemary. 1981. *Fantasy: The Literature of Subversion*. London: Methuen.

Jameson, Fredric. 1984. "Postmodernism, or the Cultural Logic of Late Capitalism." *New Left Review* 146, 53–92.

Jayanti, Vikram. 2001. "Filmed in Blood, Seminal Fluid and Napalm." *The Independent on Sunday*, "Culture," May 6, 7.

Jefferson, Thomas. 2006 [1781]. "Thomas Jefferson on the African Race 1781. Excerpted from *Notes on the State of Virginia*." http://www.historytools.org/sources/Jefferson-Race.pdf (accessed November 23, 2011).

Johnson, Barbara. 1991 [1973]. "The Frame of Reference: Poe, Lacan, Derrida." In Graham Clark (ed.), *Edgar Allan Poe: Critical Assessments*, Vol. 4, 342–374. East Sussex: Helm Information.

Johnston, Claire. 1980. "Double Indemnity." In E. Ann Kaplan (ed.), *Women in Film Noir*, 100–111. London: British Film Institute.

Kayman, Martin A. 2003. "The Short Story from Poe to Chesterton." In Martin Priestman (ed.), *The Cambridge Companion to Crime Fiction*, 41–58. Cambridge: Cambridge University Press.

Keitel, Evelyne. 1994. "The Woman's Private Eye View." *Amerikastudien/American Studies* 39, 161–182.

Kennedy, Liam. 1997. "Black Noir: Race and Urban Space in Walter Mosley's Detective Fiction." In Peter Messent (ed.), *Criminal Proceedings: The Contemporary American Crime Novel*, 42–61. London: Pluto.

Kilgour, Maggie. 1998. "The Function of Cannibalism at the Present Time." In Francis Barker, Peter Hulme, and Margaret Iversen (eds.), *Cannibalism and the Colonial World*, 238–259. Cambridge: Cambridge University Press.

Knight, Stephen. 1994. "The Case of the Great Detective." In John A. Hodgson (ed.), *Sherlock Holmes: The Major Stories with Contemporary Critical Essays*, 368–380. Boston: Bedford/St. Martin's.

Knight, Stephen. 2003. "The Golden Age." In Martin Priestman (ed.), *The Cambridge Companion to Crime Fiction*, 77–94. Cambridge: Cambridge University Press.

Knight, Stephen. 2004. *Crime Fiction 1800–2000: Death, Detection, Diversity*. Houndmills, Basingstoke: Palgrave Macmillan.

Knox, Ronald. 1946 [1929]. "Detective Story Decalogue." In Howard Haycraft (ed.), *The Art of the Mystery Story: A Collection of Critical Essays*, 194–196. New York: Grossett & Dunlap.

Lacan, Jacques. 1991 [1972]. "Seminar on 'The Purloined Letter.'" In Graham Clark (ed.), *Edgar Allan Poe: Critical Assessments*, Vol. 4, 319–341. East Sussex: Helm Information.

Läckberg, Camilla. 2010 [2004]. *The Preacher*. London: HarperCollins.

Larsson, Stieg. 2008 [2005]. *The Girl with the Dragon Tattoo*. London: MacLehose Press.

Lears, T. J. Jackson. 1983. "From Salvation to Self-Realisation: Advertising and the Therapeutic Roots of the Consumer Culture." In T. J. Jackson Lears and Richard Wightman Fox (eds.), *The Culture of Consumption: Critical Essays in American History, 1880–1980*, 3–38. New York: Pantheon.

Leitch, Thomas. 2004 [2002]. *Crime Films (Genres in American Cinema)*. Cambridge: Cambridge University Press.

"Lewis Michaux's House of Common Sense and Home of Proper Propaganda." 1964. http://www.flickr.com/photos/thefreedwomensbureau/4669273127 (accessed November 29, 2011).

Light, Alison. 1991. *Forever England: Femininity, Literature and Conservatism between the Wars*. London: Routledge.

Madden, David. 1967. "James M. Cain: Twenty-Minute Egg of the Hard-Boiled School." *Journal of Popular Culture* 1: 3, 178–192.

Madden, David. 1968. *Tough Guy Writers of the Thirties*. Carbondale: Southern Illinois University Press.

Mailer, Norman. 1961 [1957]. "The White Negro." In *Advertisements for Myself*, 281–302. London: Andre Deutsch.

Maitzen, Rohan. 2011. "Martin Beck Has a Cold." *Los Angeles Review of Books*, August 5. http://lareviewofbooks.org/post/8507768136/martin-beck-has-a-cold (accessed November 17, 2011).

Makinen, Merja. 2010. "Agatha Christie (1890–1976)." In Charles Rzepka and Lee Horsley (eds.), *A Companion to Crime Fiction*, 415–426. Chichester: Wiley-Blackwell.

Malgrem, Carl. 2010. "The Pursuit of Crime: Characters in Crime Fiction." In Charles Rzepka and Lee Horsley (eds.), *A Companion to Crime Fiction*, 152–163. Chichester: Wiley-Blackwell.

Marling, William. n.d. "Major Works: *The Maltese Falcon*, by Daniel Hammett." http://www.detnovel.com/MalteseFalcon.html (accessed November 28, 2011).

McCann, Sean. 2000. *Gumshoe America*. Durham, NC: Duke University Press.

McCoy, Horace. 1970 [1935]. *They Shoot Horses, Don't They?* Harmondsworth: Penguin.

McLaughlin, Joseph. 2000. *Writing the Urban Jungle: Reading Empire in London from Doyle to Eliot*. Charlottesville: University Press of Virginia.

Messent, Peter. 2008. "American Gothic: Liminality and the Gothic in Thomas Harris's Hanibal Lecter Novels." In Benjamin Szumskyj (ed.), *Dissecting Hannibal Lecter: Essays on the Novels of Thomas Harris*, 13–36. Jefferson: McFarland & Co.

Moretti, Franco. 1983. "Clues." In *Signs Taken for Wonders: On the Sociology of Literary Forms*, 130–156. Verso: London.

Mosley, Walter. 1992 [1990]. *Devil in a Blue Dress*. London: Pan Books.

Mosley, Walter. 1996. *A Little Yellow Dog*. New York: W. W. Norton.

Nesbø, Jo. 2010 [2009]. *The Leopard*. London: Harvill Secker.

Nestingen, Andrew. 2011. "Unnecessary Officers: Realism, Melodrama and Scandinavian Crime Fiction in Transition." In Andrew Nestingen and Paula Arvas, *Scandinavian Crime Fiction*, 171–183. Cardiff: University of Wales Press.

Nestingen, Andrew and Paula Arvas (eds.). 2011. *Scandinavian Crime Fiction*. Cardiff: University of Wales Press.

Nickerson, Catherine. 1997. "Murder as Social Criticism." *American Literary History* 9: 4, 744–757.

Nicol, Bran. 2010. "Patricia Highsmith." In Charles Rzepka and Lee Horsley (eds.), *A Companion to Crime Fiction*, 503–509. Chichester: Wiley-Blackwell.

Nielsen Bookscan. "Top 100 Books." https://docs.google.com/spreadsheet/ccc?key=0AonYZs4MzlZbdEpsS2MtbmEyU1BNVXBhMjdWcVctMFE&hl=en#gid=1 (accessed November 30, 2011).

Oates, Joyce Carol. 1995. "The Simple Art of Murder." *The New York Review*, December 21, 32–38.

Ogdon, Bethany. 1992. "Hard-boiled Ideology." *Critical Quarterly* 34: 1, 71–85.

Panek, Leroy L. 2003a. *The Police Novel: A History*. Jefferson: McFarland & Co.

Panek, Leroy L. 2003b. "Post-War American Police Fiction." In Martin Priestman (ed.), *The Cambridge Companion to Crime Fiction*, 155–171. Cambridge: Cambridge University Press.

Paretsky, Sara. 1986 [1985]. *Killing Orders*. London: Victor Gollancz.

Paretsky, Sara. 1994 [1993]. *Tunnel Vision*. London: QPD.

Paretsky, Sara. n.d. "About V I." http://www.saraparetsky.com/about-v-i (accessed November 23, 2011).

Parks, Tim. 2011. "The Moralist" [A review of the Stieg Larsson trilogy]. *The New York Review of Books*, 58: 8, 10, 12.

Peach, Linden. 2006. *Masquerade Crime Fictions: Criminal Deception*. London: Palgrave.

"People & Events: The Zoot Suit Riots of 1943." n.d. http://www.pbs.org/wgbh/amex/zoot/eng_peopleevents/e_riots.html (accessed November 29, 2011).

Pepper, Andrew. 2000. *The Contemporary American Crime Novel: Race, Ethnicity, Gender, Class*. Edinburgh: Edinburgh University Press.

Pepper, Andrew. 2003. "Black Crime Fiction." In Martin Priestman (ed.), *The Cambridge Companion to Crime Fiction*, 209–226. Cambridge: Cambridge University Press.

Pepper, Andrew. 2010a. "The 'Hard-Boiled' Genre." In Charles Rzepka and Lee Horsley (eds.), *A Companion to Crime Fiction*, 140–151. Chichester: Wiley-Blackwell.

Pepper, Andrew. 2010b. "'Hegemony Protected by the Armour of Coercion': Dashiell Hammett's *Red Harvest* and the State." *Journal of American Studies* 44: 2, 333–349.

Pérez-Reverté, Arturo. 1990. *The Flanders Panel.* New York: Harcourt Brace.

Peterson, Christopher. 2010. "The Aping Apes of Poe and Wright: Race, Animality, and Mimicry in 'The Murders in the Rue Morgue' and *Native Son.*" *New Literary History* 41: 1, 151–171.

Pile, Steve. 1996. *The Body and the City: Psychoanalysis, Space and Subjectivity.* London: Routledge.

Plain, Gill. 2001. *Twentieth-Century Crime Fiction: Gender, Sexuality and the Body.* Edinburgh, Edinburgh University Press.

Plain, Gill. 2002. Ian Rankin's *Black and Blue*: A Reader's Guide. New York: Continuum.

Poe, Edgar Allan. 1980 [1838]. *The Narrative of Arthur Gordon Pym of Nantucket.* Harmondsworth: Penguin.

Poe, Edgar Allan. 2000. *Tales and Sketches. Volume 1: 1831–1842.* Urbana: University of Illinois Press.

Porter, Dennis. 1981. *The Pursuit of Crime: Art and Ideology in Detective Fiction.* New Haven: Yale University Press.

Porter, Dennis. 2003. "The Private Eye." In Martin Priestman (ed.), *The Cambridge Companion to Crime Fiction*, 95–113. Cambridge: Cambridge University Press.

Price, Richard. 2008. *Lush Life.* London: Bloomsbury.

Priestman, Martin. 2003b. "Post-War British Crime Fiction." In Martin Priestman (ed.), *The Cambridge Companion to Crime Fiction*, 173–189. Cambridge: Cambridge University Press.

Queen, Ellery. 1947. "The Adventure of the Glass-Domed Clock." In *The Adventures of Ellery Queen.* Cleveland: World Publishing Company.

Rankin, Ian. 2006. *The Naming of the Dead.* London: Orion Books.

Rankin, Ian. 2007. E-mail correspondence. May 12.

Rankin, Ian. n.d. "Inspector Rebus Novels: *The Naming of the Dead.*" http://www.ianrankin.net/pages/content/index.asp?PageID=85 (accessed November 30, 2011).

Reddy, Maureen T. 2003a. "Women Detectives." In Martin Priestman (ed.), *The Cambridge Companion to Crime Fiction*, 191–207. Cambridge: Cambridge University Press.

Reddy, Maureen T. 2003b. *Traces, Codes, and Clues: Reading Race in Crime Fiction.* New Brunswick: Rutgers University Press.

Rosenheim, Shawn. 1995. "Detective Fiction, Psychoanalysis, and the Analytic Sublime." In Shawn Rosenheim and Stephen Rachman (eds.), *The American Face of Edgar Allan Poe*, 153–176. Baltimore: John Hopkins University Press.

Roth, Marty. 1995. *Foul & Fair Play: Reading Genre in Classic Detective Fiction.* Athens: University of Georgia Press.

Rzepka, Charles J. 2005. *Detective Fiction.* Cambridge: Polity Press.

Sayers, Dorothy L. n.d. [1923]. *Whose Body?* London: W. Collins.

Scaggs, John. 2005. *Crime Fiction.* Abingdon: Routledge.

Schmid, David. 1995. "Imaging Safe Urban Space: The Contribution of Detective Fiction to Radical Geography." *Antipode* 27: 3, 242–269.

Schmid, David. 1999. "Chester Himes and the Institutionalization of Multicultural Detective Fiction." In Adrienne J. Gosselin (ed.), *Multicultural Detective Fiction: Murder from the "Other" Side*, 283–302. New York: Garland.

Silet, Charles L. P. n.d. "The Talented – and Deadly – Mr. Ripley." www.mysterynet.com/books/testimony/ripley (accessed November 17, 2011).

Simpson, Philip. 1995. "The Contagion of Murder: Thomas Harris' *Red Dragon*." *Notes on Contemporary Literature* 25: 1, 6–8.

Sjöwall, Maj and Per Wahlöö. 2007 [1968]. *The Laughing Policeman*. London: Harper Perennial.

Smith, David. 1980. "The Public Eye of Raymond Chandler." *Journal of American Studies* 14: 3, 423–441.

Söderlind, Sylvia. 2011. "Håkan Nesser and the Third Way: Of Loneliness, Alibis and Collateral Guilt." In Andrew Nestingen and Paula Arvas (eds.), *Scandinavian Crime Fiction*, 159–170. Cardiff: University of Wales Press.

Stanford, Peter. 2006. "Kathy Reichs: The Ice Queen of Crime." *The Independent*, July 21. www.independent.co.uk/arts-entertainment/books/features/kathy-reichs-the-ice-queen-of-crime-408662.html (accessed November 17, 2011).

Stewart, David M. 1997. "Cultural Work, City Crime, Reading Pleasure." *American Literary History* 9: 4, 676–701.

Summerscale, Kate. 2008. *The Suspicions of Mr Whicher: Or the Murder at Road Hill House*. London: Bloomsbury.

Sutherland, John. 2006. "The Ideas Interview: Franco Moretti." *The Guardian*, January 9. www.guardian.co.uk/books/2006/jan/09/highereducation.academicexperts (accessed November 17, 2011).

Tapper, Michael. 2011. "Dirty Harry in the Swedish Welfare State." In Andrew Nestingen and Paula Arvas (eds.), *Scandinavian Crime Fiction*, 21–33. Cardiff: University of Wales Press.

Taylor, Barry. 1994. "The Violence of the Event: Hannibal Lecter in the Lyotardian Sublime." In Steven Earnshaw (ed.), *Postmodern Surroundings*, 215–230. Amsterdam: Rodopi.

"The Black Dahlia: Production Information." n.d. http://www.visualhollywood.com/movies/black_dehlia/notes.pdf (accessed November 29, 2011).

The Library of America. n.d. "About the Library of America." http://www.loa.org/splash.jsp?s=about (accessed November 28, 2011).

The Thrilling Detective Web Site. n.d. "Race Williams." http://www.thrillingdetective.com/race.html (accessed November 28, 2011).

Thompson, Jim. 1983 [1952]. *The Killer Inside Me*. In *Four Novels by Jim Thompson*. London: Zomba Books.

Thoms, Peter. 2002. "Poe, Dupin and the Power of Detection." In Kevin J. Hayes, *The Cambridge Companion to Edgar Allan Poe*, 133–147. Cambridge: Cambridge University Press.

Valerio, Mike. n.d. "The Great Wrong Place: Raymond Chandler's Los Angeles at 70." http://www.blackmaskmagazine.com/bm_15.html (accessed November 28, 2011).

Van Dine, S. S. 1946 [1928]. "Twenty Rules for Writing Detective Stories." In Howard Haycraft (ed.), *The Art of the Mystery Story: A Collection of Critical Essays*, 189–193. New York: Grossett & Dunlap.

Vanecker, Sabine. 1997. "V. I. Warshawski, Kinsey Millhone and Kay Scarpetta: Creating a Feminist Detective Hero." In Peter Messent (ed.), *Criminal Proceedings: The Contemporary American Crime Novel*, 62–86. London: Pluto.

Veeder, William. 1998. "The Nurture of the Gothic, or How Can a Text Be Both Popular and Subversive?" In Robert K. Martin and Eric Savoy (eds.), *American Gothic: New Interventions in a National Narrative*, 20–39. Iowa City: University of Iowa Press.

Walton, Priscilla L. and Manina Jones (eds.). 1999. *Detective Agency: Women Rewriting the Hard-Boiled Tradition*. Berkeley: University of California Press.

Wambaugh, Joseph. 2006. *Hollywood Station*. New York: Little, Brown.

Wambaugh, Joseph. 2007. E-mail correspondence. May 26 and June 26.

Whitley, John S. 1980. "Stirring Things Up: Dashiell Hammett's Continental Op." *Journal of American Studies* 14: 3, 443–455.

Widdicombe, Toby. 1981. *A Reader's Guide to Raymond Chandler*. Westport: Greenwood Press.

Willett, Ralph. 1992. *Hard-Boiled Detective Fiction*. BAAS Pamphlets in American Studies 23. Ryburn: Halifax.

Williams, John. 1973. "Chester Himes: My Man Himes." *Flashbacks: A Twenty-Year Diary of Article Writing*, 292–352. Garden City: Doubleday.

Winston, Robert P., and Nancy C. Mellerski. 1992. *The Public Eye: Ideology and the Police Procedural*. Houndmills, Basingstoke: Macmillan.

Wroe, Nicholas. 2004. "James Ellroy: Dark Star of LA Noir." *The Guardian*, "Arts," November 13, 20–23.

York, R. A. 2007. *Agatha Christie: Power and Illusion*. Houndmills, Basingstoke: Palgrave Macmillan.

Young, Elizabeth. 1991. "The Silence of the Lambs and the Flaying of Feminist Theory." *Camera Obscura: Feminism, Culture, and Media Studies* 9: 3 27, 4–35.

Žižek, Slajov. 2003. "Not a Desire to Have Him, but to Be Like Him." *London Review of Books* 25: 16. www.lrb.co.uk/v25/n16/slavoj-zizek/not-a-desire-to-have-him-but-to-be-like-him (accessed November 17, 2011).

Index

Page numbers in **bold** indicate major discussion of a topic.

The Crime Fiction Handbook, First Edition. Peter Messent.
© 2013 John Wiley & Sons, Ltd. Published 2013 by John Wiley & Sons, Ltd.